Alice Starmore's Book of
Fair Isle Knitting

Alice Starmore's Book of
Fair Isle Knitting

891017

TAUNTON
BOOKS & VIDEOS

...by fellow enthusiasts

Franklin Lakes Public Library
De Korte Drive
Franklin Lakes, N.J. 07417

©1988 by The Taunton Press, Inc.
All rights reserved

1 2 3 4 5 6 7   92 91 90 89 88

International Standard Book Number: 0-918804-97-3

Library of Congress Catalog Card Number: 88-50532

Printed in the United States of America

A THREADS Book

THREADS® is a trademark of The Taunton Press, Inc.,
registered in the U.S. Patent and Trademark Office.

The Taunton Press
63 South Main Street
Newtown, Connecticut 06470

To my mother,
Catriona Matheson

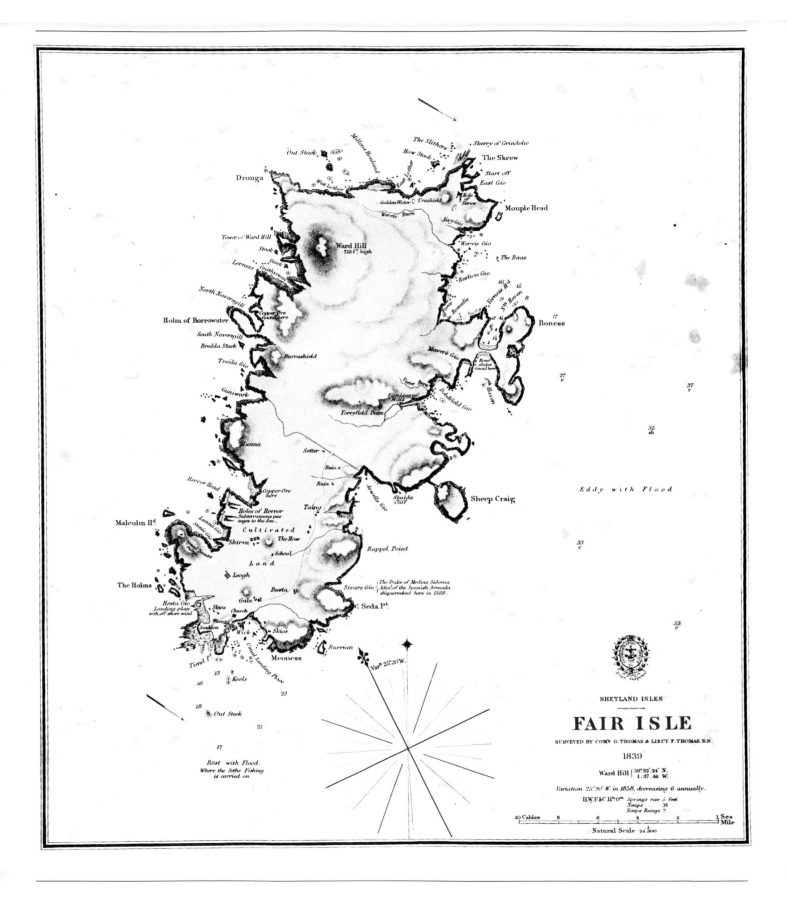

SHETLAND ISLES

FAIR ISLE

SURVEYED BY COMr. G.THOMAS & LIEUT. F.THOMAS, R.N.

1839

Ward Hill { 59°32'.24" N.
1°.37'.46" W.

Variation 25°20' W. in 1858, decreasing 6 annually.

H.W.F.&C.IIh.0m *Springs rise 5 feet*
Neaps 3½
Neaps Range 2

10 Cables   8   6   4   2   1 Sea Mile

Natural Scale 24,300

"It is remarkable that there should be lying, at no greater distance from us than half-way between Orkney and Shetland, an Isle whose inhabitants seem to be, as yet, almost in a state of nature. The account of a south-sea island could hardly attract more our curiosity....

"[The isle] rises into three very high promontories...Malcom's Head on the W., the Wart or Wardhill on the N.W., and the Sheep Craig at the S.E. extremity. This last is a stupendous and magnificent object; a huge mass of rock rising in a conical form as it were from the ocean, to a height of 480 feet, and almost entirely separated from the island, either by the force of the surrounding element or some convulsion of nature. The soil on its surface, which consists of about 12 acres, produces a kind of grass that maintains annually 24 sheep, which are as remarkable for the excellence of their wool, as for the value of their carcasses."

—*The Statistical Account of Scotland, 1791-99*

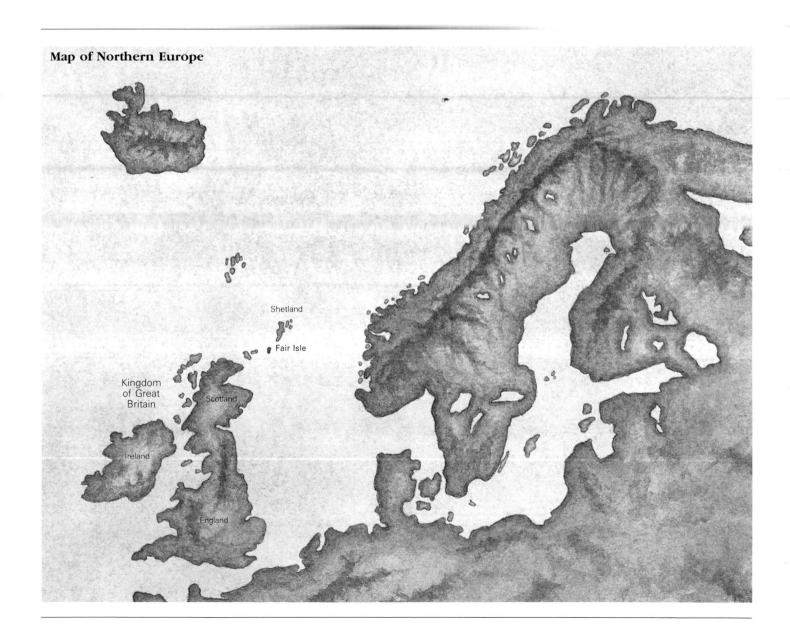

Map of Northern Europe

Shetland

Fair Isle

Kingdom
of Great
Britain

Scotland

Ireland

England

Contents

Herring packers at Lerwick harbor around 1900. Three centuries earlier, the influx of foreign fishermen into Shetland waters primed the local hosiery

A brief history

industry, which later made lace and Fair Isle garments.

If I were asked to contribute a brief definition of Fair Isle knitting to a comprehensive encyclopedia of needlework, I might provide the boxed passage on the next page. I would also point readers to an atlas of Scotland. They would find that in the group of islands known as Shetland, Fair Isle is the most southerly member, a tiny speck on the map, barely three miles long by two miles wide.

Just how this speck came to give its name to one of the best-known forms of knitting in the world is a fascinating study, part fact and part speculation. The development of this knitted art is reasonably well documented, but its origins are not definitely known. There are several theories of origin, but none of these is convincing. After carefully researching the subject, I have developed my own theory. However, before presenting it, I want to look briefly at the history of Shetland, since Fair Isle's strategic location, trade and foreign contact have all played fundamental roles in the history of Fair Isle knitting.

Knitting, Fair Isle A circular, stranded form of color knitting that takes its name from its place of origin, Fair Isle, one of a group of islands known as Shetland, which represents the northernmost reach of British soil. The exact date and circumstances of the origins of this art are unknown, though various theories have been put forward, some more fanciful than others. The earliest museum samples, however, are thought to have been knitted around 1850. These and other early examples of Fair Isle knitting are characterized by bands of geometric patterns, using two or more colors but never more than two colors in one round, or circular row.

Fair Isle knitting was considered quaint and outlandish until about 1900, when it was adopted by the knitters of mainland Shetland, developed and successfully commercialized. These knitters added more patterns from a variety of sources. The advent of chemical dyes around the turn of the century led knitters to use a great many more colors in their work, but they steadfastly adhered to the rule of no more than two colors per round.

Since the 1920s, Fair Isle knitting has enjoyed considerable commercial success, though in recent years the industry again suffered setbacks. The art is now widely copied by manufacturers around the world, and as a result, the overall quality of the work has suffered. Nonetheless, genuine Fair Isle knitted garments remain highly desirable.

Shetland	
Number of islands	more than 100
Total population	22,500
Land area	552 square miles
Length of coastline	900 miles
Main town	Lerwick, 60° 9′ N
Industries	Fishing, farming, knitwear, oil-related industries

The harsh, windswept coast of Fair Isle, the most southerly of the Shetland islands.

Shetland, a brief history

"A race of fishermen who happen to be farmers." This brief, anonymous quotation sums up the economic history of Shetland, or Zetland. Or rather, it did until the 1970s, when the discovery of oil in the North Sea had a radical impact on Shetland life and livelihood. Note, however, that the oil came from under the sea, not from the land—in keeping with the history of Shetland, where ploughing the land has always been secondary to ploughing the sea. The sheep that for centuries have cropped the Shetland heather may be the basis for the story of knitting, but the sea is all-important to the story of these islands. No part of Shetland is more than three miles from the sea, a fact that statistics alone fail to convey.

Nor can statistics capture the fact that for the British, Shetland is the epitome of "the back of the beyond," that is, to use its American equivalent, "nowheresville." I have even known fellow Scots (at least, Lowland Scots) to confuse Shetland with my own native Western Isles. To many Britishers, Shetland forms a kind of peripheral northern blur, synonymous with remoteness and wild weather. Shetland does not even fit on the standard school map of Britain, but instead is usually found in its own little box, towed down to ride at anchor near the Scottish mainland.

While Shetlanders would agree that their weather is wild—a gale in London would constitute only a slight breeze in Shetland—they take great exception to the portrayal of their islands as remote, provincial and rarely visited. They know that they are members of a busy, bustling community with a strong sense of identity and boundless vitality. Although landsmen view the sea as a barrier that cuts off and isolates what it encircles, this community of seafarers understands that the sea also serves as the highway that has made their strategically located islands a center of traffic over the centuries.

Bressay Sound, the natural harbor on which Shetland's main town of Lerwick stands, has seen through the years a constant flow of vessels from all maritime nations. These ships have come for various reasons—trade, fishing and war. A Royal Navy fleet of 94, for example, looked in on Shetland while searching for the Dutch during the first Anglo-Dutch War of 1653. Then in 1702, the French burned a Dutch fishing fleet in Shetland waters, making a grim but spectacular sight. During the Napoleonic Wars, the dreaded Press Gang of the Royal Navy haunted Shetland's shores in search of island men, who, long known for their seamanship, were pressed into service against the French.

The traffic to Shetland began with the Vikings in the ninth century, when King Harald the Fairhair of Norway brought Shetland under Norse control. For the next few hundred years, the islands changed hands— though seldom peacefully—from one Norse earl to another. Throughout this period, the islands were used as the base for Viking raids down both coasts of Britain and even as far south as the Mediterranean Sea.

In 1648, Shetland was pledged as part of the collateral to the Crown of Scotland for the dowry in a political marriage between James (later James II) of Scotland and Margaret of Denmark and Norway. Because the dowry was never paid, Shetland was annexed into Scottish rule. In the years that followed, life for the islanders was made miserable by the misrule of a series of Scottish earls. The most notorious of these was Patrick Stewart, unaffectionately known as Black Pate, who

used forced labor to quarry stone for the building of his castle at Scalloway in 1600.

The Act of Union of 1707 made the islands firmly British, a designation that today still upsets many Shetlanders who feel strongly about their Norse heritage. That heritage runs through the place names of Shetland, such as Unst, Fetlar, Yell, Whalsay, Bressay, Papa Stour, Foula and Fair Isle.

Where does Fair Isle fit into the picture of Shetland? Though one of the most remote islands of the group, it has seen plenty of seaborne traffic through the centuries. Among a surprising number of visitors to the island, more than one sea captain, a famous novelist and several church ministers have left us firsthand accounts of life in Fair Isle in the eighteenth and nineteenth centuries. That life can be summed up in one word: hard!

Although limited agriculture and sheep raising were important to life on Fair Isle, a family's sustenance came from the sea. To work their fishing grounds, the menfolk rowed fragile boats over some of the roughest seas in the British Isles.

> Their boats, which are 14 in number, lie on the SW shore…from which they go with only 2 or 3 men in them…and, with an oar in each hand, row over immense billows, in a short time, to a great distance. In these pitiful skiffs in which a landsman would scarcely trust his

A Fair Isle fishing boat and crew in the early 1900s.

Cliffs along the coast of mainland Shetland.

life across a river, they fly to the fishing ground, almost out of sight of the island, where they catch plenty of fine code, ling, tusk, skate, holibut, mackerel, cyth, and other fish of inferior quality. These together with their hens, chickens, sheep, eggs &c. they afterwards carry to ships which they observe in the offing...and barter them to great advantage, for various articles of food and clothing.
—*Statistical Account, 1791-1799*

This seaborne barter was dangerous but vital, as it brought the islanders nails, tools, various luxuries and other articles that they otherwise had no hope of obtaining. The supply of these items, however, was subject to the course of political events, as noted by the novelist Sir Walter Scott in *Northern Lights,* his account of a visit to the island in 1814:

The women knit worsted stockings, nightcaps and other similar trifles, which they exchange with any merchant vessels that approach their lonely isle. In these respects they greatly regret the American war [of 1812] and mention with unction the happy days when they could get from an American trader a bottle of peach brandy or rum in exchange for a pair of worsted stockings or a dozen eggs.

The inhabitants of Fair Isle were experts in the art of survival and made the most of their scarce resources. Blessed with excellent pastures for sheep, they wasted not one bit of available land, even if, like Sheep Craig, it was cut off from the island and surrounded by a precipice. Sir Walter Scott also noted that "the natives contrive to ascend the rock by a place that would make a goat dizzy and then drag the sheep up by ropes, though they sometimes carry a sheep up on their shoulders."

In the massive cliffs surrounding the island, the Fair Islanders found another natural resource—the nesting sites of various seabirds. To obtain eggs and young birds for the pot, the islanders became expert cragsmen. The Reverend James Kay, whose parish of Dunrossness in Shetland included Fair Isle, observed this hazardous and occasionally lethal occupation in the 1680s, noting that "instead of catching the prey, they sometimes catch a slip, whereby they are either crushed on the rocks, or drowned in the sea." The islanders accepted this activity as a necessary part of life, and the danger they faced daily became routine.

The Fair Islanders were indeed survivors. The Reverend John Brand, member of a special commission appointed by the Church of Scotland to inquire into the state of religion and morals in the Northern Isles, recorded in 1701 that "death hath almost depopulated the isle, the Small Pox having lately raged there, and swept away two-thirds of the Inhabitants." By the 1790s, however, the Statistical Account reports a population of 220 and rising, noting that "in the last 8 years, there have been 11 marriages, 64 births and only 27 funerals." Sir Walter Scott reports a population of 250 in 1814, and by mid-century it had reached 360—apparently too crowded for some, however, since 137 people are shown in census figures to have emigrated to Nova Scotia around 1860.

As the changing climate and competition from larger fishing boats deteriorated the islanders' fishing income, many families moved to the mainland. Population again declined as the twentieth century began and World War I took its toll. Although the population of Fair Isle has continued to decrease throughout this century, it has now stabilized at about 70 inhabitants. This stability is due mainly to the fact that in 1954 the island was taken over by the National Trust for Scotland (the equivalent of the National Park Service in the U.S.), which improved communication and transportation between Fair Isle and mainland Shetland. The Trust has established a bird observatory on the island, which studies the vast number of migrants passing over its shores and itself attracts numerous unfeathered visitors.

Today, Shetland remains a fishing and farming community, despite the recent incursion of the oil industry into the economy (see pp. 26-31). Shetland fishermen still plough the seas, although their vessels nowadays are equipped with computers and sonar. The shell of Black Pate's castle still stands at Scalloway, but its gaunt, glassless windows look out on a giant wind turbine and comfortable modern homes with new Ford automobiles in their driveways. One feature of the Shetland landscape, however, remains unchanged: Shetland sheep still crop the heather on hill and moorland as they have for centuries.

Plain knitting in Shetland

Plain knitting, mainly in the form of stockings, has been an important and continuous thread in much of the history of Shetland. The wool for this knitting came from the small but sturdy breed of Shetland sheep, which are capable of withstanding both the islands' harsh climate and limited moorland pasture.

> The sheep of the Shetland Islands are of a peculiar and indigenous breed—very small, very wild, and very hardy....The animal is distinguished also by a soft, fine, short wool, of a variety of shades of colour, from a black to a light brown or a silvery grey, some are even piebald. Two circumstances are supposed to cause its silky softness, besides peculiarity of breed: first, the coarse but often aromatic pastures; and secondly, the mode in practice of pulling the wool from the animal, instead of shearing it.
>
> *—Anonymous resident of Shetland, 1861*

Although the soft wool produced by Shetland sheep is too weak for weaving, it is excellent for knitting. Given the fineness of the wool and the handsome array of its natural hues, it was inevitable that sooner or later the women of Shetland would take up the art of knitting (only rarely did the men knit, which is still true today). The first recorded evidence of Shetland knitting dates to the sixteenth century; by the seventeenth century the craft was practiced everywhere in the islands.

During the seventeenth and eighteenth centuries, hand-knitted hosiery became the islands' main manufacture. According to the Statistical Account of 1791-1799, the island knitters spun "excellent linen yarn, and discover[ed] much dexterity in manufacturing their fine soft wool into stockings, gloves,

Shetland sheep, noted for their fine wool, graze on a hillside.

nightcaps, and other wearing apparel." Local eighteenth-century physician and historian Dr. Arthur Edmondston noted that this industry generated about £17,000 a year in the 1790s. The reasons for the industry's healthy growth were the proximity of raw material and a ready market for the goods.

The manufacture of knitwear by hand was a five-step process: plucking the wool, known locally as "rooing" the sheep; teasing and removing the coarse wool; carding, or combing, the wool to straighten the fibers; spinning the wool; and knitting it on fine needles, or "wires." All these processes were performed by hand until about 1890, when the raw wool began to be sent to Scottish mills for the middle three stages.

On mainland Shetland the stockings were often bartered with local shopkeepers for commodities like tea, snuff, tobacco and cotton drapery goods. In fact, said Dr. Edmondston, the stockings "form a principal article of exchange in the country." The main market for knitted goods, however, was not the locals but rather the hordes of foreign fishermen who came annually to the islands in search of herring.

The Hollanders also repair to these Isles in June for their Herring Fishing, but they cannot be said so properly to Trade with the Countrey, as to fish upon their Coasts, and they used to bring all sorts of Provisions necessary with them, save some fresh Victuals, as Sheep, Lambs, Hens &c. Which they buy on shore. Stockins are also brought by the Countrey People from all quarters to Lerwick and sold to these fishers, for sometimes many thousands of them will be ashore at one time, and ordinary it is with them to buy Stockins to themselves, and some likewise do to their Wives and Children; which is very beneficial to the Inhabitants, for so Money is brought into the Countrey, there is a Vent for the wooll, and the Poor are employed.
     —*Reverend John Brand, 1701*

Reverend Brand was describing the annual influx of Dutch herring fishers, who worked the Shetland waters throughout the seventeenth century and until about 1711, when a combination of war and a high duty on curing salt finally broke their monopoly. It is the sheer scale of the herring operation that impresses today. In 1653, one Captain Smith estimated the fleet at about 1,500 fishing vessels, each with a crew of about 15 men, plus 20 "wasters," that is, escort vessels, each with some 20 guns. The ships used the township of Lerwick and the sheltered Bressay Sound as their base. Since Shetland had a guaranteed

A woman's Fair Isle gansey (traditional pullover sweater with gussets under the arms), dated 1910.

annual market of this size and a healthy supply of raw material, it is little wonder that the cottage hosiery industry grew dramatically at this time, reaching its zenith around 1700.

The Shetland hosiery trade began to decline a decade later, and plummeted in the early 1800s. By 1809, Dr. Edmondston reported that the value of annual sales had fallen to about £5,000. "This deficiency," he noted, "is in part due to the interruption which the war has given to the Zetland trade with the Dutch and German fishermen; but a great failure has also occurred in the demand for Zetland stockings all over Britain."

The falling demand for Shetland hosiery resulted from both the dramatic rise in sheep farming in Scotland and England and the mechanization of stocking manufacture. The Shetland hosiery trade never recovered, and in time the islanders took up new types of knitting, mainly lace. But that is another story.

Theories of origin

For many people, Fair Isle knitting once constituted a paradox: a rich, exotic art with a wealth of pattern and color, famous the world over, yet produced by an uneducated people in remote isolation, harsh physical conditions and extreme poverty. Add to this paradox the fact that Fair Isle knitting exhibits a host of design elements regarded by many as cryptic symbols, and it's easy to see how the seeds of mystery have been sown amidst speculation about the origins of this art.

Where do the patterns come from? What do they mean? For many, it is rather like contemplating the pyramids or the mysterious geometry of Inca walls. Some of the ideas on the subject are therefore obviously fanciful, but more realistic, scholarly approaches have also been marked by a gentle astonishment at the art. In the end no one knows for certain what the missing link in this story is.

After presenting the major theories to date, I'll conclude with my own views on the subject. What I hope to show is that far from being mysterious or astonishing, the origins of Fair Isle knitting are logical and natural.

The Spanish connection

One memorable accident here occurreth; namely, that the Duke of Medina, Admiral of that formidable Spanish Armada (in ye reign of Q. Elizabeth an. 1588) here made Ship-

wrack in a Creek on the East side of this Isle, where the ship split: but the Duke wt 200 men came to shore alive, & wintered here in great misery.

—Reverend James Kay, in Description of Ye Countrey of Zetland by Parish Ministers &c, circa 1680

The unfortunate duke in question was Admiral Juan Gomez de Medina and his hapless ship, the 650-ton *El Gran Grifón,* the flagship of the Armada, which carried 38 guns and 286 men. The duke had fled north from the English Channel during the Anglo-Spanish War following a disastrous defeat by the English fleet under the command of Sir Francis Drake. On August 17, 1588, the Spanish ship was wrecked on the rocks of Fair Isle. Kay's description of the number of survivors and their immediate fate is believed to be accurate. His account goes on to describe how the Fair Islanders, fearing that this sudden influx of unwelcome visitors would cause famine, hid most of their food and animals. As a result, many of the bedraggled Spaniards died of starvation. Others were so weakened that they were easily set upon by the islanders and hurled over the high cliffs into the sea. Eventually a small boat was sent to mainland Shetland for help, and the duke and his surviving crew were returned to Europe.

Is there any connection between this event and knitting? If there is, the first written mention of it appeared in 1856.

It is believed the Duke of Medina Sidonea, Admiral of the Spanish Armada, and his followers, whose ship was wrecked on Fair Isle, and who afterwards wintered in Shetland, were the first that taught these islanders the art of knitting. Certain it is that the painted-like manufacture of the Fair Isle people at this day, is quite similar to what is made in the South of Spain.

—Eliza Edmondston, in Sketches & Tales of the Shetland Isles, 1856

Once suggested, the Spanish connection captured the imagination of visitors to the Shetland Isles. With its Spanish Duke, the Armada and a shipwreck, the Spanish connection had all the requisite ingredients of local lore and was consistently mentioned in travel books and magazines throughout the remainder of the nineteenth century.

In the 1920s, Jessie Saxby, author of a pamphlet entitled "Shetland Knitting," continued the legend of the Spanish connection: "It is known that this peculiar work—Moorish in its lavish richness of colouring, Arabesque in its quaint, intricate tracery— was taught by Shipwrecked Spaniards, of Moorish origin, a remnant of the Great Armada which found temporary refuge on Fair Isle."

The Spanish connection even has its champions today. In *Creative Dressing* by Kaori O'Connor (1980), Heinz Edgar Kiewe claims first that the seafaring Vikings sported a type of Fair Isle sweater with motifs copied from North African carpets. He goes on to state:

> In 1588, some ships of the Spanish Armada were blown off course and wrecked off the Shetland Islands. The Armada sailors were found to be wearing patterned sweaters and scarves, the heritage of the centuries when Spain was ruled by the Moors of North Africa —the Spanish equivalent of the Northern Fair Isle knits. The islanders copied the designs, and added them to their repertoire of traditional patterns.

There is no evidence whatsoever to support Kiewe's claim that the Armada sailors wore patterned sweaters and scarves. This is pure fiction. Nonetheless, this and earlier references to Fair Isle knitting are instructive, however inaccurate they may be. This knitting is described in various references as "peculiar," "quaint," "intricate" and "lavish," and as containing "varied bright colours" and even "mongrel Highland tartans." This language is strong. Clearly the patterns caught the eye and invited comment, even if it was not because they were admired but because they were regarded as outlandish curiosities from an outlandish locale.

It is surprising, therefore, that these patterns, which are supposed to have been around since 1588, are not mentioned at all by the numerous visitors to Fair Isle and Shetland who recorded their observations in the three centuries before Eliza Edmondston suggested the Spanish connection in 1856. This lack is particularly striking since nearly every written account of Fair Isle and Shetland after 1856 contains descriptions of Fair Isle knitting. Did visitors before the middle of the nineteenth century consider the patterns unworthy of note? Did they not see the Fair Isle patterns? Or were the patterns simply not around to be seen—had they not yet been invented?

Certainly if the patterns had existed before the mid-nineteenth century, the novelist Sir Walter Scott would have included some reference to them in his work. He had a keen eye for detail and was always on the lookout for local color for his book in progress. Yet the only observation on knitting he offers in the account of his 1814 Shetland travels is a passing reference to the fishermen's striped worsted caps.

Given these various written accounts, the inescapable conclusion is that what we know as Fair Isle knitting originated between the time of Scott's visit and the 1856 mention of the patterns by Eliza Edmondston. It is virtually impossible to pin down an exact date. The earliest pieces held in the National Museums of Scotland in Edinburgh are dated around 1850, but the museum's information is limited to that given at the time of an artifact's donation. The dates attributed to an artifact may therefore not be entirely reliable. Certainly these and other Fair Isle pieces, whether now lost or in private collections, may have been made in the 1850s or even slightly earlier.

Even if the origins of Fair Isle knitting must necessarily remain mostly a matter of speculation, I feel confident that the Spanish connection belongs to the realm of fairy tale. It is entertaining and picturesque, but it owes more to the imagination than to the facts available.

An exotic import?   The theory of the Spanish connection may not stand up to close examination, but this does not mean that the wreck of the Armada's flagship was an unimportant event in Fair Isle's history. On the contrary, this event vividly illustrates how the inhabitants of this remote island came into contact with seaborne traffic from around the world. The point is important because it provides the backdrop for the one element that is shared by most of the theories of origin: that the patterns were copied from some foreign source. Some people theorize further that this source was a woven shawl brought to Fair Isle by a foreign visitor or perhaps by a Fair Isle seaman returning from another land. Yet it seems to me that this object might just as well have been another woven textile, a piece of knitting or perhaps even a piece of pottery.

The premise of this theory is unarguable. As I have pointed out, there has been no dearth of visitors to Fair Isle's shores. The Vikings, French privateers, the Royal Navy and legions of Dutch herring fishermen all arrived

FRANKLIN LAKES PUBLIC LIBRARY **A brief history** 11

at one time or other at the islanders' doorstep. The Fair Islanders, in turn, rowed out to meet their boats to transact their trade. This contact with the outside world may have been informal and sporadic over the centuries, but it was contact just the same.

More formalized trade with North European merchants (principally German) occurred throughout the seventeenth and eighteenth centuries. These merchants came for fish to feed a hungry Europe. They arrived in May and set up booths at various points around Shetland, including Fair Isle. In exchange for fish, these merchants traded the necessities and luxuries the islanders otherwise did without—fishhooks, nets, muslin and fine linens, wheat flour, brandies and beers. The foreign influence on Shetland was so great that it even drew the attention of *London Maga zine,* which ran a feature on the subject in May 1752, mentioning that "the coast towns of Shetland are enriched by this confluence of foreigners who continually go on shore both to buy and sell."

Foreign contact increased still further in the eighteenth century, when various wars between Great Britain and other European nations made travel in the English Channel dangerous. To protect their cargo—and themselves as well—merchants avoided the English Channel in favor of the longer but safer passage north through the Atlantic. This passage took them by Shetland and Fair Isle, the latter, according to Reverend Brand in 1701, "being seen by them [approaching ships] at 14 or 16 leagues distance [and serving] in a clear day...as a myth or mark for directing their courses."

Dubbed the "Passage North About" (see the map below), this route principally served Dutch merchants traveling between Holland and the East Indies, but there was also a large amount of traffic bound for North America, and from the 1780s onward, considerable traffic between England and the Baltic countries of Sweden, Finland and Estonia. Even when the Napoleonic Wars ended in 1815 and the Passage North About was no longer crucial, Shetland remained a crossroads for trade between Europe and North America.

Given Fair Isle's extensive contact with the outside world, it's entirely possible that the

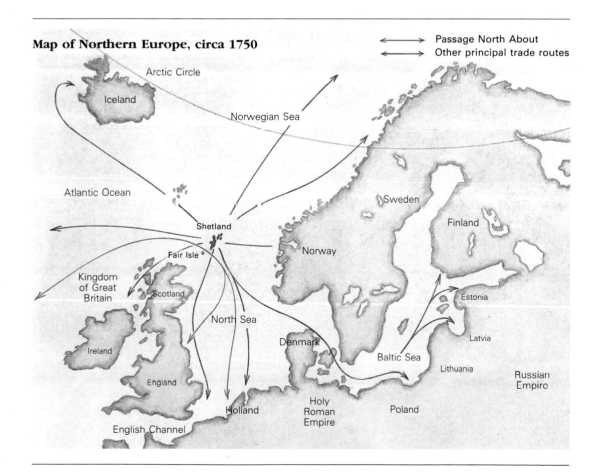

Map of Northern Europe, circa 1750

← → Passage North About
← → Other principal trade routes

Arctic Circle

Iceland

Norwegian Sea

Atlantic Ocean

Shetland

Fair Isle

Kingdom of Great Britain

Scotland

North Sea

Ireland

Sweden

Finland

Norway

Estonia

Latvia

Lithuania

Russian Empire

Denmark

Baltic Sea

England

Holland

Holy Roman Empire

Poland

English Channel

Traditional OXO pattern

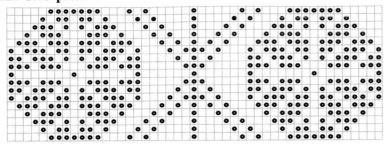

This detail of a Shetland pullover from the 1940s shows a sophisticated use of the OXO pattern—two stylized, lozenge-shaped letter O's separated by the letter X.

source of the Fair Isle patterns was external. If that source were a single object, however, where did that object come from? It could have come from anywhere—from the Old World or the New World, from the East or the West. But if that source were a particular object, it certainly has never been found.

Realistically, I question whether it's likely that all the early Fair Isle patterns were conveniently drawn from a single source, which then inconveniently vanished without a trace. Although I subscribe to the maxim "Never say never," I remain unconvinced.

Religious signs or symbols? The art of Fair Isle knitting serves as a storehouse of rich and varied geometric designs. All the early samples of Fair Isle knitting are based on what is called the OXO pattern, a pair of stylized, lozenge-shaped letter O's separated by the letter X (see the chart and photo at left). It is within these lozenges that often appear the patterns that some people regard as religious or cryptic symbols. Among the crosses that frequently fill these spaces is the Moorish Cross (see the chart at the bottom of the facing page), which provides additional evidence for some believers in the Spanish connection.

Among current writers who subscribe to the religious or mystical theory of origin is Heinz Edgar Kiewe, who, in *The Sacred History of Knitting* (1971), says of the Fair Isle patterns that "spiritual men and women, working together to produce the religious symbols and abstract forms, come nearer to their one God and closer together in their community." Sarah Don in *Fair Isle Knitting* (1979) states definitively that "Fair Isle designs are composed of ancient religious and national symbols."

Can Fair Isle patterns really be attributed to such religious, mystical or symbolic origins? I think not. Although the Fair Islanders were certainly religious, they were first and foremost a practical people who led difficult lives in harsh circumstances. Their daily work, produced under a conflicting array of pressures in the home and in the fields, was not, I think, a mindful celebration of God or country. Rather it was the dogged perseverance that survival entailed. Where that work involved the practical mastery of knitting techniques, the Fair Islanders more than survived; they succeeded masterfully.

These patterns all share a principal characteristic: They have at least two, and commonly four, lines of symmetry. In other words, the patterns reflect both from side to side and from top to bottom. Furthermore, these lines are perpendicular to one another and meet at the exact center of symmetry, about which the entire motif can be rotated, as shown in the drawing below. This simple fact means that the patterns are ideally suited to the knitting technique, since they are easy to remember and produce. The knitter simply works with exact repetitions or their inverse, and the first complete pattern row acts as a guide for what follows.

For a knitter, the advantages of using a small pattern with at least two perpendicular lines of symmetry are twofold: ease and greater speed of construction. Such patterns also have the advantage of eliminating long loops of yarn on the back of the piece and accommodating other technical concerns as well (see pp. 33-34). The patterns are in fact not mystical, but rather they are practical—like the Fair Islanders themselves.

With this discussion of lines of symmetry, I do not mean to suggest that the Fair Isle knitters themselves would have conceived of these patterns in such abstract, mathematical terms. An expert knitter's instinct alone would have sufficed.

In the course of researching and writing this book, I by chance discovered an interesting parallel between the Fair Isle patterns and the series of designs shown in the drawing at right. Several of these designs have long been used in Shetland, and one of them is from the Western Isles.

As with the Fair Isle patterns, one could long puzzle over the significance and origin of these motifs. Why are they so shaped? Where do they come from? What do they mean? Are they religious in nature? They can be viewed either as the Christian cross or, rotated 45°, as the diagonal cross of Saint Andrew, the national symbol of Scotland.

Actually, these designs were found on the heads of plungers from upright milk churns, circular devices used for centuries in Scotland and elsewhere to make butter. Each represents the response of a different craftsman to the same practical problem: how most effi-

Heads of milk-churn plungers

North Ulst, Western Isles

Papa Stour, Shetland

Fetlar, Shetland

Dunrossness, Shetland

Burwick, Shetland

Lines of symmetry

A shape is symmetrical if it can be cut in half exactly and both halves are mirror images. Some shapes have more than one line of symmetry, that is, they can be symmetrically cut in half along more than one axis.

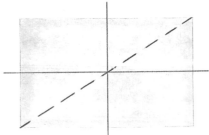

A rectangle has two lines of symmetry, vertical and horizontal. A rectangle cut diagonally does not produce halves that are mirror images.

A square has four lines of symmetry.

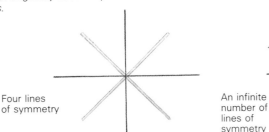

Four lines of symmetry

An infinite number of lines of symmetry

While several letters of the alphabet have two lines of symmetry, X and O are the only letters with four or more lines of symmetry.

Moorish cross

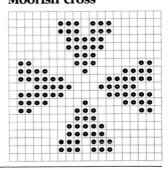

Design experiment

ciently to agitate the milk over the entire interior of the churn. In each case, the problem has been adequately and aesthetically solved. To read symbolism into these designs—or into the Fair Isle patterns—is, in my view, romantic nonsense.

Spontaneous development? Must the Fair Isle patterns have derived from a specific source, or is it possible that they may have arisen spontaneously? I explored the idea that the patterns might have developed on Fair Isle itself by conducting an experiment.

I enlisted the aid of a small secondary school on the Isle of Lewis, my home. All of the 78 pupils, 11 to 13 years old, were given a sheet of graph paper and told to produce bands of repeating designs. They were given no limitations on what they could produce. They could ignore the squares on the paper or use color if they wished. The only rule was that they were not to confer with one another on the designs.

The task was given to the pupils with no advance warning and with no time for preparation. The work was conducted in the school science lab, where there were no reference materials whatsoever on the tables or the walls.

Some students worked faster than others, producing about eight or nine designs, and only three students were unable to create any motifs at all. The average was four patterns per student. When the children were told to stop working after half an hour, they had produced a total of 245 different patterns, a few of which are shown on the facing page. Of these, there were 30 pictorial designs, 34 asymmetrical abstract shapes, 79 designs with one line of symmetry, 70 patterns with two lines of symmetry and 32 with four or more lines of symmetry.

I was surprised to find that only 30 pictorial patterns were produced. These and the 34 abstract asymmetrical shapes accounted for only 26% of the total. The tendency toward symmetry was overwhelming in this admittedly informal experiment.

I am sure that many readers will raise the valid objection that 78 high-tech kids, brought up on television and video games, hardly constitute a model for the Fair Islanders of the 1840s. And, to be sure, many of the designs were Space Invaders and other derivatives of the Computer Age. Yet an equal number of the designs were timeless geometric patterns, elegant in their simplicity. The cross in all its variations was a recurring theme, and although some people would argue a religious influence, it might just as well indicate an obvious starting point for a symmetrical design.

Endless argument might also ensue about the source of the patterns, but it would doubtless result in an inconclusive nature vs. nurture dispute. Do the patterns stem from an inner sense of geometry, or are they a rehash of every piece of imagery the children have soaked up? The truth probably lies halfway between.

The last pattern shown on the facing page, by the way, is a cheat. I saw it in a Navajo sand painting on my last trip to the United States and threw it in to show how this simple geometric pattern is equally at home in two different cultures. It is, in fact, a recognized Fair Isle pattern.

The conclusions I drew from this experiment were the following:

First, many people find pleasure in decorative symmetry and can, if they make the effort, quickly produce copious amounts of symmetrical patterning.

Second, since the children in the experiment produced an extensive body of designs in just half an hour, it seems possible that the Fair Isle patterns could have been independently developed by an island knitter or knitters who combined creative energies with borrowings from varied sources, whether domestic or exotic.

However, the one serious flaw in this theory of spontaneous development is that it assumes that the general technique of stranded color knitting was in use on Fair Isle at the time these patterns were being developed. Yet there is not one shred of evidence to this effect. There are simply no known examples of other, simpler types of stranded Fair Isle knitting that predate these patterns.

This theory also assumes a developmental period during which both the patterns and the technique of stranded knitting reached perfection. However, as you'll see in the next section, one of the most interesting features of the earliest examples of Fair Isle knitting is that they contain very sophisticated patterns. Any trace of experimentation with pattern occurs in pieces done in later years. The theory of spontaneous development—seemingly a promising candidate—is therefore out of the running.

An alternative theory of origin

Now that the various theories of the origin of Fair Isle knitting have been presented, I want to set forth my own views on the subject. But first, let me recap the significant facts about Fair Isle in the 1840s. This island had:

—a geographical position at the confluence of important shipping lanes as well as an economic history of seaborne barter, which brought exposure to influence from around the world;
—agricultural conditions favoring sheep farming and the production of first-rate yarn;
—a population necessarily practical in outlook and adept at making the most of its scarce resources;
—a centuries-old tradition of plain knitting.

In addition, Fair Isle was located on the fringes of the countries surrounding the Baltic Circle—Norway, Sweden, Finland, Latvia, Lithuania and Estonia (the last three are now part of the U.S.S.R.). Around 1800, a color explosion took place in the knitting of northern Europe, particularly in the Baltic Circle countries. The beginning of this boom in stranded knitting is comparatively easy to date because a vast amount of material is preserved in the collections of museums throughout the region.

The large range of surviving examples indicates a tradition of plain knitting (sometimes with embroidered decoration) up to about 1800, and, from then on, a rapid development in stranded knitting. Owing to the ongoing exchange of textiles among the Baltic Circle countries over the centuries, many of the patterns in the preserved garments are similar. The charts below illustrate the diversity of the Baltic Circle patterns. As you examine and compare these patterns with the Fair Isle fragments, remember that there was an upsurge in Baltic trade with Shetland that began around 1800 and increased throughout the nineteenth century.

Fair Isle fragments—historical evidence
Throughout the ages, knitwear has been created mainly for one reason: to be worn until worn out. It is therefore not surprising that few old pieces remain and that our information on this most prosaic of crafts is scanty. In the case of the Fair Isle museum pieces, the

Examples of early Baltic Circle patterns

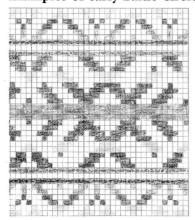

Chart 1
Early 19th-century Estonian pattern

Chart 2
Typical Norwegian pattern, circa 1800

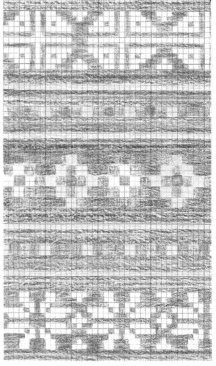

Chart 3
Early 19th-century Finnish pattern

only information available is that given by the donors, but, for the most part, the dating can be considered reasonably accurate. The photographs and charts that follow give a representative sampling of Fair Isle pieces held by the Shetland Museum in Lerwick and the National Museums of Scotland in Edinburgh. They also provide compelling evidence for my own view of the origin of Fair Isle knitting—that the patterns originated in the Baltic countries and were imported to Fair Isle in the first half of the nineteenth century.

The earliest dated Fair Isle pieces in these museum collections are a silk smoker's cap and matching pouch and a woolen cap and pouch, all dating to around 1850 (see the photo below). Each piece is sophisticated in design, featuring highly developed OXO bands and displaying no trace of experimentation. The woolen cap and pouch also feature an openwork pattern identical to that used on the cuffs of many Finnish and Estonian stranded knitted gloves produced from 1800 onward; and the color pattern on the cap's rib is the same as that found on the ribbing of many Baltic pieces in museum collections. Finally, it is important to note that neither of the woolen pieces is knitted in Shetland yarn.

In contrast, all subsequent Fair Isle pieces in these two museums (see the charts on p. 18) *are* knitted in Shetland yarn and display clear evidence of experimentation with the design elements of the 1850 pieces. For example, highly sophisticated OXO bands contrast sharply with neighboring bands of small, simple and often rudimentary patterns.

The fact that the 1850 pieces display extreme sophistication in design and all the confidence of a well-established art and that the subsequent pieces are far more experimental and less assured indicates a complete reversal of how a technique normally develops. In fact, no major development or change took place in Fair Isle knitting during the remainder of the century, and nothing matched the precision of the 1850 samples until after 1900.

The color in these pieces also provides interesting clues to the origin of Fair Isle knitting. We know that various local plants were used to produce yellow dye and that madder (red) and indigo (blue) vegetable dyes were imported to the island. Indigo in particular was difficult, and therefore expensive, to pro-

The earliest examples in the National Museums of Scotland of Fair Isle knitting, all dating to around 1850. The woolen cap and pouch on the left and the silk cap and purse on the right may have been made in one of the Baltic Circle countries.

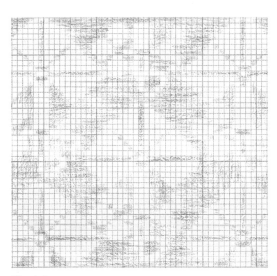

Chart 4
Early Swedish pattern

Charted patterns from early Fair Isle garments

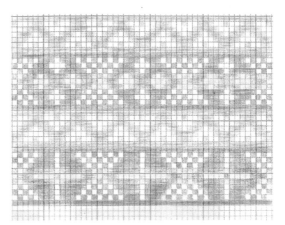

Chart 3: *Patterns from a Shetland wool gansey, dated 1895. The small, simple OXO bands repeat continuously throughout the garment.*

Chart 1: *Patterns from a cap, dated 1860 and knitted in Shetland wool. The design is made of sophisticated OXO bands separated by small, simple pattern bands (the lower lozenge is the same as the lozenge that is second from the top on the 1850 silk cap in the photo on p. 17).*

Chart 4: *Patterns from a gansey, dated about 1900 and knitted in Shetland wool. This gansey is a busy mix of large and small OXO bands and various smaller patterns, each used only twice throughout the garment.*

Chart 2: *Patterns from another cap, also dated 1860 and knitted in Shetland wool. The bands are composed of three different sizes of lozenges, the X's having been replaced by small diamond motifs.*

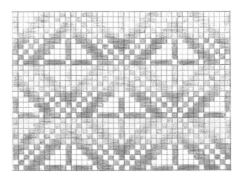

Chart 5: *Pattern from a gansey, knitted in Shetland wool and dated 1919. An allover pattern, similar to pieces from Estonia and Finland dated about 1800. The colors do not follow the symmetry of the pattern but rather change every five rows.*

duce, which explains its limited use and replacement by natural dark brown in almost every piece until the 1920s. Interestingly, the 1850 pieces made liberal use of blue, which supports the thesis that they were produced in a place other than Fair Isle, a place where indigo was common and relatively inexpensive.

The 1850 samples display color changes in tune with the symmetry of the OXO pattern—that is, the color bands are spaced symmetrically across the top, middle and bottom of the OXO. This technique is seen on most examples of large OXO bands throughout the remainder of the nineteenth century. However, the small OXO and non-OXO bands developed from 1850 to 1900 do not display the same color symmetry. Color changes in these bands are not in tune with the symmetry of the pattern, occurring rather in either the top or bottom of the pattern rows, as seen in Charts 4 and 5 on the facing page. It looks as if the knitters were able to copy an existing technique, but could not manipulate color with the same sophistication in the patterns they created themselves.

Now I am ready to draw some conclusions. First, given that no examples of other kinds of stranded knitting have survived from Fair Isle and that no other type of complex patterned color knitting has been described in the early written accounts of the island, I conclude that stranded knitting was introduced to Fair Isle simultaneously with the development of the OXO patterns.

Second, given that there are no surviving examples of Fair Isle knitting or descriptions of it before the 1850s, that stranded knitting had been well established in Baltic Circle countries since about 1800, and that there was regular passage of Baltic Circle ships around Fair Isle throughout the nineteenth century, I conclude that samples of Baltic Circle stranded knitting reached Fair Isle. These provided islanders with the impetus to try the technique and the patterns.

What knitted garments could have reached Fair Isle from the Baltic Circle countries? A scan of early nineteenth-century knitting from this region reveals that the chances of its being an OXO pattern are very high. I will go further, however, and conclude that the 1850 Fair Isle museum pieces—the silk set and the woolen cap and pouch—are not from Fair Isle at all but were imported to Fair Isle from somewhere in the Baltic Circle, probably Finland or Estonia. The evidence for this

conclusion is compelling: the extreme sophistication of these pieces compared with subsequent Fair Isle examples; the similarity of their designs to those found in Baltic Circle stranded knitting from 1800 on; the fact that the woolen pieces are not made of Shetland wool; and their liberal use of indigo dye, so rare on Fair Isle that natural brown was substituted in later examples. The openwork pattern on these woolen pieces, however, is the most important clue to support my thesis since this pattern appears with great frequency on early nineteenth-century Finnish and Estonian examples of complex, stranded patterns. Insofar as Fair Isle knitting is concerned, apart from these 1850 pieces, the openwork pattern is never seen again.

Geometric progression Could the early repertoire of Fair Isle patterns really have developed from a single starting point like the OXO band on the 1850 cap or similar garment? Some people may find it incredible, but the answer is plainly yes. If the Fair Isle patterns are regarded as a fixed body of static designs, a single point of departure does seem unlikely, but the patterns are not at all static. Rather they represent a related series or progression—the result of simple, experimental variations on a given starting point, within certain geometric and technical constraints.

This concept of geometric progression is central to the development of the Fair Isle patterns. The starting point is the lozenge of the OXO motif, and the constraints are created by the need for symmetry and the lozenge's shape. For a pattern to be large enough to fill the lozenge efficiently and yet be symmetrical, it must be an octagon or a cross.

This sounds complicated, but look at the charts on p. 21, and you will see that it is quite simple. This progression is nothing more than a series of slight, developing changes in a symmetrical design.

The best proof is to try it. Take some graph paper, draw several crosses or octagons, as shown, and make a pattern. Then create a series of new patterns, making small changes each time. Within half an hour you will see all the early Fair Isle patterns emerge, from the Moorish cross to all manner of cryptic-looking symbols. But there is nothing Moorish or cryptic about these patterns. They are logical developments—variations on a theme. This is the sort of progression that naturally comes about as a knitter tires of one pattern and begins to make minor changes. It is impossible to know whether this development took place as the knitter worked or if there was any preplanning.

How many women founded the art, we will never know. It could have been a group of knitters or one particularly talented individual who inspired the others. From one viewpoint, these knitters could be accused of timidity in their rigid adherence to a limited geometric format. Yet they showed quiet common sense in working with a technique totally suited to the art of knitting and with which they created a body of work with a definite identity. The dazzling illusion of complexity in this work is achieved by juggling a very small number of variables.

A foreseeable objection to my theory might be that since mainland Shetland had even more direct connections with the Baltic countries than Fair Isle and had equally expert knitters, why didn't a similar kind of stranded knitting develop there? The answer has to do with economics. The knitters of mainland Shetland had suffered from the slump in the hosiery market around 1800. About 1839, efforts began to be made to find a suitable alternative by promoting and marketing Shetland lace knitting in the south of England. The venture was highly successful, and mainland Shetlanders had no need to look beyond this proven successor to hosiery. Remember also the lowly, uncouth status of Fair Isle, which was probably an important factor in the development of its art. Remote from the market forces, the islanders had more freedom to experiment than their mainland cousins.

Although my own theory of the origin of Fair Isle knitting cannot be proved for certain, those who disagree with it should now be in an excellent position to develop their own hypotheses. My theory does not allow for any element of surprise, mystery or cryptic symbolism. It does, however, acknowledge a hardworking, practical people with generations of knitting expertise who lived in proximity to an area where a stranded-knitting revolution took place. That the Fair Isle women came in contact with this development is logical, not surprising. That such avid knitters tried stranded knitting was inevitable. That they should eventually give their island's name to an entire style of knitting is a tribute to their skill and tenacity—and to a master stroke of marketing that will be described shortly.

The color of money

Except perhaps a few individuals in the town of Lerwick, the Shetland girls do not prosecute knitting as a trade or means of livelihood. They have many other things to do.... Each family has with the cottage, a small croft or farm of four to six acres; the work belonging to which is done, in by far the larger proportion, by the females. The produce of the soil may in favourable seasons, maintain the family in oatmeal, potatoes and milk. Every other comfort or necessity is produced by the labour of spinning and knitting, while fishing generally pays the rent. You will never see a Shetland female without knitting in her hand—while talking to you she is busy working.
—*Anonymous Shetlander, 1861*

And it hardly ever happens that the poor people see the colour of money. They have to take out the value of their manufactures in goods, so that the merchant or shopkeeper may have a double profit on the transaction.
—*Benjie's Tour in Shetland, 1870*

These two quotations summarize the economic system of Shetland throughout the last century—a system in which the staples of fishing, crofting and knitting frequently yielded goods instead of "the color of money." This method of barter was often made compulsory by the local merchants and was known as the Truck System.

The system was simple. A knitter who had made a shawl, for example, took it to a local merchant, who appraised its value. She received goods (usually groceries, clothing or fabric by the yard) equal to the shawl's value. If she did not then take the full amount of goods due her, she took an IOU, which could be exchanged later for whatever she needed.

This system drew mixed response among knitters. It was hated by some and tolerated by others, depending on the individual's financial situation. The merchants believed that the system was vital. They claimed that because they were generous in appraising the knitters' work, they made no profit whatsoever by trading it to city dealers. Their only profit, they said, came on the goods sold or exchanged over their counters. Certain influential Shetlanders found the merchants' claims difficult to believe and delivered evidence to the government-appointed Truck Commission that "the existence of Truck in an oppressive form is general in all the staple trades in the

The OXO framework

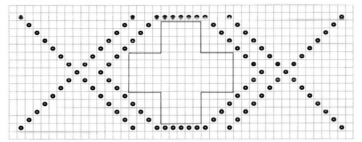 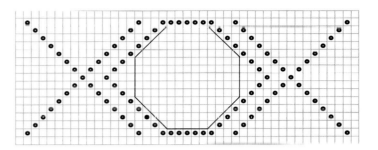

In order to fill the lozenge of the OXO framework (shown in blue above) and have the required symmetry, the motif has to have either a cross or an octagonal framework. This is the starting point for geometric progression. The charts below are examples of a series of designs developed from the cross (above) and the octagon (right).

Geometric progression

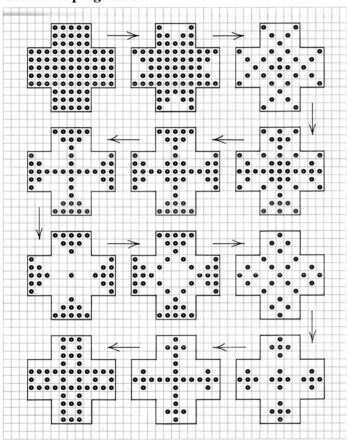 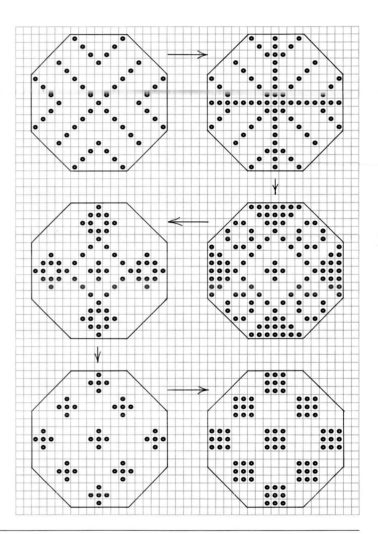

Shetland woman knitting while carrying peat in a creel for heating.

needed food. The merchant IOUs became a secondary form of currency in Shetland.

This may not be the only courtroom drama about knitting, but it certainly has to be the most serious and vital in the issues it raised. Ironically, the report yielded by the investigation caused the immediate demise of the Truck System in the fishing trade but not in the knitting industry, where it lingered on until World War II.

The century turns

As the twentieth century began, Fair Isle knitting was still regarded as a curiosity by the outside world—outlandish souvenirs for travelers to take home. The marketing of this knitting was localized and haphazard, its commercial value small, and its status as fashionwear nil. Yet 25 years later, Fair Isle knitting was worn by royalty and the "bright young things" of the Flapper Era. It gained cult status among the smart set at the universities of Oxford and Cambridge. And it came to dominate the Shetland knitting scene in the 1920s, which caused the terms *Fair Isle knitting* and *Shetland knitting* to become almost synonymous. The uncouth country cousin had, in effect, become the head of the family.

Three things account for this turn of events. First, the popularity of Shetland knitted lace, which had fully occupied the mainland knitters from around 1840 to the turn of the century, began to decline in the early 1900s. By 1910, the ready availability of less expensive machine-made lace erased the demand for all but the very finest handmade lace from the island of Unst. The mainland knitters were faced with dwindling orders and the need to find a successor to lace knitting.

Second, there was a fundamental change in fashion just after World War I. Stiff collars and corsets were shed in favor of more comfortable, practical clothing and the liberated styles of the 1920s. The fisher gansey, for example, previously regarded as strictly a working man's garment, became the basis for a full range of leisure sweaters for the wealthy and middle classes.

Third, given this change in fashion, an important marketing event took place in 1921. The Lerwick draper James A. Smith presented HRH The Prince of Wales with a Fair Isle pullover, which he wore at the St. Andrews Golf Club (see the top photo on the facing page). This gift was a conscious effort to stimulate

Islands." The result was a special investigation rigorously pursued by Sheriff W. Guthrie of Glasgow, who chaired hearings throughout Shetland in 1872.

Sheriff Guthrie's questioning of about 270 witnesses revealed much of interest about the role of knitting in Shetland in the late nineteenth century. Evidence presented at the hearings showed that there were girls in Lerwick who were penniless and without food other than tea and bread but nonetheless magnificently dressed in clothing they had received in payment for their knitting. Women equally well dressed occasionally drifted into casual prostitution due to lack of money. Women from Lerwick would traipse about the island, trying to barter the tea that they had obtained for their knitting for much-trade since it was known that the youthful Prince of Wales made it his mission to "meet the people" and that his personality and position guaranteed worldwide fascination with every aspect of his life. Circling the globe in the 1920s, he was considered by many the British Empire's premier traveling salesman!

The Prince's ability as a salesman was not restricted to textiles. The proprietor of the financially beleaguered Café de Paris, for example, telephoned and begged the Prince to make an appearance to boost business. The Prince complied, and the place became fashionable again overnight. His wearing of a Fair Isle pullover had the same effect on the Shetland knitting industry. This was undoubtedly the single most important event in the commercialization of Fair Isle knitting.

The Prince's golfing outfit of a Fair Isle pullover and plus fours became so popular among undergraduates at Oxford and Cambridge that it was considered almost a uniform. By the late 1920s, Fair Isle pullovers, cardigans, gloves and tams were worn by all. This commercialization of the industry marked the adoption and development of the Fair Isle technique by the mainland Shetland knitters.

From its beginnings to the 1920s, Fair Isle knitting had changed very little. In the 1920s, however, the mainland Shetland knitters were quick to experiment with both color and pattern. Chemical dyes had become widely available in the 1920s, and the Prince of Wales' pullover is a good example of the Shetlanders'

Above, the portrait by John St. Helier Lander of HRH The Prince of Wales in his Fair Isle pullover. The sweater uses typical OXO bands set between small block-and-wave patterns. At left, a Fair Isle sweater, dated 1903, originally a gansey and later made into a cardigan, which shows sophisticated experimentation with small OXO's and peeries.

experimentation with color. It introduced orange and green, setting them against an innovative fawn background.

New patterns appeared throughout the 1920s, most of them either small peerie patterns (one to seven rows) or border patterns (nine to thirteen rows). Examples of these are shown on pp. 36-37. Many of these patterns were identical to embroidered sampler patterns, which proliferated from the late nineteenth century on. Drapers stocked embroidery pattern books, and knitters either copied or adapted the more symmetrical patterns, along with some small asymmetrical patterns, like the anchor, heart, crown and clover leaf. Although experimentation with peerie and border patterns dominated, there was also some development in allover patterns during this period.

While knitters were adding more colors to the patterns in the 1920s, they continued to work them in tune with the symmetry of the pattern. This practice is apparent from the knitted Fair Isle samplers, like those in the photo below, kept by shop merchants to indicate to their knitters the requirements for individual orders.

The influence of the local merchant was paramount in the development of the technique. It was he (note the gender) who set the high standards of quality. (Contemporary knitter Nancy Johnson, from Cunningsburgh, Shetland, who learned the Fair Isle technique in the 1920s, recalls the local merchant in-

Reproductions of merchant samplers from the 1920s, below, show the early and crude use of chemical dyes as well as new border patterns, many copied from embroidery patterns popular at the time. On the facing page, a Fair Isle pullover from about 1925, which emphasizes the natural white background in its design.

structing her so well that when she *did* make an error, she thereafter "never made the same mistake again.") It was also the merchant who kept abreast of the market demands of the southern wholesaler and provided the knitters with exacting specifications of style, pattern and color for their orders. He did not, however, provide the knitters any written instructions for the garments. To this day, a Shetland knitter has only her collection of pattern graphs by way of written instruction. The idea of working from step-by-step patterns is completely alien to these knitters.

The knitters' skill is not surprising, since Shetland girls learned to knit from as early as four years of age, and by six often produced small articles for sale. In time, many knitters were able to work more than 100 stitches a minute with no loss in quality. Their remarkable speed resulted from the fact that in the average crofting family, the girls were relied upon to provide "goods for the table."

Although payment through the Truck System was miserly, it was so vital to the family economy that many knitters were obliged, in addition to their daily chores, to complete one Fair Isle sweater per week. To do this, the knitter had to finish the garment by Friday evening at the latest to allow time for it to be dressed, that is, washed and dried on the woolly board (see pp. 108-109) and ready for the merchant on Saturday.

Just as World War I had benefitted the Shetland knitters by heralding lasting changes

Doubtless dictated by the merchant samplers, the patterns on this Shetland piece from the 1930s, shown in the photo at top, are typical of commercial work of the period. The back of a V-neck vest from the late 1940s, above, shows a Norwegian tessellated pattern, a popular design after World War II.

in fashion, World War II brought them further economic benefits. With Shetland and its surrounding waters of strategic importance, the islands once again saw a "confluence of foreigners," this time in the form of naval servicemen with money to spend on presents for their families. The servicemen placed private orders with the knitters and paid them fairer sums in cash, so the merchants were forced to improve their pay to the knitters. This development almost instantly killed the truck system. By the 1940s the knitters were on a par with—and sometimes better off than—the women who worked in the banks and offices of Lerwick.

As well as forcing economic improvement for the knitters, private commerce gave them an artistic freedom that they had rarely enjoyed before and furthered their mastery of pattern and color combination. World War II also contributed to the expanding body of patterns by introducing several new ones, principally in the form of stars and some tessellated patterns, brought directly from Norway by sailors and refugees.

Although royal patronage and wars seem unlikely influences, they were nonetheless critical forces in Fair Isle knitting's artistic and commercial success in the world. The next major influence on Fair Isle knitting was even more improbable. By the 1970s, the Shetland waters were again found to contain riches much in demand by the world, hungry this time not for fish, but for oil.

Into the Oil Age

For Shetland knitters, the postwar era was the age of the machine. In the late 1950s, the hand frame-knitting machine became available for home use. Within a few years many Shetland knitters had invested in a machine to keep up with the mass production of knitwear, which was then in full swing. The immediate result of this was the introduction of the circular-yoke sweater. This garment was an ideal combination of machine and hand knitting. It was quick to produce, yet still retained the hand-knit touch.

Unfortunately, these sweaters did not reflect Fair Isle knitting at its best. Color was used in a more limited and less imaginative way; patterning was usually a single border in a peerie frame, or a large star separated by trees. The monotonous designs were the very antithesis of the Fair Isle tradition. These mass-produced, circular-yoke sweaters were particularly popular in France, and by the early 1970s the great bulk of Shetland production was geared to this market. This overspecialization was unfortunate since the French market declined drastically in the same decade. The Fair Isle knitting industry again found itself in trouble.

Even more drastic events were on the horizon. The waters east of Shetland were being explored, since undersea oil had been discovered there in the early 1970s. Suddenly oil development took command of the entire scene, and once again Shetland played host to a confluence of foreigners—this time with names like Conoco, Amoco, Mobil and Texaco. As the oil fields opened, Bressay Sound again became crowded—not with fishing boats, but with oil-rig supply ships. Supply bases mushroomed at Lerwick, the airport at Sumburgh was upgraded to international standards, and work on a huge oil refinery was begun at Sullom Voe. Construction workers flooded in, and "The Voe" became legendary for the size of its pay packets.

The mid-1970s were boom years. Workers descended on Lerwick from all over Great Britain, and its streets and bars hummed with the same sort of activity as when the Dutch fishing fleets arrived in the eighteenth cen-

A detail of a circular-yoke sweater, knitted in 1986 by machine and hand, in the bland, mass-produced style typical of the 1960s and 1970s.

Signs of the times: the Oil Age comes to Sullom Voe in the 1970s. The discovery of North Sea oil brought prosperity to Shetland's economy and, for a time, a sharp decline in the local knitwear industry.

tury. The Sullom Voe field came on line in 1978, and within seven years Shetland accounted for 2.5% of world oil production.

Some Shetlanders cursed the oil and all it brought. The sound of Chinook helicopters mingled with the bleating of sheep on the hill. Suddenly a pint of beer in even the most modest Lerwick bar cost the same as in an expensive London hotel. Nonetheless, no one can deny that there have been benefits. Roads have been upgraded to a standard that amazes visitors from other Scottish islands. In a time of savage cuts in education budgets, Shetland schools are abundantly supplied with new books and equipment. Shetland unemployment is among the lowest in Scotland.

The effect of Shetland's oil boom on knitting was considerable. Knitters—or their husbands—could find well-paid employment in oil-related industries, and many gave up knitting commercially. Young people, like most kids today, with their high hopes and expectations, found that the financial rewards of knitting paled in comparison to the possibilities in the oil fields.

Despite this turn of events, the spark did not fully go out. Shetland primary schools have taught Fair Isle knitting technique since the early 1960s, and the skill of some girls has proven remarkable. Sheep farming in Shetland

also rose steadily during this period, from 264,779 animals in 1971 to 329,912 in 1986. In the same year, wool production stood at about 300,000 kilograms, or 661,300 pounds.

At the same time that the oil industry was luring knitters away from their handiwork, however, hand knitting suddenly became fashionable in Great Britain. The pages of British *Vogue* magazine were crowded with the "ethnic look," which prominently featured handmade knitwear; and for the first time hand knits retailed for high prices in London and other cities. With Fair Isle knitting in high fashion, many small producers sprang up all over Britain, claiming to produce Fair Isle garments. Some used the very latest in industrial technology—machines that produced "Fair Isle" patterns—but the quality and artistry of the results were usually vastly inferior to the genuine article.

Shetland joined this knitwear boom, and new businesses, from one-person operations to substantial factories, produced a range of traditional and contemporary styles, most of them made by machine. In 1986, there were about 50 such Shetland businesses, which produced about 450,000 garments, worth about £6.4 million wholesale. About half this total production came from one large Lerwick factory with electronic machines. Significantly, only 5% of the total was knitted by hand. In fact, the number of Shetland home knitters decreased from 2,268 in 1971 to just 1,200 in 1981. Since then the number has risen slightly and in 1986 stood at around 2,000. This rise, however, reflects an increase in domestic machine knitting rather than an upsurge in hand knitting.

An initiative to revitalize the Shetland knitting industry began in 1983 with the establishment of the Shetland Knitwear Trades Association. This association, financed by local government, is a marketing and promotional organization that aims to introduce Shetland knitwear into new markets, like Japan. While such markets will doubtless prove profitable, they nonetheless call for products standardized in color, size and design, which leaves little room for individual artistry.

Among the first problems the association addressed was the misuse of the terms *Shetland* and *Fair Isle*. The former is often found on labels of garments produced as far away as Japan simply because they contain a percentage of Shetland wool; the latter is frequently applied to any kind of stranded knitting. The

Two Lerwick boys in machine-made Fair Isle sweaters unknowingly keep the tradition alive. In 1986, machine-knitted garments accounted for about 95% of Shetland's total commercial knitwear production.

new association has countered such misuse by introducing a new trademark, The Shetland Lady, which is to be carried only on garments genuinely produced in Shetland.

Some hand knitters see these developments as part of the inevitable march of progress; others are saddened by them and feel that the factories are pirating the hand knitters' hard-won reputation. As a result, some knitters have struck out on their own and produce private orders using their own labels.

Today Shetland is at a crossroads. The first flush of the oil boom is over, and no one is sure what the future holds. In recent years, Shetland has seen its first air and tanker disasters, the latter causing massive destruction of wildlife. As I write this, the radio brings news that a Chinook has crashed into the sea near Sumburgh, with the loss of more than 40 lives— Europe's worst helicopter disaster ever.

Today in Lerwick, past and present mingle in a fascinating mix. Along the same narrow streets where women once traded their knitted handiwork for bread and tea, you now see groups of self-confident, young Shetland girls with punk hairdos, laughing together on a Saturday afternoon. Nearby, merchants' signs announce the presence of drapers in the same buildings their grandfathers occupied a hundred years before them. Just a few yards away, you can buy goods of every description: a Fair Isle sweater, an electric guitar, a pair of oil-rig boots, a Nikon camera, a Chinese meal or a badge protesting against the nuclear reprocessing plant that may soon be polluting Shetland waters.

Bearing testimony to the fact that the Oil Age has not entirely extinguished the genuine art of Fair Isle knitting, this 1986 sweater, designed by Annabel Bray, displays an elaborate use of border patterns, some of them asymmetrical.

Down at the harbor's edge, among the nets and large, modern fishing boats, seagulls dive over the same Bressay Sound where Norse battle fleets, Dutch herring boats, English men-of-war and French privateers lay at anchor. Look around, and there is the Lerwick motorbike contingent, clad in denim and leather, sitting astride Hondas and Yamahas while eating fish and chips. But under the leather jacket of one of these bikers, beneath the trendy black coat of one of the spikey-haired teenage girls, on a fisherman at the harbor or on any Shetlander going about the day's business, there might be an example of the art that originated on the small island just a few miles away. Many of the Fair Isle garments one sees these days may well be machine made or a little disappointing in quality, but every now and then there will be an example that strikes the eye and proclaims that, with someone, somewhere, the art is alive and well. The aim of this book is to make that someone be you.

Scenes of Shetland today, where past and present mingle, including the remains of Scalloway Castle (below left), built in the 1600s for Scottish earl and notorious despot Patrick Stewart ("Black Pate").

Pattern and color are the hallmarks of Fair Isle knitting. Patterns can be traditional, like the OXO patterns in the swatch above, or they can be

Pattern

variations on the classics or entirely original.

During the 140 or so years that Fair Isle knitting has been practiced, a wealth of patterns has emerged. Some of these—like the Fair Isle OXO's, certain border and peerie patterns, Norwegian stars and the tessellated allover patterns—have become classics. Most knitters keep their own personal collections of patterns, which include not only these classics and their endless variations but also original patterns created from experimentation with geometric shapes (see pp. 19-20) and patterns copied or adapted from any suitable source.

In order for a pattern to qualify for inclusion in the Fair Isle repertoire, it must satisfy two important practical requirements. First, the pattern and background yarns—there will be only two colors used in any one row—must change frequently along each row. The reason for this is simple. In stranded knitting, the yarn that is not being used is carried, or "stranded," across the back of the work (see the drawing on p. 95). In order to produce a firm, even fabric of double

Charted patterns from 1850 museum pieces

These patterns are drawn from two 1850 museum examples of Fair Isle knitting (see also p. 17). In the top pattern, the O's and X's of each band are placed one directly above another. In the bottom example, the O's and X's are transposed.

	white
o	red
●	blue
▪	gold

Pattern with vertically aligned OXO's

Pattern with transposed OXO's

thickness, the strands should be short. Changing frequently from pattern to background yarns along each row ensures short strands, and therefore most Fair Isle patterns have a maximum stretch of seven stitches in one color. It is possible to have a pattern with a longer run of one color—13 stitches would be the limit—but such runs would be confined to one or two rows within the whole pattern. (For a run longer than seven stitches, the yarn not in use would need to be woven in at the center stitch of the run, as shown on p. 96, to avoid an excessively long strand.)

The second requirement of a Fair Isle pattern is that it contain diagonal lines, which are especially important in large patterns. Tension is created between pattern and background yarns at the points in the row at which the yarns change. Diagonal lines of color distribute this tension by varying the change-over points of the yarns from one row to the next. Consequently, patterns with diagonal lines produce a fabric that is firm, but elastic. By contrast, in a pattern with vertical blocks of color, the tension builds up at the consistent changeover points, producing a fabric that is less elastic. Vertical lines should therefore be kept to a minimum in Fair Isle patterns, and when used, should be broken up after a few rows.

In addition to these two characteristics, most Fair Isle patterns have an odd number of rows and are symmetrical. Although pattern symmetry does not affect the structure or quality of the fabric, it produces aesthetically pleasing results and has practical advantages. These patterns are easier than asymmetrical ones to create, vary, memorize and knit.

The best examples of patterns combining diagonal lines with frequent changes of yarn in each row are those found in the earliest Fair Isle garments, charted at left (see also p. 17 for a photo and full description of these pieces). These patterns are all based on the OXO form, which has four lines of symmetry—that is, this form produces an exact mirror image when cut in half vertically, horizontally and diagonally (see p. 13). The chart at the top of the facing page shows the basic OXO form and how it is used as a basis for a Fair Isle pattern.

Patterns with little or no symmetry also work well for Fair Isle knitting, provided the two fundamental requirements are observed, as they are in the two examples in the middle of the facing page. The first chart shows a pattern of stylized flower vases and crowns, a nice example of a pattern with one line of symmetry. The second chart illustrates a good asymmetrical pattern. You can see that the asymmetry of the base of the repeat and scrolled element on either side of the "star" preclude any mirror images in this pattern. While patterns with little or no symmetry often produce visually pleasing results, they are more difficult to remember and therefore slower to knit than symmetrical patterns.

Types of patterns

Fair Isle patterns fall into one of several broad categories, based on the number of rows that make up the pattern and on the pattern's use. The groupings include large Fair Isles (OXO's), peeries (small patterns used in arrangements with other patterns), borders (used singly or in combination with other patterns), seeding (small filler patterns), waves and peaks (patterns used to shade and set off the patterns they surround), Norwegian stars (large patterns shaped, as their name suggests, like stars), and allover (tessellated) patterns. In addition to the charted pattern examples presented in each of the categories below, you will find an ample library of patterns at the end of this chapter.

Large Fair Isle patterns These are the original, elaborate OXO patterns that marked the beginning of the art on Fair Isle. They are worked over 17 or 19 rows and consist of six-sided or eight-sided lozenge shapes (O), linked horizontally by crosses (X). These large Fair Isle patterns can be worked in either of two ways. The lozenge can be defined in the pattern color, with the inner design worked in the background shade, as shown in the first half of the bottom chart at right (this was the most common style used on Fair Isle). Alternatively, the lozenge can be worked in the background color, with the inner design knit in the pattern shade, as shown in the second half of the same chart.

Large Fair Isle patterns are traditionally used in horizontal bands, placed either directly one above the other or transposed, as in the charted patterns on the facing page. One solid row of the background color is generally worked before and after each pattern band. Large Fair Isle patterns are also often worked with small peerie patterns between the horizontal bands.

Basic OXO form (shaded) with a typical OXO pattern

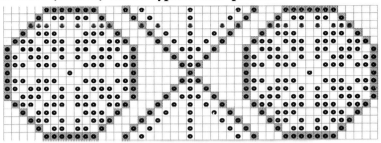

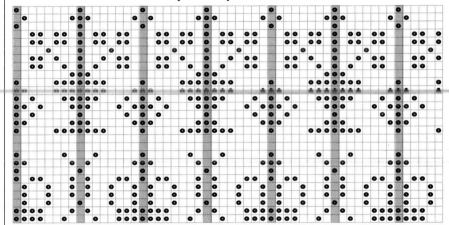

Patterns with one line of symmetry

Shading represents one line of vertical symmetry.

Pattern with no lines of symmetry

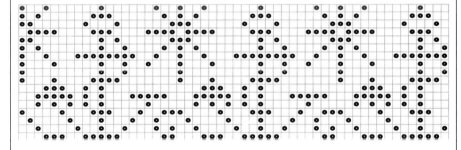

Inner lozenge design worked in background color   **Inner lozenge design worked in pattern color**

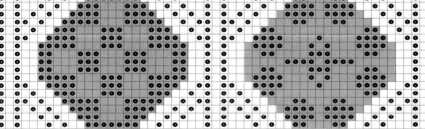

Peerie patterns *Peerie* is a Scottish word meaning "small," hence the name given to the smallest Fair Isle patterns, which consist of one to seven rows. In addition to separating large Fair Isle patterns, peeries are often used in horizontal arrangements with border patterns (see the charts below and on the facing page). Peeries can also be used vertically in panel arrangements with border patterns. (See, for example, the panel arrangement on p. 39 of peerie, border, seeding and Norwegian star patterns.)

Border patterns Border patterns have 9 to 15 rows. Many are based on the OXO form and are found in early examples of Fair Isle knitting. Many other borders, both symmetrical and asymmetrical, have been added over the years.

As their name suggests, these patterns are often used as single bands on garment borders. However, they are most frequently used in horizontal arrangements with peerie patterns, repeated throughout a garment, as in the chart below. They can also be used in vertical arrangements.

The horizontal border-and-peerie format offers great scope in terms of design, from a

Peerie pattern

Popular border pattern

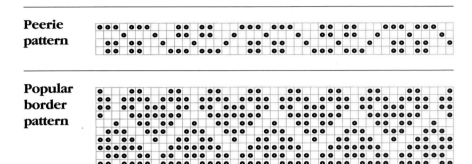

Repeated peerie-and-border pattern arrangement

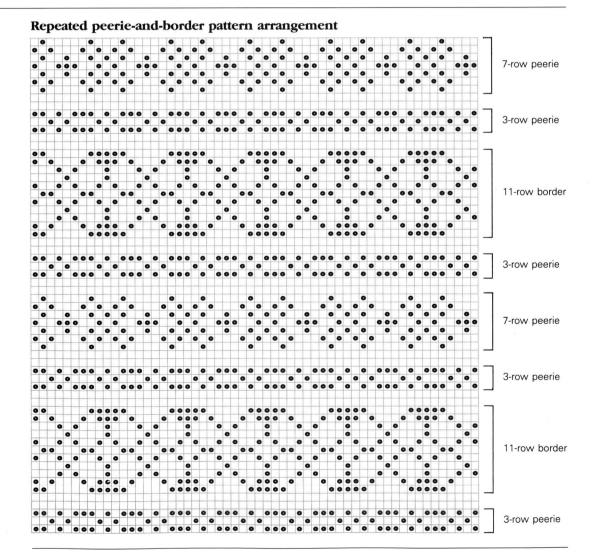

7-row peerie

3-row peerie

11-row border

3-row peerie

7-row peerie

3-row peerie

11-row border

3-row peerie

single border alternating with a single peerie to much more complex arrangements. The chart at the bottom of the facing page, for example, illustrates an arrangement of a 3-row peerie / 11-row border / 3-row peerie / 7-row peerie, repeated throughout. Other possible configurations could be slightly more complex, for instance, a 1/9/1/3/13/3 repeat, as shown in the chart below, or as complicated as a 1/7/1/5/9/5/1/7/1/3/13/3 repeat. Large OXO patterns can also be worked with a peerie-and-border arrangement, as for example, in a 5/13/5/19 repeat or a 3/15/3/1/17/1 repeat.

Still further variation can be added by working a different pattern on some or all the patterns at each repeat. In the chart below, different 9-row and 13-row patterns are worked throughout. The border patterns could also remain the same throughout, with a different peerie pattern used at each repeat, or all the patterns could change. This last alternative, however, is best kept to fairly simple arrangements. Complex arrangements will be more aesthetically unified if there is some pattern repetition—for example, if the same peerie is used throughout the piece.

Peerie-and-border pattern arrangement with changing border pattern

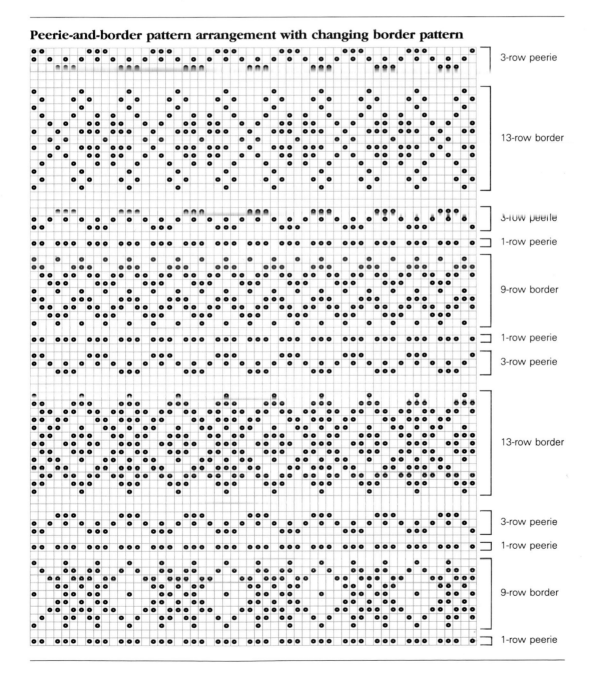

A typical seeding pattern

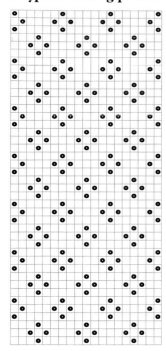

Seeding These small patterns, like the ones in the chart at left, are used mainly on the palms of gloves and mittens, or between the larger patterns of panel garments. Rather than serving as patterns in their own right, seeding serves as filler, keeping both pattern and background yarns in use between larger patterns. However, this does not mean that seeding is unattractive as a design element. It warrants careful consideration when planning a pattern arrangement.

Waves and peaks Waves and peaks are used to shade colors from light to dark and from dark to light. This makes it possible for the patterns around them to appear on alternating dark and light backgrounds. Border and peerie patterns are most commonly used with waves and peaks.

The chart below left shows a waved pattern with an 11-row border worked on the light ground and a 5-row peerie worked on the dark ground. The chart below right illustrates a peaked pattern with the same 15-row border worked on both light and dark ground. If you study these charts carefully, you will see that waved patterns are shaped, as their name suggests, like waves; peaked patterns are diamond-shaped. While waves and peaks never change shape (and hence are not included in the Pattern Library at the end of this chapter), they can be enlarged. Generally speaking, they are used at the scale presented here and are varied by combining them with different border and peerie patterns.

Because waved patterns repeat over four stitches, they are best combined with patterns that also repeat over four, or a multiple of four, stitches. The border and peerie patterns in the chart below left, for example, repeat over 12 stitches.

Since peaks repeat over six stitches, they work best with patterns that likewise repeat over six, or a multiple of six, stitches. The border patterns in the chart below right, for example, repeat over 18 stitches.

Waved pattern with border and peerie patterns

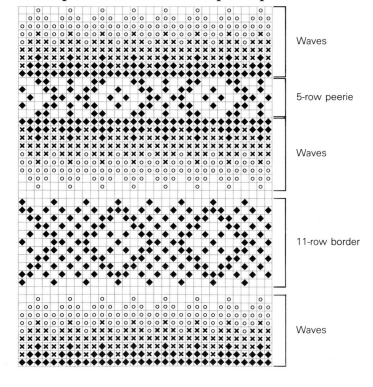

Waves

5-row peerie

Waves

11-row border

Waves

Peaked pattern with border pattern

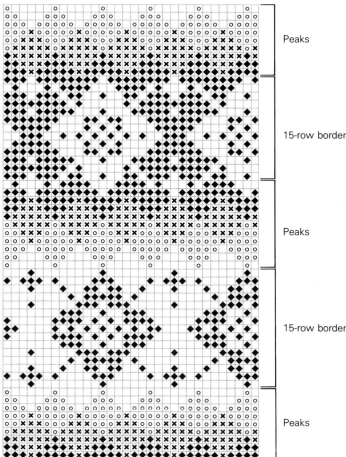

Peaks

15-row border

Peaks

15-row border

Peaks

FRANKLIN LAKES PUBLIC LIBRARY

Norwegian stars Norwegian stars are always worked over the same number of rows as stitches, usually 25, 27 or 31. They are used primarily to decorate the backs of gloves and mittens or as the main design element in circular-yoked garments. The most inventive use of Norwegian stars is in vertical panels, as the main, often central pattern in "panel garments" (see pp. 116-118 and pp. 136-139).

The chart below illustrates a pattern arrangement for a panel garment with Norwegian stars, peeries, borders and seeding. This type of arrangement can also be used horizontally, with the stars forming the yoke of the garment.

A typical Norwegian star

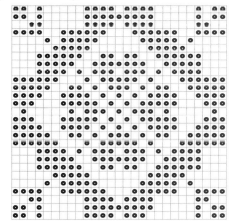

Pattern arrangement for panel garment

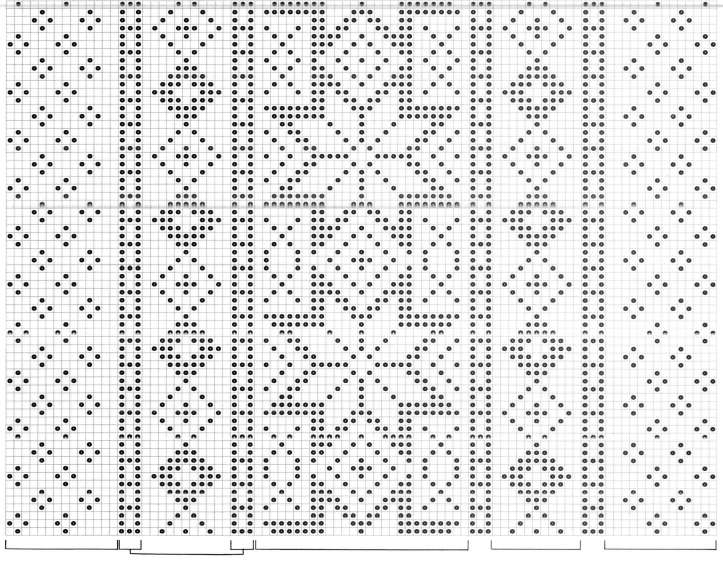

| Seeding | Peerie patterns | Norwegian star | Border pattern | Seeding |

Allover pattern 1

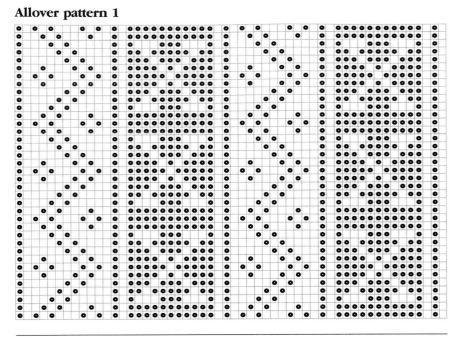

Allover pattern 2

Allover patterns *Allover* is the term used to describe the tessellated patterns that repeat continuously in both vertical and horizontal directions. They vary in size from small "diced" and Argyle patterns to the familiar larger configurations, most of which originated in Selbu, Norway.

The charts at left illustrate two popular allover patterns. It is interesting to note that the zigzag lines in the top chart may have evolved from working with OXO bands placed directly one above the other, as in the top chart on p. 34. Similarly, the pattern in the bottom chart may trace its origins to working with transposed OXO bands, as shown in the bottom chart on p. 34.

Reading pattern charts

Patterns are charted on graph paper, with each square representing one stitch and each horizontal row of squares representing one row or round of knitting. The marked squares indicate the pattern color; the empty squares indicate the background color. To knit from a chart, view it as the right side of a piece of knitting and read from right to left and from bottom to top.

To integrate individual patterns into a full garment, the size and shape of the final piece must be taken into consideration. The technical aspects of adjusting patterns to fit a given measurement are discussed below, and the entire process of designing garments is fully explored in Chapter 6.

Stitch repeats Patterns repeat horizontally over a certain number of stitches, and this number can vary widely from pattern to pattern. To chart a pattern for knitting, the horizontal stitch repeat must be identified, and the repeat should start at a central point in the pattern. In the chart at the top of the facing page, the central points are marked with arrows.

In the case of OXO patterns, the lozenge is always seen as the main feature of the design, and the X as simply a device to link the lozenges. The lozenge should therefore be placed at the center of the repeat, and the repeat should begin at the center of the X, as shown in the top chart on the facing page. With this stitch designated as stitch number one, count the stitches up to the next same,

Counting stitch repeats

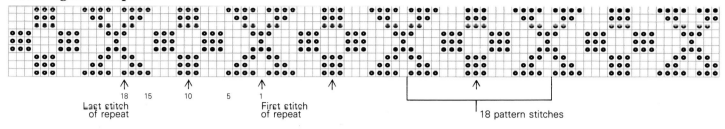

18   15   10   5   1
Last stitch   First stitch
of repeat   of repeat

18 pattern stitches

central stitch. The resulting number—in this case, 18—is the stitch repeat.

For circular knitting, stitch repeats should divide exactly into the total number of stitches in the round, so that the pattern forms a continuous circle. For example, for the pattern repeat charted at top right to be used successfully for a garment knitted in the round, the total number of stitches in the round should be exactly divisible by 18, the stitch repeat.

For flat knitting, the pattern should be centered on the work so that the first and last stitches (each side of the opening) are the same. (Cardigans fall into the flat category, since, although they are knitted in the round, the steeks—carried strands or extra knitted stitches at the front and arm-hole openings that allow the work to proceed in the round [see pp. 100-104]—are later cut open, which makes the knitting discontinuous.)

The pattern for flat knitting should be charted as shown in the middle chart at right, with an extra stitch added at the end of the round or row to complete it. If you choose not to adjust the pattern for a flat piece to fit exactly into the total number of stitches, center it, as shown in the bottom chart at right, with the extra stitches placed at each side, to be knitted at the beginning and end of the row or round.

Adjusting stitch repeats Some individual patterns or complex arrangement of patterns may have stitch repeats that do not fit exactly into the total number of stitches in the round. Usually these patterns can be adjusted to fit. OXO patterns are particularly well suited for adjustment because the O and X can be moved closer together or farther apart, as the situa-

Charting stitch repeat for circular knitting

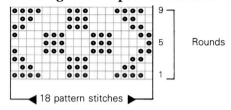

9
5   Rounds
1

◄ 18 pattern stitches ►

Charting stitch repeat for flat knitting

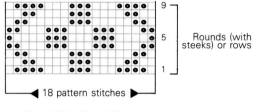

9
5   Rounds (with
    steeks) or rows
1

◄ 18 pattern stitches ►

Last stitch of round/row

Charting unadjusted stitch repeat for flat knitting

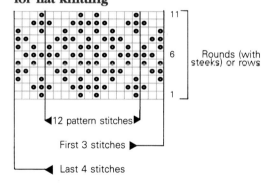

11
6   Rounds (with
    steeks) or rows
1

◄ 12 pattern stitches ►

First 3 stitches ►

◄ Last 4 stitches

tion warrants, and the X can be made larger or smaller.

The OXO pattern in the first chart below, for example, has a 34-stitch repeat. To make this repeat larger, the O and X can be moved farther apart, as shown in the second chart below. In this example, the O and X have moved one stitch farther apart, producing a 36-stitch repeat. The consequently larger space has been neatly filled with a small motif to avoid a long stretch of one color of yarn. Alternatively, the X can be redesigned and made wider, as shown in the third and fourth charts below, which produces 38-stitch and

Increasing stitch repeats

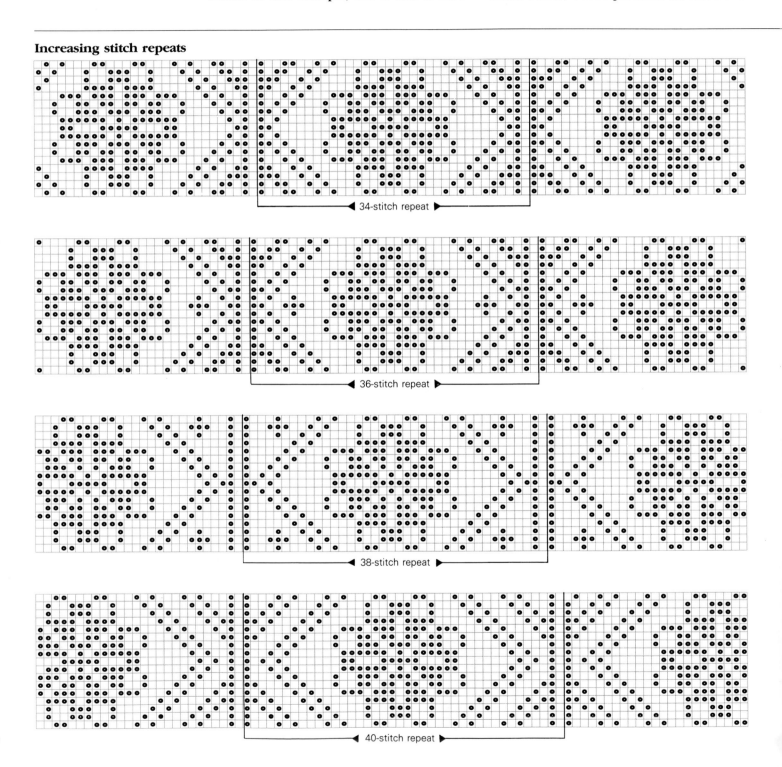

◀ 34-stitch repeat ▶

◀ 36-stitch repeat ▶

◀ 38-stitch repeat ▶

◀ 40-stitch repeat ▶

40-stitch repeats. When making pattern repeats larger, be careful to redesign them so that both background and pattern colors change frequently on each row.

To make the repeat smaller, the X can be redesigned and made narrower, as shown in the first chart below. The X can also be nar-rowed to one stitch at its center and the O moved one stitch closer, as shown in the second chart below. (This is as close as the O and X can get without merging.) In the third chart below, the X's have been reduced to shallow V's, and as a result the O's are closer together. In the fourth chart, the O's have

Decreasing stitch repeats

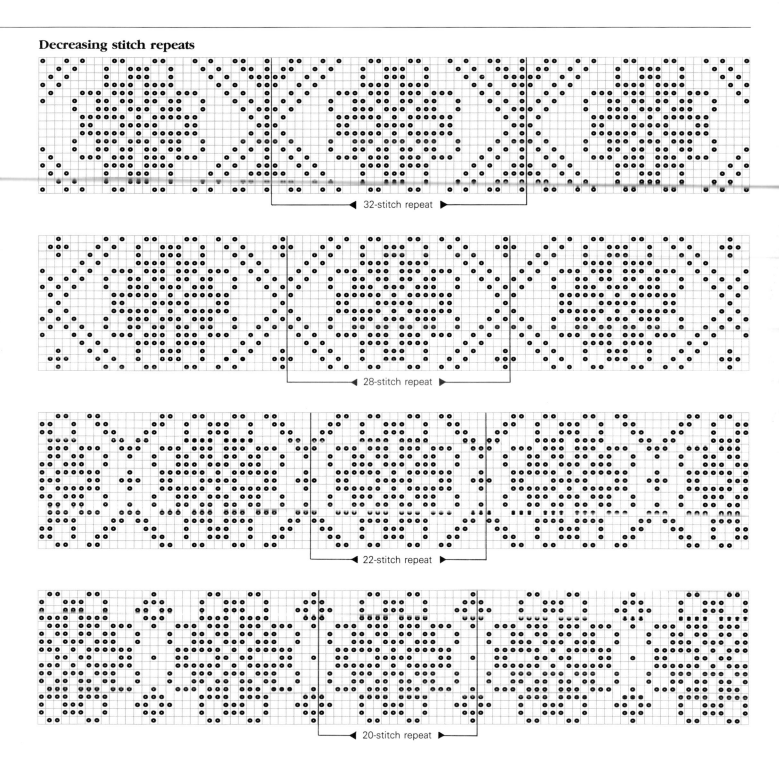

◀ 32-stitch repeat ▶

◀ 28-stitch repeat ▶

◀ 22-stitch repeat ▶

◀ 20-stitch repeat ▶

been moved still closer, and the X's are replaced with small diamond motifs. This last pattern moves farther away from the appearance of the original 34-stitch repeat and, indeed, can no longer be described as an OXO. Yet it is still an excellent pattern and a good example of how variations can come about.

Creating patterns

It is very easy to create patterns by varying a basic shape. The most obvious route to take is the one that I am convinced was taken by the first Fair Isle knitters, namely, geometric progression (see pp. 19-20). The only important points to bear in mind when varying or creating patterns are those I outlined at the beginning of this chapter: Change the pattern and background colors frequently along each row, use diagonal lines in your pattern and avoid strong verticals.

If you want to begin simply, try a diamond shape, which inherently conforms to the second rule above. The patterns shown in the chart below were constructed easily and quickly from the basic shape, keeping in mind

Creating patterns through geometric progression

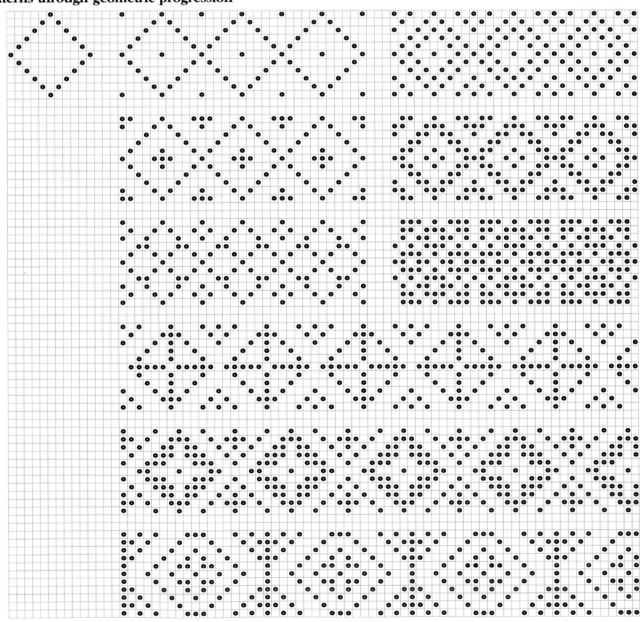

the first rule. I am sure that you can add many more patterns to this series.

Once you begin to experiment, you will quickly realize how interesting the process can be. The starting points for geometric progression can be found in amazingly diverse places. Consider the patterns shown here. I found the inspiration for the one at right on a quiet roadside near my home on the Isle of Lewis. The wildflower we call ragged robin caught my eye among the tall roadside grasses and buttercups, and I photographed it. Using graph paper and pen, I later recreated the image in this allover pattern.

The pattern below was inspired 5,000 miles from Lewis, on the other side of the Atlantic Ocean. In the aftermath of Mardi Gras, the Garden District of New Orleans was just as quiet as that Lewis roadside. The source of inspiration, however, was very different. In the ornate wrought-iron fence and vines around an old plantation house, I found the source of this highly original Fair Isle pattern.

These examples are worlds apart, but they illustrate the principle of designing Fair Isle patterns: Follow the rules, and anything goes. The Pattern Library that follows is drawn from my own collection and includes some classics, variations on these classics, and my own creations. I hope that they will inspire you to branch out in your own direction.

Overall pattern inspired by ragged robin

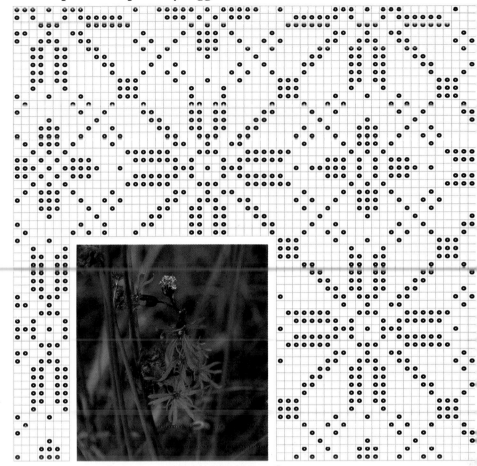

Ragged robins and buttercups along a Lewis roadside.

Pattern inspired by ironwork fence

Wrought-iron fence in the Garden District of New Orleans.

Pattern library

Peerie patterns

1-row peeries

2-row peeries

3-row peeries

49

4-row peeries

5-row peeries

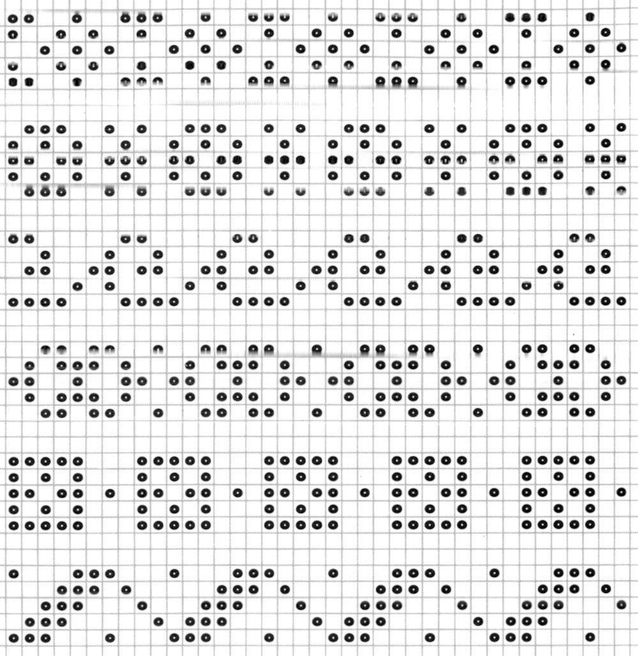

6-row peeries

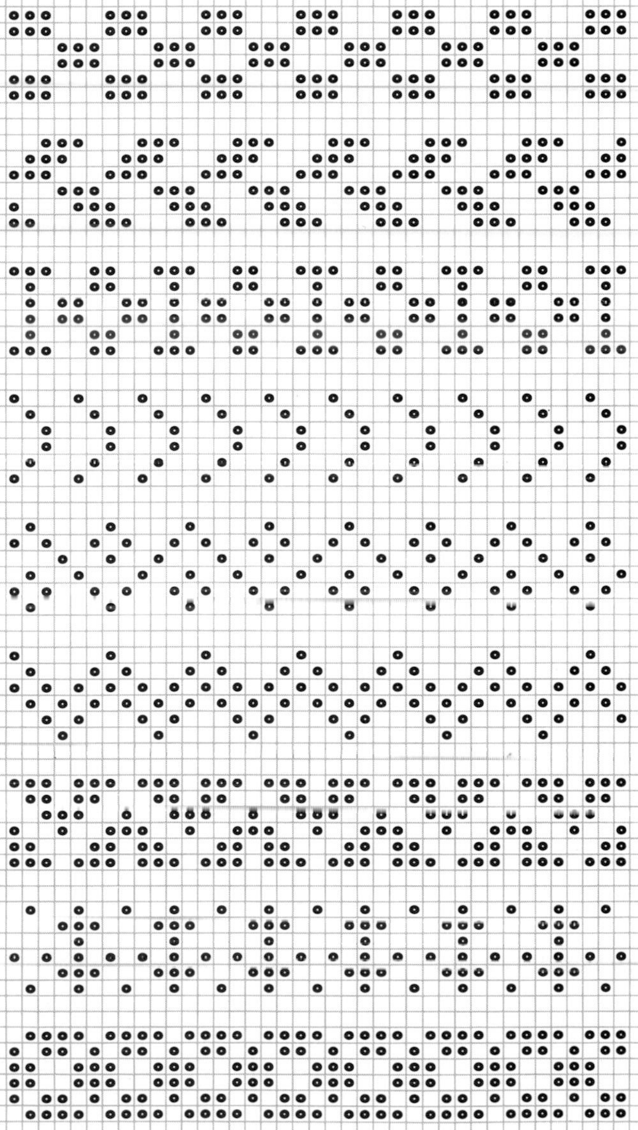

7-row peeries

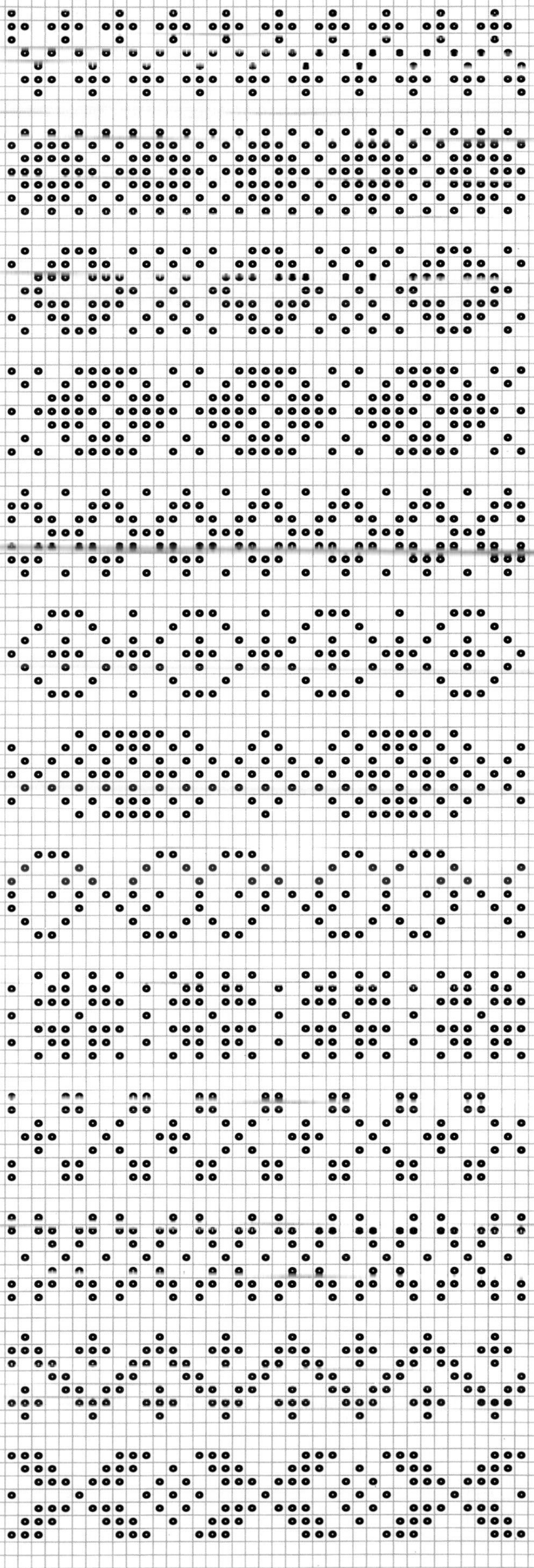

51

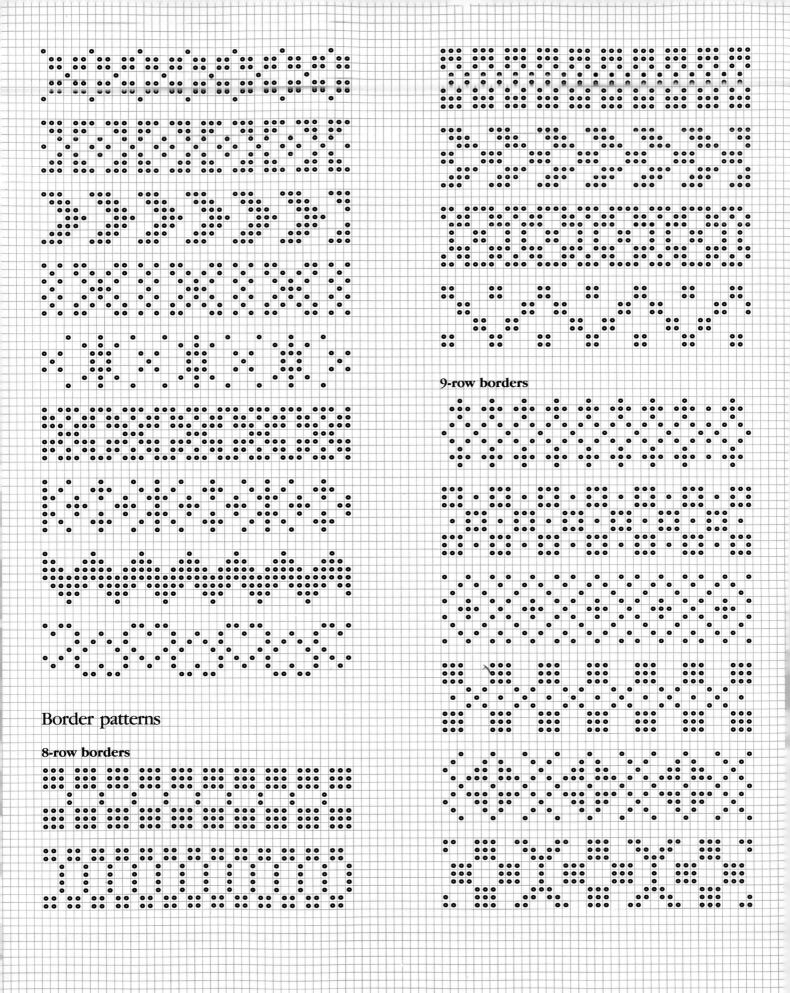

Border patterns

8-row borders

9-row borders

10-row borders

11-row borders

54

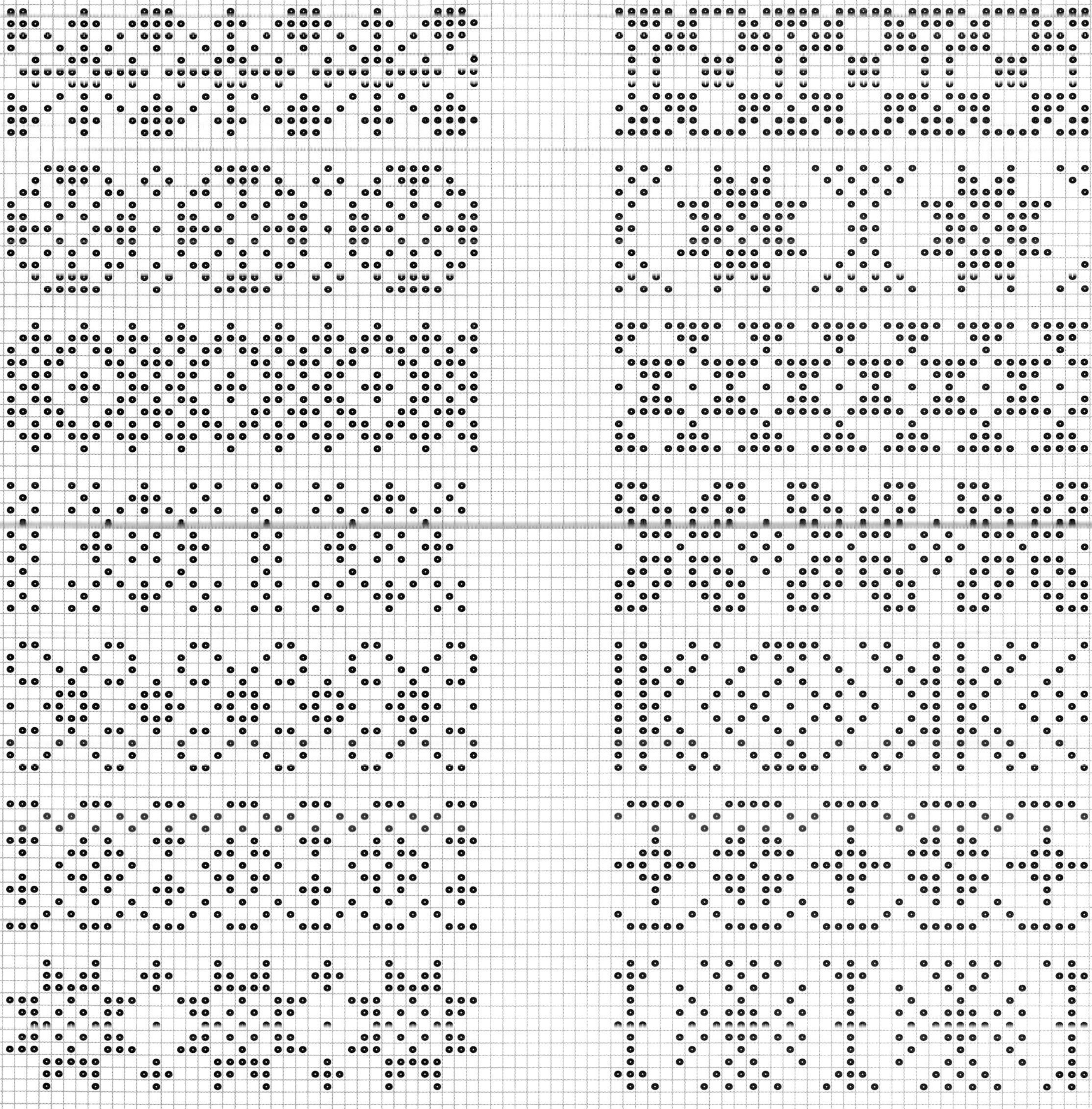

15-row borders

57

Large Fair Isle patterns

17-row patterns

19-row patterns

Allover patterns

Diced and Argyle patterns

Norwegian star patterns

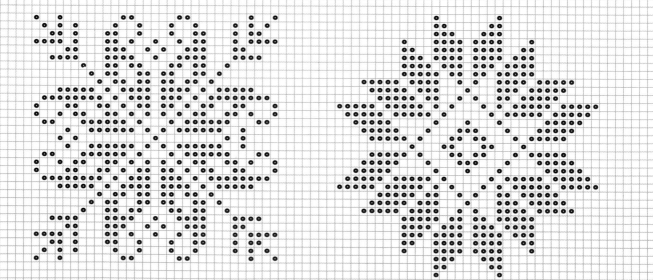

Seeding patterns

Inspiration for color and pattern in Fair Isle knitting can be found in everything that surrounds us. Sunset over Loch Achmore on the Isle of

Color

Lewis inspired the swatch above.

Mention Fair Isle knitting, and color is the first element that springs to mind. "Polychromatic," "bright, varied hues," and "painted manufacture" are some of the words and phrases used in the earliest descriptions of the art, indicating that color has been a vital feature from the outset.

In Fair Isle knitting, there is only one absolute rule about the use of color: No more than two colors—a pattern and a background color—are ever used in any one row. The reasons for this rule are both practical and aesthetic. First, given that we have only one pair of hands, restricting the colors in a row to two makes the knitting easier and faster than if many colors were used. Second, carrying more than two strands in a row produces an uneven, bulky and unattractive fabric.

The rule about color may seem severely limiting, but this is hardly the case. Both the pattern and background colors can change from row to row, and there are infinite possibilities for creating unique color schemes. Although both

Color and design

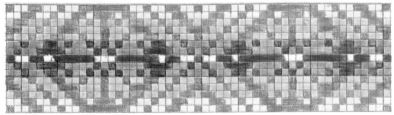

Chart 1

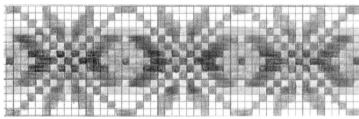

Chart 2

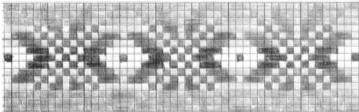

Chart 3

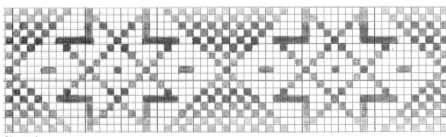

Chart 4

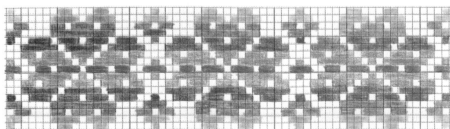

Chart 5

colors can be varied on every row of a garment, it is unnecessary to go to this extreme to create very colorful effects.

Traditionally, the use of color in Fair Isle knitting has been quite controlled; that is to say, the colors change in perfect step with the symmetry of the patterns, as in the earliest dated examples of Fair Isle knitting in museum collections (see p. 17). Although some later examples in these collections display a less sophisticated use of color (see p. 18), the practice of matching symmetry in pattern and color became fairly standard. Even when the advent of chemical dyes around 1900 made available a broader range of colors, knitters continued to observe this tradition. Today it is still a hallmark of Fair Isle knitting.

Chart 1, at left, illustrates the traditional use of color in a 15-row pattern using eight colors. Both the background and pattern colors are mirrored on either side of the center row, which itself is knitted in vividly contrasting shades. This visual emphasis on the center row or rows (sometimes there are three) is

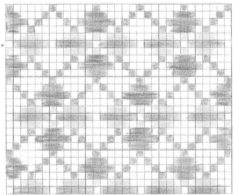

Chart 6

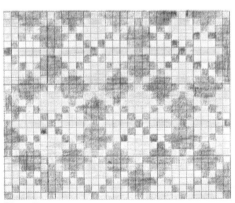

Chart 7

also a common practice, though by no means a hard-and-fast rule.

Another effective practice is the shading of colors in a pattern from light to dark and dark to light. The background in Chart 1, for example, moves from light yellow through gold to chrome toward the center. This treatment adds depth and interest to the color scheme. Chart 2 illustrates a subtle, harmonious scheme based on violet and grey, where the background is shaded from white through silver to medium grey, and the pattern from light violet through red violet to deep violet. Because the level of contrast between the background and pattern colors is fairly constant throughout, the scheme is balanced, and the pattern shows up well.

Reversing the background shading in the same design, however, produces severely unbalanced results. In Chart 3, the medium-grey background and light-violet pattern colors at the top and bottom are so similar in value that the pattern effectively disappears at these points. At the same time, the stark contrast between the white background and deep violet pattern colors at the center of the pattern makes this area appear to leap out. The lesson here is always to make sure that the level of contrast between background and pattern is sufficient but not extreme, so that the pattern remains distinct and balanced throughout.

A given color scheme can also produce different effects from pattern to pattern. Charts 4 and 5 illustrate the varying results created by the same colors used in two different 17-row patterns. In the first pattern, which consists of narrow lines, the background domiwith an overall light, delicate effect. In the second example, the solid pattern areas dominate, producing a strong, bold effect.

Colors can also be combined to convey a strong sense of mood, as seen in charts 6 through 10, which use different color schemes with the same pattern. In Chart 6, clear, light colors on a white background produce a fresh, clean image. The chalky pastels on a dusky indigo background in Chart 7 create a subtle, dreamy mood. In Chart 8, bold primary col-

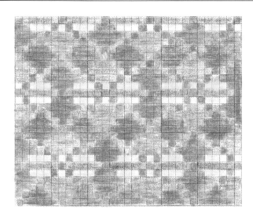

Chart 8

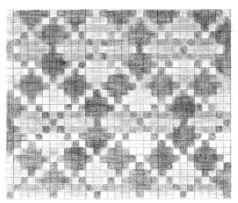

Chart 10

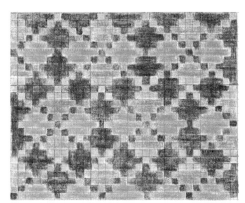

Chart 9

A color scheme does not need to be complex to be interesting. A simple scheme used deftly with an appropriate pattern, like the examples above and on the facing page, can be quite effective.

ors convey a sizzling carnival atmosphere. In Chart 9, a feeling of quiet strength and stability is produced through the use of subdued, earthy tones. In Chart 10, bright colors on a dark background create a bold, aggressive mood.

These are just a few examples of the effect of color on design. Colors can be combined in an infinite number of ways, and a single scheme can be significantly altered by changing just one or two colors. For example, a quiet, neutral scheme can be brightened by accenting the center pattern row or rows with one or two contrasting colors; bright, brash colors can be toned down with a neutral background. Colors used in combination can often affect each other in surprising ways. This phenomenon can be frustrating at times, especially for the beginning Fair Isle knitter, but it is also the very element that makes working with color so exciting.

It is also worth noting that color schemes do not have to be complex to be effective. A simple scheme combined with a suitable pattern can work very well. In the swatch at left, for example, the scheme uses only two basic colors, white and turquoise. The diced pattern at bottom, center and top (see p. 40) emphasizes the shading of turquoise from a light hue through mid-range to a dark hue, and vice versa. The border patterns are highlighted by the contrast of deep turquoise on white and, alternately, of white on deep turquoise.

The same idea is employed in the swatch shown on the facing page, which uses softer, natural colors in a waved pattern (see p. 38). Because the colors are closely related, they produce a subtle, shaded effect. Interest is added by working different patterns on the light and dark grounds.

It is quite understandable that many knitters become confused and intimidated by the prospect of combining colors. They seem to believe that only the few people born with a natural gift for working with color are able to do so and that everyone else is incapable of learning. Yet this is simply not the case. While it is true that some people are lucky enough to be born with a wonderful natural sense of color, it is equally true that a good color sense can be developed. The Shetland knitters themselves are clear evidence of this since they certainly were not all endowed with a natural gift for color. Many of them developed this skill through constant experimentation and practice.

Three basic requirements are vital to developing a skill for working with color in Fair Isle knitting. First, collect yarns in as wide a range of colors as possible (see Sources of Supply, p. 194). Find a manufacturer with a broad spectrum of yarns, purchase a ball of each color available, and experiment with various color combinations by knitting swatches. Make a point of knitting swatches whenever you have a spare moment. The more you knit, the more you will learn about color.

Second, get into an experimental frame of mind. In other words, have patience and be prepared to work at it. I suspect that even the world's greatest colorists have hurled a few abortive attempts into the nearest wastebasket. Lessons can be learned from all mistakes, however, so no effort is in vain.

Third, have fun. Searching out color schemes is a thoroughly enjoyable process, which can sharpen your perception of all that surrounds you, both natural and manmade.

I live on a wild and windswept island, very similar to Shetland. The moors, hills, lochs and sea are my main sources of inspiration, but inspiration can come from anywhere. Nature, of course, provides us with endless, beautiful colors, and art and textiles offer a similar wealth of inspiration. But look, too, for inspiration in unexpected places—a passing truck, or graffiti on a wall. You might find it on your own block, or inside your own house. You certainly do not have to travel to find stimulating combinations of colors. But if you do travel, go with an open mind and a ready camera, which will serve as a passport to continued explorations when you return home.

The photographs that follow were taken of a variety of objects and places, but they share one common feature: They each served as my inspiration to explore color and pattern. The Fair Isle swatches the photos inspired display a representative sampling of my work and choices about color, but they are intended, above all, to help you begin to explore color and develop your own style. As you explore, I would suggest a rule of thumb: Be like the Shetland knitters—if a combination of colors works, use it.

Veins of quartz running through a layer of blue gneiss, and seaweed inspired the swatch at right.

Rocks upon the shore were translated into the knitted sample at right.

Driftwood, seaweed and pebbles inspired two interpretations. The swatch at right focuses on the pebbles, while the one at the bottom of the page explores the driftwood and seaweed.

Autumn scenes interpreted in Fair Isle swatches.

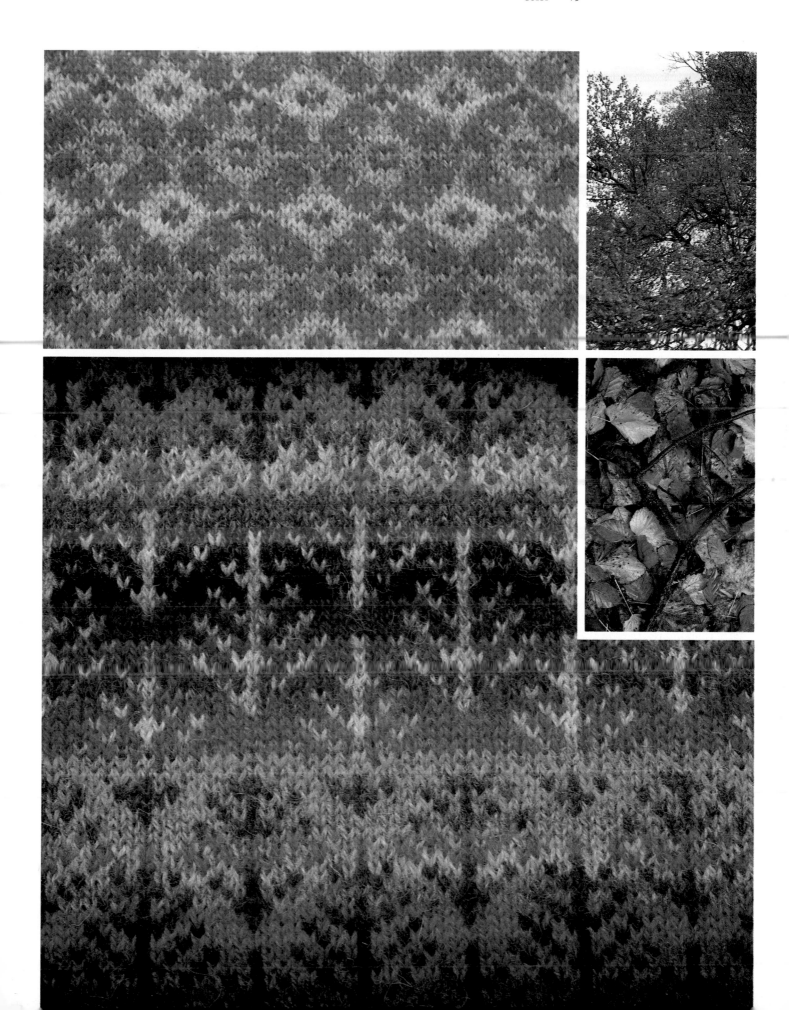

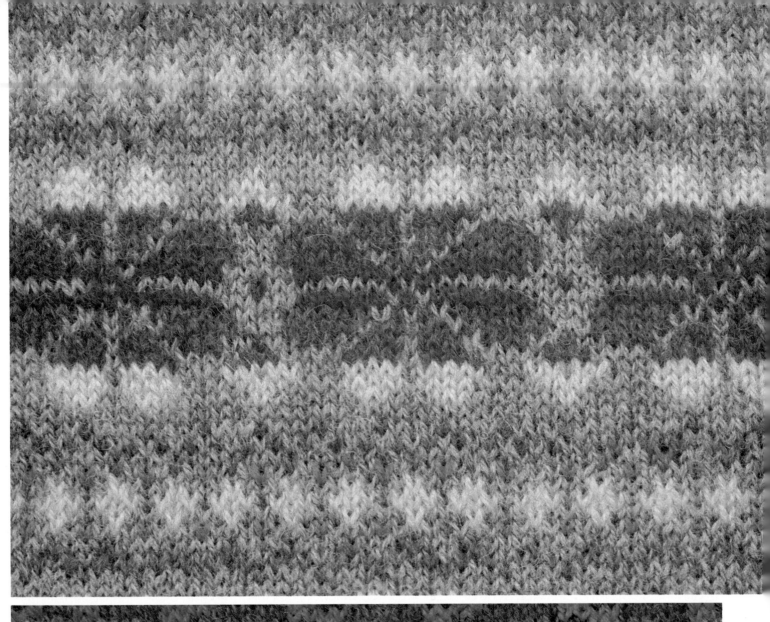

The swatches on the facing page were inspired by wild poppies in a potato patch, below left. Below, a seaside meadow, with yellow dandelions and blue harebells.

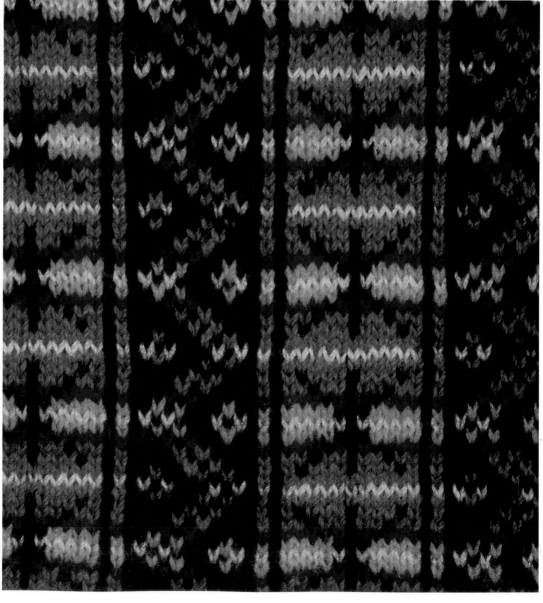

American taxis and trucks, with their Fair Isle translations at right.

Shells from the Atlantic shore of Lewis.

Carnival colors at Mardi Gras in New Orleans inspired the swatches at left and below. Facing page, beads thrown from Mardi Gras floats.

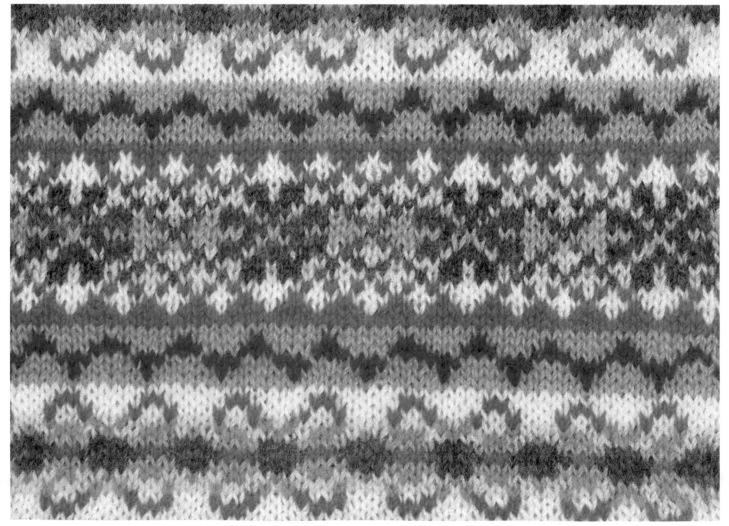

Spray-painted graffiti on a white marble monument, weathered to an almost impressionistic blur. Close examination of the paint reveals the decidely existentialist statement, 'I woz ere.'

A gift box with bright red printed paper was the inspiration for the sweater shown at right.

Below and left, moorland
bogs in summertime.

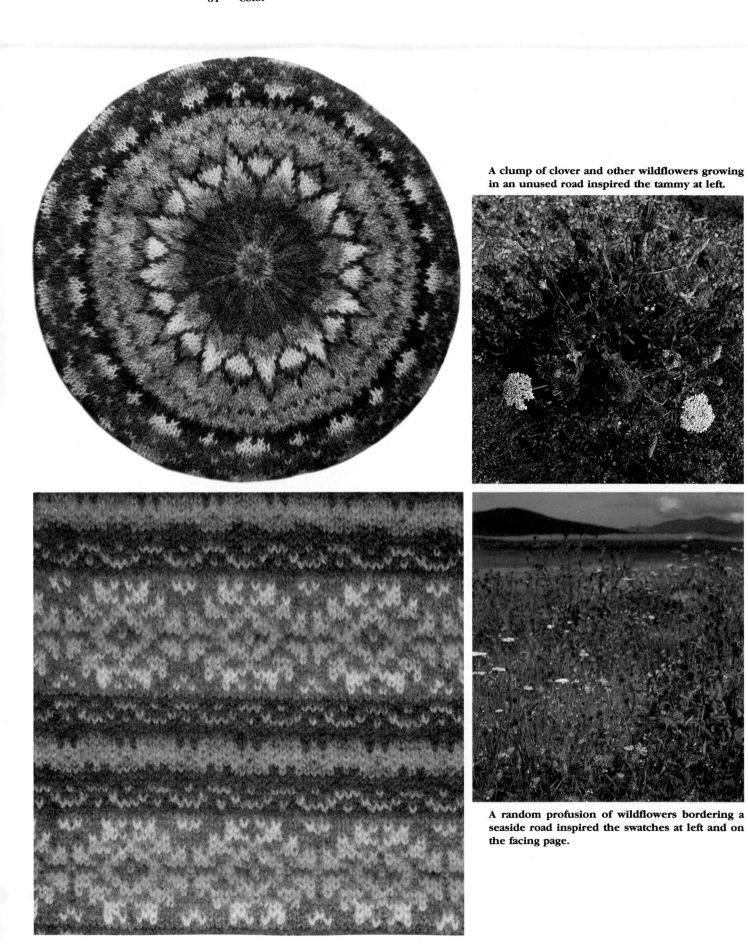

A clump of clover and other wildflowers growing in an unused road inspired the tammy at left.

A random profusion of wildflowers bordering a seaside road inspired the swatches at left and on the facing page.

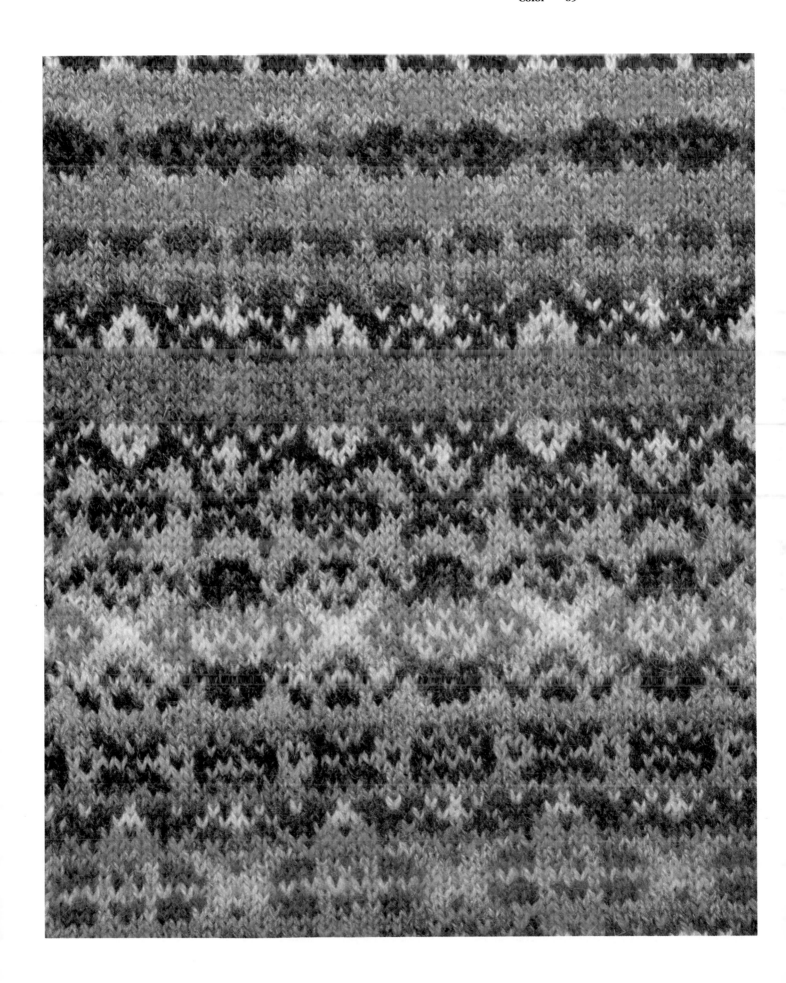

A knitting belt, a leather pouch stuffed with straw or horsehair, holds the right-hand needle and supports the weight of the knitting,

Technique

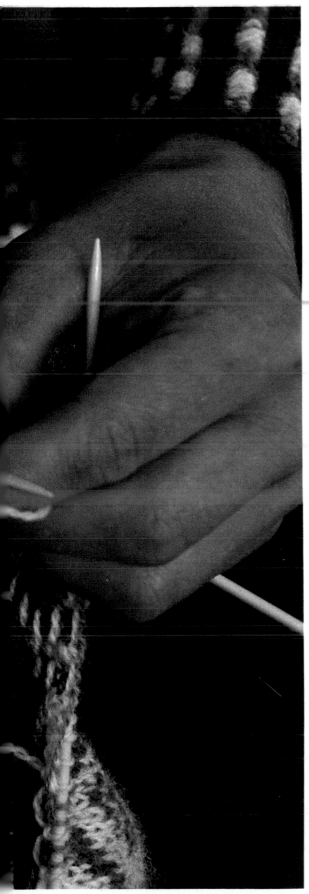

so the knitter can knit while sitting, standing or walking.

For Fair Isle work, the circular method of knitting has several important advantages over flat knitting. Shetland knitters have always recognized the ease, speed and excellent results this method produces and have employed it whenever possible. There are three reasons for the superiority of this method. First, the right side of the work always faces the knitter, which means that the pattern can be seen at all times. Second, all pattern rounds are worked in knit stitch, making manipulation of the yarns easier and faster, and also producing a more uniform gauge. Finally, this method eliminates seams, which saves time and produces a neater, better garment.

The Shetland knitter works in the round even when the garment is to have armholes or a cardigan-front opening. Such openings are bridged by working a "steek"—a series of unknitted lengths of yarn or extra knitted stitches that allow the knitting to proceed in the round (see pp. 100-103). On parts of the garment, where a steek may make the work awkward to handle, such as a neck opening, the piece is worked flat on two double-pointed needles, on the right side only. The Shetland knitter never turns and purls the back of the stockinette fabric when working a Fair Isle pattern. This means that the yarns must be broken off at the end of every row and joined afresh on the right side of the next row.

Knitters unfamiliar with circular knitting often imagine that this method has limits with regard to shaping garments, yet this is not the case. Increases and decreases can be used effectively to produce any number of sophisticated shapes.

Traditional gansey knitting plan

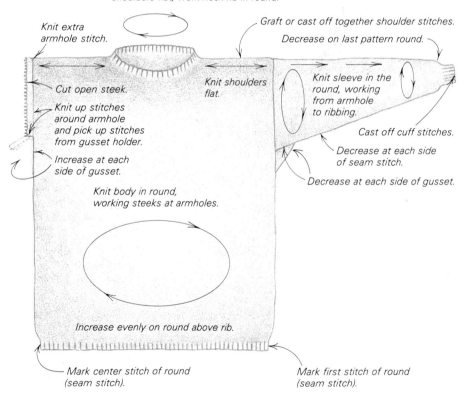

= Work in the round.

After putting neck stitches on holders to knit shoulders flat, work neck rib in round.

Knit extra armhole stitch.

Graft or cast off together shoulder stitches.

Decrease on last pattern round.

Cut open steek.

Knit shoulders flat.

Knit sleeve in the round, working from armhole to ribbing.

Knit up stitches around armhole and pick up stitches from gusset holder.

Cast off cuff stitches.

Increase at each side of gusset.

Decrease at each side of seam stitch.

Knit body in round, working steeks at armholes.

Decrease at each side of gusset.

Increase evenly on round above rib.

Mark center stitch of round (seam stitch).

Mark first stitch of round (seam stitch).

Circular knitting, an overview

The drawing at left illustrates the circular method of knitting applied to a traditional gansey shape. The body is worked in circular fashion, with an increase round immediately above the ribbing. The gussets are formed under the armholes by increasing regularly on each side of the seam stitches (the first and center stitches of the beginning round of the body). At each armhole, the gusset stitches are placed on holders, an extra "edge" stitch is cast on at each side of the armhole, and the armholes are bridged by working steeks. The body then continues to be knit in the round up to the neck opening.

The shoulder pieces are worked flat on double-pointed needles, on the right side only. On completion of the body, the shoulder stitches are either grafted or cast off together (see pp. 104-105), thus eliminating seams. The neck stitches are picked up and the neckband is worked in the round. The steeks are next cut open, and the sleeves are worked by picking up and knitting stitches into the edge stitch around the armhole and picking up the gusset stitches. The gusset is completed by decreasing regularly at each side until only the seam stitch remains. The sleeve continues to be shaped by decreasing at each side of the seam stitch. A decrease round is then worked above the cuff. The cuff is ribbed and then cast off. Finally, all loose yarn ends are sewn in on the wrong side of the garment.

The drawing on the facing page illustrates the circular method applied to a cardigan with shaped armholes. A steek is worked at the front opening, from cast-on edge to neck opening. Stitches are placed on holders at the underarms, underarm steeks are worked and the armholes shaped by decreasing at each side of the steeks. The neck and front-band ribs are worked flat.

Gauge, or tension

Whether you are working with a commercial pattern or your own design, it is absolutely essential to determine your knitting gauge by knitting a swatch with the yarn and needles intended for the work. A gauge swatch establishes the number of stitches and rounds or rows to a given measurement. In commercial patterns and in those in this book, the required gauge is stated before the knitting instructions begin. Because every knitter knits with a different tension, however, you must always knit a gauge swatch to determine if your gauge matches that required for the pattern. If it does not, you will need to adjust the size of the needles until you achieve the correct gauge before embarking on the project. Otherwise, the garment will not be the right size. In patterns of your own design, you need to establish the gauge in order to work out the number of stitches and rounds or rows required to produce the given measurements for all the garment's parts.

The gauge swatch can be worked on the right side only as a flat piece with two double-pointed needles. Knitting on the right side only requires breaking off the yarns at the end of each row and rejoining them on the right side of the next row. Alternatively, the swatch can be worked in circular fashion as a tubular piece. Whichever method is chosen, the piece should measure at least 4 in. (10cm) in width and length when laid flat.

To calculate the gauge, lay the finished swatch on a flat surface and pin it down at the edges, being careful not to pull it out of shape. Lay a firm ruler on the fabric and count the exact number of stitches to a 2-in. (5cm) width, and the exact number of rows to a 2-in. (5cm) depth. Remember to count half-stitches and half-rows—half a stitch in 2 in. means ten stitches in a 40-in. width.

If you are trying to produce the gauge required for a given design and yours is too tight—that is, you have too many stitches to a given measurement—correct by working another swatch on larger needles. If necessary, keep changing to larger needles until you produce the correct gauge. Conversely, if your gauge is too loose—that is, if you have too few

stitches to the given measurement—change to smaller needles that produce the right gauge.

When creating your own designs, there is, of course, no "correct" gauge to use as a reference (unless you intend to copy an existing knitted fabric as part of your design). You must simply establish the gauge of your own knitting, using the yarn and needles intended for the project. Obviously, it is important to suit the size of the needles to the type of yarn and to experiment with needle size (if necessary) until you are content with the gauge of the fabric produced. You can also use the swatch to experiment with colors and patterns.

Cardigan knitting plan

A cardigan with shaped armholes is worked the same as the traditional gansey shown on the facing page, with the exceptions noted below.

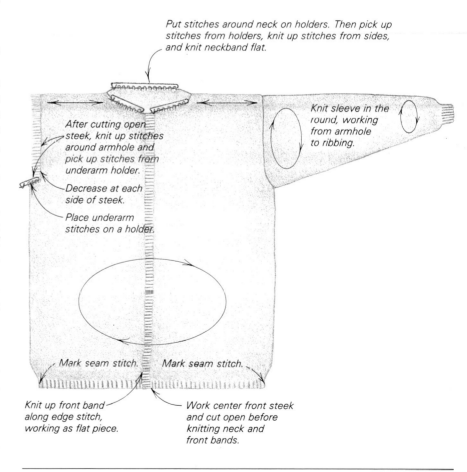

Put stitches around neck on holders. Then pick up stitches from holders, knit up stitches from sides, and knit neckband flat.

Knit sleeve in the round, working from armhole to ribbing.

After cutting open steek, knit up stitches around armhole and pick up stitches from underarm holder.

Decrease at each side of steek.

Place underarm stitches on a holder.

Mark seam stitch.   Mark seam stitch.

Knit up front band along edge stitch, working as flat piece.

Work center front steek and cut open before knitting neck and front bands.

Making a cable-edge cast-on

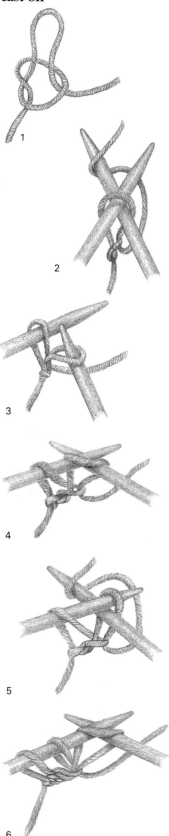

1

2

3

4

5

6

Casting on

The most suitable method of casting on for circular knitting is the cable-edge cast-on, shown in the drawing at left. The cable-edge cast-on produces a firm, elastic edge. Work the cable-edge cast-on with two double-pointed straight needles or with circular needles. Begin by making a starting loop (see Step 1 in the drawing). Place this loop on a needle, and hold this needle in your left hand. (The technical directions in this chapter are given for right-handed knitters. Left-handed knitters will have to reverse the instructions.) Insert the point of the right-hand needle through the loop, from front to back, and pass the yarn around the needle (2). Then pull a loop through (3).

Put this loop on the left-hand needle, turning it so that it lies correctly, as shown in the fourth drawing at left, and withdraw the right-hand needle. Two stitches are now on the left-hand needle. Finally, insert the right-hand needle between the two stitches, pass the yarn around the needle (5) and pull a loop through. Put this loop on the left-hand needle, turning it so that it lies like the second stitch (6). Then repeat this process of inserting the right-hand needle between the last two stitches on the needle and making a new stitch until the desired number of stitches has been cast on.

Make sure that you cast on evenly and not too tightly. The edge should be firm but elastic. Be certain to work in the front of the cast-on stitches on the first round.

Working on a set of four needles When you are working on a set of four double-pointed needles, cast on the total number of stitches required, distributing them as equally as possible over three of the needles. Make sure that the cast-on edge is untwisted, and draw up the last stitch on the third needle so that it meets the first stitch on the first needle, forming a triangle. Then, using the fourth needle, close the triangle as shown in the drawing below, by knitting through the

Casting on with a set of four double-pointed needles

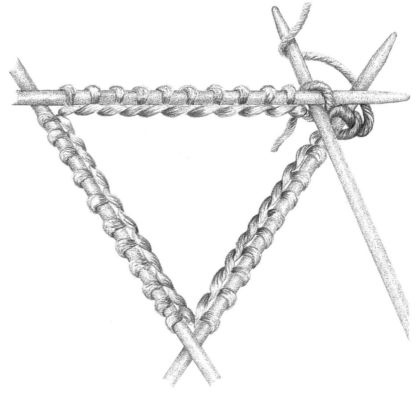

The required stitches are cast on three needles, which are drawn together to form a triangle. The fourth needle is used to close the triangle and knit in the round.

first stitch on the first needle, and begin knitting in the round. Continue knitting to the end of the first needle, which is then free to work the stitches on the next needle, and continue in this manner.

There are a couple of useful points to remember. First, always mark the initial stitch of the round with a stitch marker or a short length of different-colored yarn. Marking is necessary to keep an accurate count of rounds worked and to know where patterns and colors should change at the beginning of a new round.

Because the distance between stitches enlarges between the last stitch on one needle and the first stitch on the next, the thread between each of the three needles tends to be looser than the rest of the knitting. To compensate for this looseness, work the first stitch on each needle with slightly more tension, being careful, however, not to pull the yarn too tight. To avoid undesirable vertical lines of loose stitches between the needles, move one or two stitches on each round to the adjacent needle to vary the changeover points from round to round.

Be sure to use needles that are suitable in length for the width of the planned work; otherwise the stitches will tend to slip off the ends of the needles. When you are working a wide garment, it may even be necessary to use five needles instead of four. (In this case, cast on the requisite number of stitches over four needles and knit with the fifth needle.) Although Shetland knitters always use 14-in. steel needles, even for small articles, most knitters find that it's easier to reserve the long needles for large pieces and use shorter needles for small items.

When working on a set of double-pointed needles, Shetland knitters often use a tool called a knitting belt, shown in the photo on pp. 86-87. The knitting belt is a leather pouch, stuffed with straw or horsehair, pierced with small holes and attached to a leather belt that is buckled around the waist. The right-hand needle is inserted into the hole in the pouch that holds the knitting in the most comfortable position for the knitter, whether she is sitting or standing. This needle is held secure and rigid by the pouch and therefore removes the weight of the knitting from the right hand and arm.

The knitting belt has always been a vital tool for knitting while standing or walking (see the photo on p. 22). It is particularly helpful when knitting in Continental fashion (see pp. 92-93), which requires the yarn to be held in the left hand.

Working on a circular one-piece needle
Using the cable-edge cast-on technique (see the drawings on the facing page), cast on to a circular needle the total number of stitches required (see Step 1 in the drawing below). Reverse the work and, making sure that the cast-on edge is not twisted, knit into the first stitch, as shown in Step 2. Then proceed to knit continuously in the round.

As when working on a set of double-pointed needles, always mark the first stitch in the round. Also check the length of your needle to make sure that it is not too long for the number of stitches. If the needle is long and the knitting narrow, the stitches may not fit around the needle, making it impractical or even impossible to knit in the round. Therefore, when working narrow pieces like sleeves, use a very short one-piece needle or change to a set of four double-pointed needles.

Casting on with a circular one-piece needle

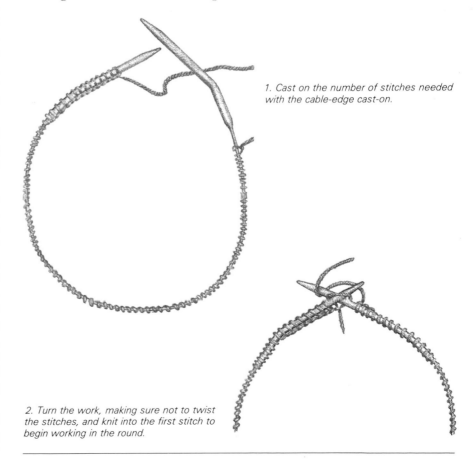

1. Cast on the number of stitches needed with the cable-edge cast-on.

2. Turn the work, making sure not to twist the stitches, and knit into the first stitch to begin working in the round.

Knitting methods There are two basic methods of knitting. In the English method, the yarn is held in the right hand; in the Continental method, the yarn is held in the left hand. Although the methods differ, the results are the same. The Continental method, however, is faster, because the yarn does not have to be passed around the needle before pulling the loop through (see the drawing on the facing page).

As a rule, most Shetland knitters use the Continental method and work Fair Isle knitting with both the pattern and background yarns held in the left hand (you will learn in a moment how they manage to keep the strands of yarn untangled).

English knitting method

In the English method of knitting, the yarn is held in the right hand. A new knit stitch is formed by inserting the right needle into the first stitch on the left needle from front to back, passing the yarn around the right needle (1) and pulling a loop through (2).

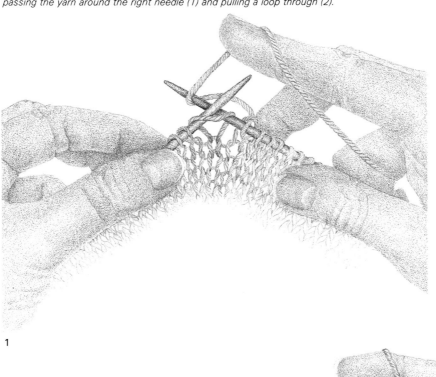

1

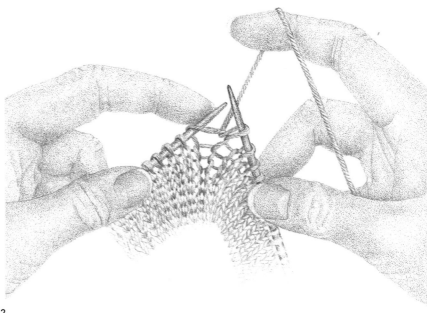

2

To knit by the English method, hold the yarn in the right hand. Insert the right-hand needle through the first stitch on the left-hand needle, from front to back (see the drawing on the facing page). Pass the yarn around the point of the right-hand needle, pull a loop through the stitch and slip the stitch off the left-hand needle.

To knit by the Continental method, hold the yarn in the left hand, as shown in the drawing below. Then insert the right-hand needle through the first stitch on the left-hand needle, from front to back. Using the point of the right-hand needle, pull a loop through the stitch and slip the stitch off the left-hand needle.

Continental knitting method

In the Continental method of knitting, the yarn is held in the left hand. After inserting the right needle into the first stitch on the left needle from front to back (1), a new stitch is formed by pulling a loop of yarn through (2) and slipping the old stitch off the left needle.

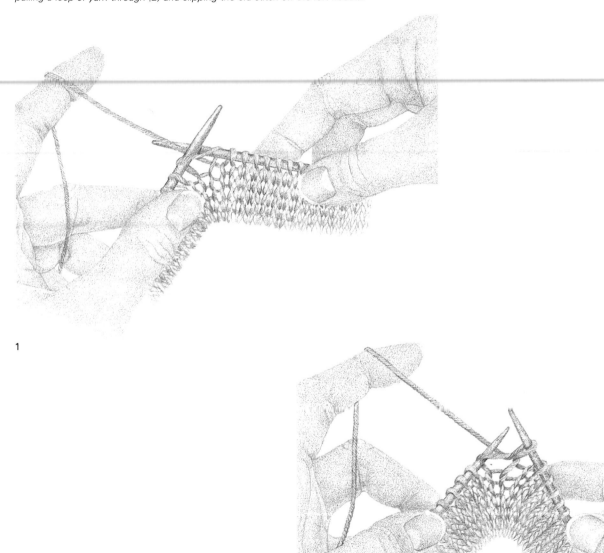

1

2

Stranded knitting

Fair Isle patterns are created by knitting with two colors in the same round—a background color and a pattern color. Although a single round never contains more than two colors, one or both colors may change at the beginning of each new round. The color not in use is carried, or stranded, across the back of the work. Great care must be taken not to strand the yarn tightly because this will cause the work to pucker. On the other hand, the yarn should not be stranded so loosely that it hangs. The stranded yarn should lie flat, relaxed and even across the back of the work (see the photos below). Stranding is not a difficult technique, but it takes some practice to achieve perfection.

In stranded knitting, the yarn not in use is carried loosely across the back of the work and should lie flat so that the fabric does not pucker. The photos below show the right and wrong sides of a stranded Fair Isle swatch.

An excellent method of working stranded knitting is to hold one yarn in each hand, thus combining the English and Continental methods (see the drawing below). At first, whichever method you are unused to will seem awkward, and you may find the tension difficult to control. However, rest assured that control will come with practice and that the result will be well worth the effort.

To avoid tangling the two yarns as you work, always change from pattern to background yarn, or vice versa, by stranding the right-hand yarn over the left-hand yarn and the left-hand yarn under the right-hand yarn, as shown below. Whichever knitting method you use, if you observe the rule of consistently stranding one yarn over and the other under, the yarns will remain untangled.

Stranded knitting

Combine the English and Continental methods by working with a yarn in each hand. To avoid tangling the yarn, consistently strand the right-hand yarn over the left-hand yarn (1), and the left-hand yarn under the right-hand yarn (2).

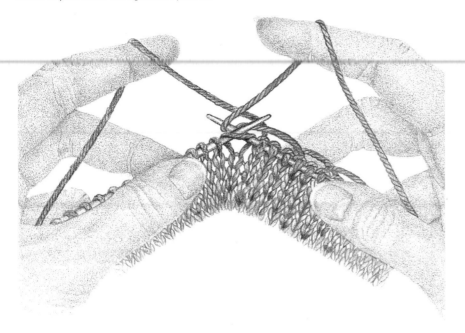

1

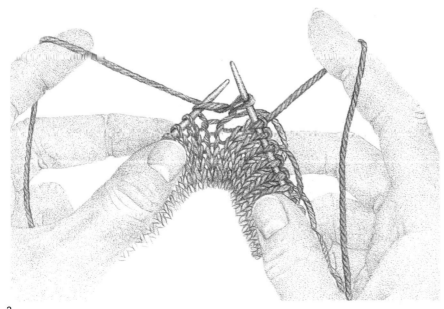

2

Weaving in a strand

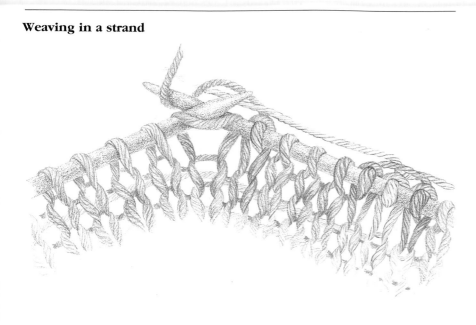

In a long run of one color, the yarn not in use is woven in at the center of the run. To weave in the yarn, simply carry it over the yarn in use before knitting the next stitch.

Corrugated ribbing

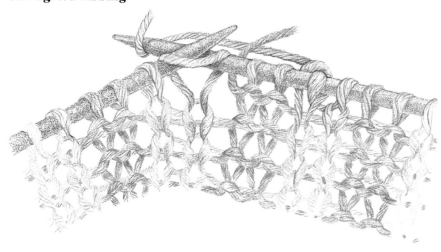

In corrugated ribbing, the knit stitches are worked in one color and the purl stitches in another. The same two colors can be used throughout the ribbing, or they may change at the beginning of any round.

Weaving in strands Weaving in strands on the back of the work as you knit is done only very occasionally. Because Fair Isle patterns are usually small and colors change frequently, the strands being carried are not very long. However, if the pattern includes a row with a long run of one color, say, 11 or more stitches, it is acceptable to weave the yarn in once at the center of the run.

The drawing at top left illustrates weaving in the pattern yarn at the center of an 11-stitch block of background color. To weave in, strand the yarn not in use over the yarn in use before knitting the next stitch. Then knit the stitch as usual, without pulling through the woven strand. If the yarn woven in is the one usually stranded under, as shown in the drawing, then it is important to remember to disentangle the yarns after working the weave-in.

Corrugated ribbing Corrugated ribbing is the name often given to the two-color rib stitch used on many Fair Isle garments. The stitch is generally a K2, P2 (or less often, a K1, P1) rib, with the knit stitches worked in one color and the purl stitches worked in a second color (see the drawing at bottom left). As with stranded knitting, no more than two colors are used in the same round, and the yarn not in use is stranded across the wrong side of the work. The same two colors may be used throughout the rib, or one or both colors may change at the beginning of any new round. Worked on smaller needles than the main pattern, this rib is firm, hard-wearing and less elastic than ordinary ribbing.

Corrugated ribbing is much easier to work if the knit stitches are produced with the Continental method and the purl stitches with the English method. Remember to take the yarn to the back of the piece after working the purl stitches.

On cardigan necks and front openings, work the rib flat, turning to work the wrong-side rows. On these wrong-side rows, remember to take the yarn to the front after working the knit stitches.

Increases and decreases

A lifted increase (M1) should be used wherever stitches must be added. It is neat and virtually invisible. To increase by this method, knit into the stitch below the next stitch to be knitted, making a new stitch (see the drawing at right). Then knit into the original stitch as usual.

There are four methods of decreasing, each with its own characteristics: knit two together (K2tog); slip, slip, knit (SSK); mitered double decrease (SL1-K2tog-PSSO); and vertical double decrease (SL2tog knitwise-K1-P2SSO).

The first method, knit two together (K2tog), is shown in the drawing below. It decreases one stitch, with the decrease slanting to the

The lifted increase (M1)

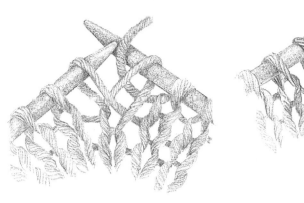

1. To produce a lifted increase, first knit into the stitch below the next stitch on the left needle.

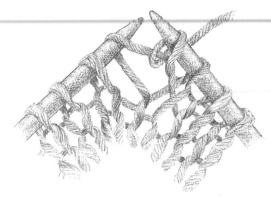

2. Then knit the next stitch on the left needle and slip it off the needle.

Knit two together (K2tog)

1. In a knit-two-together decrease, insert the right needle through the next two stitches, front to back, and knit the stitches.

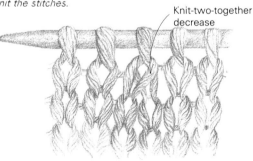

Knit-two-together decrease

2. This decrease eliminates one stitch and slants to the right.

Lifted-increase stitch

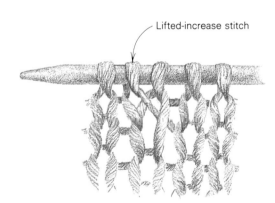

3. The increase produced is effectively invisible.

Slip, slip, knit (SSK)

1. Slip two stitches knitwise from the left to the right needle.

2. Insert the left needle into the fronts of the slipped stitches and knit them together.

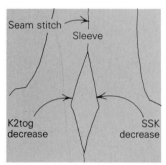

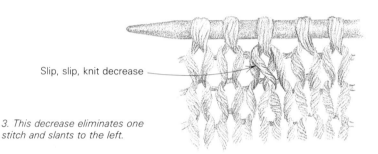

Slip, slip, knit decrease

3. This decrease eliminates one stitch and slants to the left.

To balance the decreases on this sleeve, a K2tog decrease, which slants to the right, is used on the left side of the gusset and seam stitch, and a SSK decrease, which slants to the left, is used on the right side.

right. To decrease by this method, insert the right-hand needle through the next two stitches to be knitted, from front to back, and knit as usual.

The slip, slip, knit (SSK) method also decreases one stitch, but this decrease slants to the left. To work this decrease, slip two stitches knitwise, one at a time, from the left-hand to the right-hand needle (see the drawing above). Then insert the point of the left-hand needle into the fronts of these two stitches, and knit them together.

When decreases are required on both sides of a center stitch or stitches, for example, on either side of the gusset or sleeve-seam stitch, the knit-two-together and slip-slip-knit decreases are used on alternate sides. This combination makes the decreases symmetrical, as shown in the photo and drawing at left.

The mitered double decrease (SL1-K2tog-PSSO) decreases two stitches and is most commonly used to shape the crown of caps and tammies. As shown in the top photo on the facing page, the mitered double decrease produced the left-slanting stitches radiating from the center of the tammy through the six sections of its wheel.

To highlight the decrease, as shown in the photo, work the stitch to be slipped in a col-

The top of the tammy in the photo at top is shaped with a mitered double decrease (the broken lines at the center of the star points). The tammy in the photo above is shaped with a vertical double decrease (the raised vertical lines at the center of the star points).

or that contrasts with the stitches on either side. This must be done on the round before the decrease.

To work the decrease, slip one stitch knitwise, from the left-hand to the right-hand needle (Step 1 in the drawing at right). Insert the right-hand needle through the next two stitches and knit these two stitches together (2). Then insert the left-hand needle though the slipped stitch, pass the slipped stitch over the stitches knit together (3) and drop the slipped stitch from the needle.

The vertical double decrease (SL2tog knitwise-K1-P2SSO), like the mitered double decrease, decreases two stitches and is also used to shape the crown of caps and berets (see the photo above). It creates a vertical, slightly raised stitch. Because this method

Mitered double decrease (SL1-K2tog-PSSO)

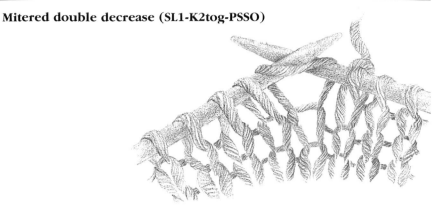

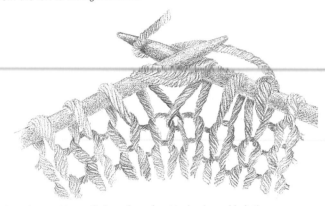

1. Slip a stitch knitwise from the left to the right needle.

2. Insert the right needle into the next two stitches, from front to back, and knit these stitches together.

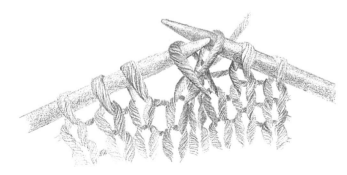

3. Pass the slipped stitch over the stitch produced by knitting two stitches together, and drop the slipped stitch.

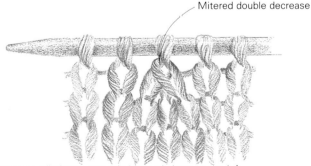

Mitered double decrease

4. The mitered double decrease eliminates two stitches and slants to the left.

Vertical double decrease (SL2tog knitwise-K1-P2SSO)

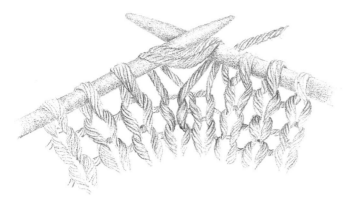

1. Insert the right needle through the next two stitches on the left needle, from front to back, and slip these stitches off the left needle.

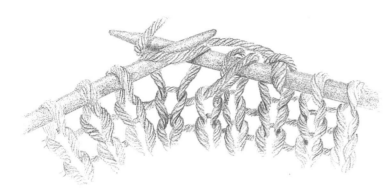

2. Knit the next stitch on the left needle.

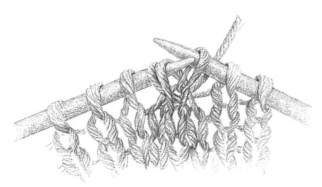

3. Pass the two slipped stitches over the knit stitch and drop them off the needle.

Vertical double decrease

4. This decrease eliminates two stitches and produces a slight vertical ridge.

produces a vertical rather than a slanted decrease, it is also very good to use at the center front of V-neck ribs.

To decrease by this method, insert the right-hand needle through the next two stitches on the left-hand needle, from front to back, and slip the two stitches together to the right-hand needle (see Step 1 in the drawing at left). Knit the next stitch as usual (2). Then insert the left-hand needle through the two slipped stitches from the left, pass the slipped stitches over the knit stitch (3) and drop the slipped stitches off the needle (4). The dominant vertical line of this decrease can be highlighted by working all three stitches in a contrasting color to the stitches on either side, and thereafter working the stitch directly above the decrease in the contrast color.

Steeks

Steek is a Scottish word meaning "to fasten or close." It is the name often given to the method of bridging an opening, such as a cardigan front or an armhole, when knitting in the round so that the work may proceed uninterrupted. There are two types of steeks—wound steeks and knitted steeks. Both serve the same function, but the knitted steek has an important advantage over the wound steek: The finishing process does not involve the tedious sewing in of yarn ends at every round.

To make a wound steek, wind both pattern and background yarns loosely around the right-hand needle several times at the intended opening (see the drawing on the facing page). On the next round, drop the previous set of loops before making a new set of loops. Continuing this process forms a wide ladder of yarn, which, when the knitting is completed, is cut at the center, leaving the yarn ends to be darned in on the wrong side (see the photo on the facing page).

To allow for picking up and knitting the stitches for a sleeve or front band on a cardigan, always work an extra edge stitch on either side of the opening. Remember to work the steek on every round; otherwise it will be impossible to cut it open without destroying the knitting.

To make a knitted steek, cast on an extra ten stitches at the required opening. The first and tenth stitches are the edge stitches, and the center eight stitches form the steek. On two-color rounds (patterns may contain some single-color rounds), work the eight

Wound steek

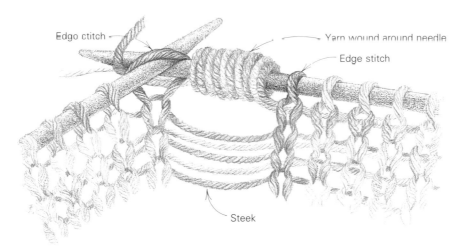

Edge stitch

Yarn wound around needle

Edge stitch

Steek

To make a wound steek, wrap pattern and background yarns loosely several times around the right needle at the desired opening. On the next round, drop the wrapped yarn off the needle before winding on a new set of yarn loops.

The wound steek at the armhole of this gansey is cut open after the body of the sweater is completed. The yarn ends are eventually darned in on the wrong side.

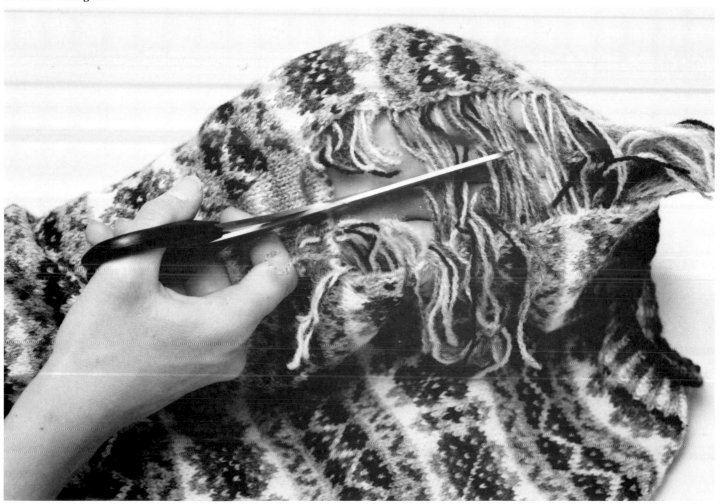

Knitted steek

To make a knitted steek, cast on and work a total of ten extra stitches at the desired opening—eight for the steek and two for later picking up stitches.

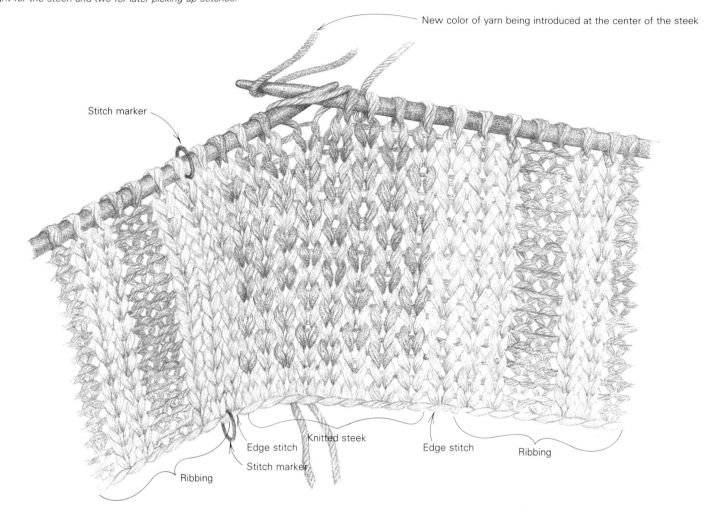

New color of yarn being introduced at the center of the steek

Stitch marker

Edge stitch

Knitted steek

Stitch marker

Ribbing

Edge stitch

Ribbing

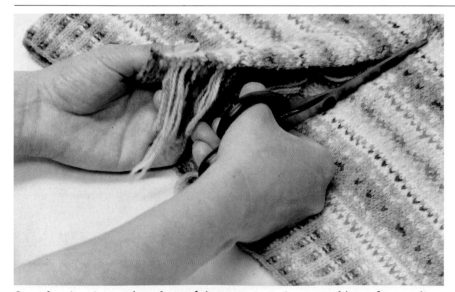

Once the piece is complete, the steek is cut open up the center (above, for a cardigan front). The bands or sleeves are knitted up from the edge stitch. The knitted steek is then trimmed to a two-stitch width (facing page) before being sewn on the wrong side.

steek stitches in alternating colors throughout, that is, in a basic seeding pattern. The drawing above shows a knitted steek being worked for a front opening, with the beginning of the ribbing indicated by orange markers.

When working knitted steeks, note that color changes for new rounds should take place at the center of the steek, that is, on the fifth stitch, as shown in the illustration. The colors are changed at the center of the steek so that the yarn ends will fall at the opening when the steek is cut and thus will not need to be sewn in separately.

Once the knitting is completed, the knitted steek is cut up the center, between the fourth and fifth stitches (see the photo at left). Some knitters may be nervous at the prospect of cutting into knitted fabric, but you need not worry since the raw edge will not unravel easily. After knitting the sleeves or cardigan bands, the steek is trimmed and stitched in place, as described below.

Knitting up stitches Stitches are picked up and knitted around the necks or armholes or along the front opening in order to avoid having to knit the neckband, sleeve or front band separately. This technique, which is referred to simply as knitting up stitches, eliminates seams.

For neckbands, the stitches held at the front and back of the neck on holders are picked up, and additional stitches are knitted up along the left and right sides of the neck. These stitches are then knitted in ribbing, either in the round for a pullover sweater or as a flat piece for a cardigan.

In the case of sleeves and front bands, the steeks that bridge these openings are cut before any stitches are knitted up. Stitches for the sleeve or front band are then knitted up into the edge stitch at each side of the steek and worked in the round or flat respectively.

To knit up stitches, slip the point of the needle through the inside loop of the edge stitch, pass the yarn around the needle and pull a loop through (see the drawing at right). When the required number of stitches has been knitted up, the stitches are then worked in the desired pattern on the neckband, sleeve or front band. When knitting up stitches, use the color of yarn that will predominate in the first round or row to be worked in the sleeve or ribbing.

Finishing off a steek After completing the sleeves or ribbing, the steek must be finished off. In the case of a wound steek, each yarn end must be darned into the back of the fabric. A knitted steek must be trimmed to a two-stitch width (see the photo at right), folded back and hand-stitched in place. To reduce the bulk, stitch the steek, if possible, with a finer yarn than you are using to knit. If you are using a 2-ply jumper-weight Shetland wool, for example, a lace weight is ideal for stitching steeks. If a finer yarn is not available, cut suitable lengths of the yarn you are using and split the plies.

To stitch the trimmed steek in place, thread a darning needle and secure the thread at the beginning of the steek. Then insert the needle through the strands of the garment on the wrong side—be careful not to stitch through

Knitting up stitches

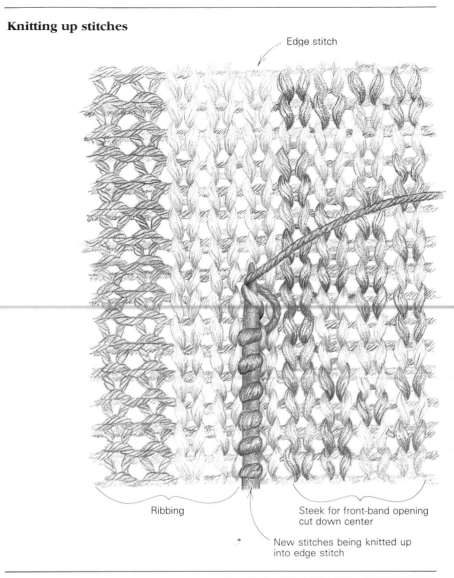

Edge stitch

Ribbing

Steek for front-band opening cut down center

New stitches being knitted up into edge stitch

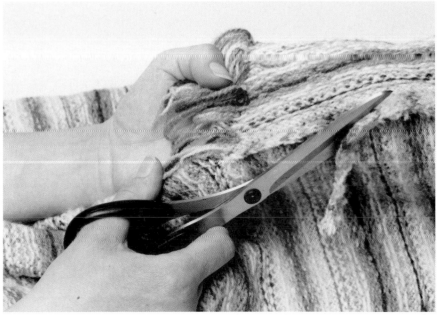

Stitching a knitted and trimmed steek in place

After folding back the trimmed steek, stitch it in place with a darning needle and yarn preferably lighter in weight than that used for knitting. First overcast the edge (1), catching the yarn into the stranded back of the fabric. After sewing to the end of the steek, reverse the process, creating cross stitches (2).

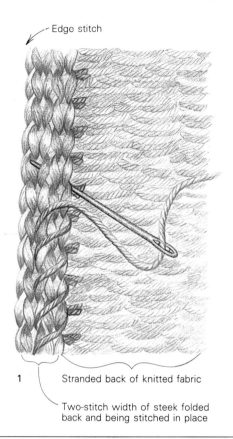

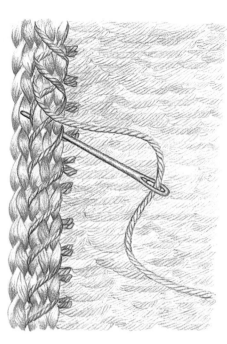

Edge stitch

1

2

Stranded back of knitted fabric

Two-stitch width of steek folded back and being stitched in place

Grafting

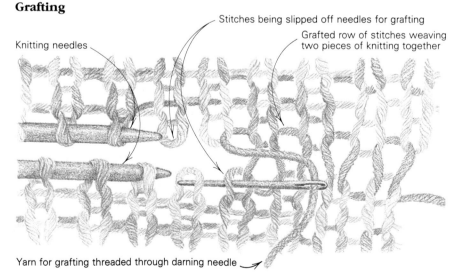

Knitting needles

Stitches being slipped off needles for grafting

Grafted row of stitches weaving two pieces of knitting together

Yarn for grafting threaded through darning needle

To join two pieces of knitting by grafting, place the needles side by side and slip off a few stitches at a time from each needle. Weave the stitches together as shown, with yarn threaded through a darning needle.

to the right side. Next insert the needle into the inside stitch of the steek and overcast the edge, as shown in the drawing above, sewing to the end of the steek. Then reverse the process, sewing in the opposite direction and slanting the stitches to the other side to form cross stitches. Finally fasten off the thread securely and cut off the excess.

Joining two pieces of knitting

There are two methods for joining pieces of Fair Isle knitting: grafting and casting off stitches together. In grafting, the two pieces of knitting are joined by working a new row of stitches with a darning needle, which creates an invisible seam. To graft pieces together, place the two needles side by side, as shown in the drawing at left, and slip the stitches off both needles a few at a time. Thread the darning needle with a length of yarn approximately four times the length of

FRANKLIN LAKES PUBLIC LIBRARY

Casting off stitches together

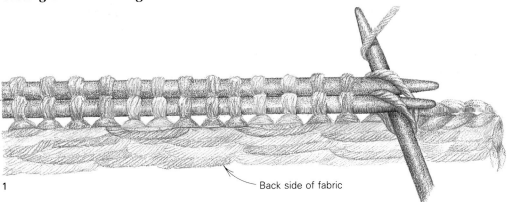

1

Back side of fabric

Holding two needles side by side with the fabric face to face, knit through two stitches from front to back (1).

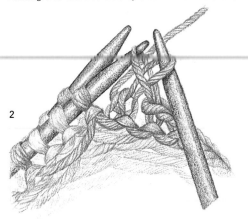

2

After repeating the first step, slip the first knit stitch over the second (2) and off the needle (3).

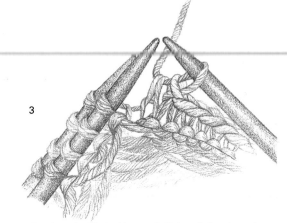

3

Continue in this fashion until all the stitches have been cast off, and pull the yarn through the final stitch.

the seam and weave the yarn through the stitches as illustrated. For purposes of clarity in the drawing, the grafted row is shown in a contrasting color. In reality, the yarn should be one of the two colors used in the rows being sewn together.

As you can see in the drawing, the stitches slipped off the needles do not lie directly opposite each other but instead are staggered. This means that the pattern will be half a stitch out of line, but the offset will not be strikingly noticeable.

Casting off stitches together is an alternative way of joining two pieces of knitting, and with this method the stitches do lie opposite each other. The cast-off stitches form a ridge, which can be worked on the right or wrong side of the garment, depending on whether the ridge is to be incorporated into the garment as a design feature.

To cast off stitches in this way, hold the two needles together in your left hand. Insert the third needle through the first stitch on both needles, from front to back, and then knit the stitches together (see the drawing above). Repeat this once again. Then pass the first stitch on the third needle over the second stitch and off the needle, thus casting it off. Continue in this manner until all the stitches are cast off. Finally, pull the yarn through the last stitch to fasten the seam.

Be sure to avoid casting off too tightly, or the work will pucker. If you have difficulty casting off, use a third needle that is a size or two larger than the other two.

Trimmings

There are a number of trimmings that can be incorporated into Fair Isle garments. Those most often used are buttonholes, pompoms, fringes and cords. By following these basic instructions, you will be able to make trimmings for your own garments.

Buttonholes   For a small round buttonhole, first work a yarn over (yo) and knit two together (K2tog). Then knit the next row as usual. The drawing below illustrates working a small buttonhole, first after a knit stitch, and then after a purl stitch. In the first case, the yarn has to be brought forward before it is passed over the needle. In the second case, the yarn is already in front of the needle and is simply passed over it. When you are making small buttonholes in front-band ribbing, work them in the knit stitches rather than the purl stitches, as shown in the second part of the drawing.

To make a large horizontal buttonhole, cast off the number of stitches required for the buttonhole's width. Then on the following round, simply cast on the same number of stitches over the stitches cast off and continue knitting as usual.

Pompoms   In traditional Fair Isle knitting, pompoms are used mainly on tammies. To make a pompom, cut two cardboard circles of the same size, with diameters equal to that of the finished pompom. Then cut a small hole in the center of each card about one-quarter the size of the finished pompom, as shown in the top drawing on the facing page. Next, thread a darning needle with a long length of yarn. Then, with the two cards placed together, wind the yarn around them and through the center hole, continuing to wrap the cards until the hole is completely filled. Cut the yarn at the outer edge of the cardboard between the two circles. Insert a length of yarn between the cards and tie it tightly around the pompom, leaving enough yarn to sew the pompom on the garment. Then remove the cards and trim the pompom to give it a round shape.

Making a buttonhole

Making a buttonhole after a knit stitch

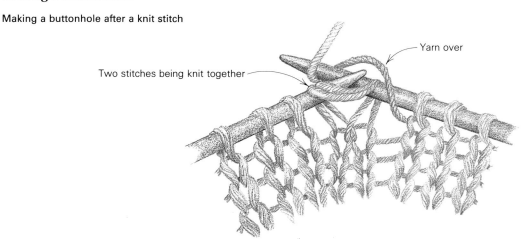

Two stitches being knit together

Yarn over

Making a buttonhole after a purl stitch

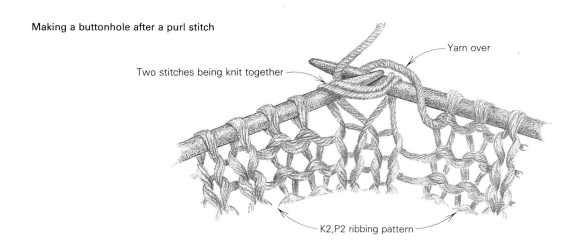

Two stitches being knit together

Yarn over

K2,P2 ribbing pattern

Tasseled fringe Cut pieces of yarn twice the desired length of the finished tassel. One or more strands can be used for each tassel, depending on how thick you want it to be. Gather up the number of strands needed and, with the wrong side of the edge being fringed facing you, insert a crochet hook through the fabric from front to back. Fold the strand or strands of yarn in half, put the fold on the crochet hook, and pull the loop through (see the bottom drawing below). Without removing the crochet hook from the loop, catch the loose ends of the tassel around the hook and pull them through the loop. Then pull the ends taut to tighten the knot.

Cord Cut two lengths of yarn about four times the desired length of the finished cord, and knot each pair of ends together. Then, with the help of another person, insert a pen-

Making pompoms

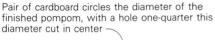
Pair of cardboard circles the diameter of the finished pompom, with a hole one-quarter this diameter cut in center

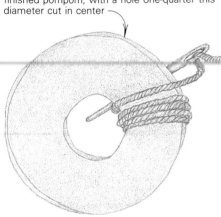

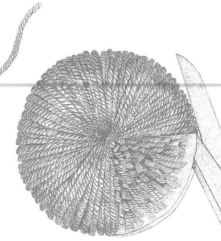

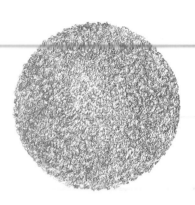

1. With the cardboard circles held together, wind the yarn through the center hole and around the cardboard until it is completely filled.

2. When the cardboard is filled, cut the yarn between the circles at their outer edge. Insert a length of yarn between the two circles and tie it tightly around the yarn, leaving enough length to sew the pompom on the garment.

3. Remove the cardboard circles, fluff up the pompom and trim it to shape.

Making tasseled fringe

Wrong side of fabric

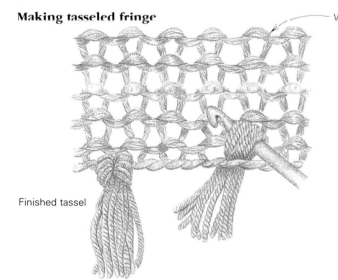

Finished tassel

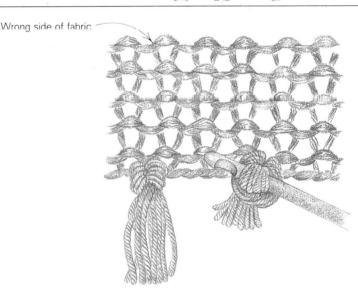

1. With the wrong side of the fabric facing you, insert a crochet hook through the fabric to the right side, place the strands of yarn folded in half on the hook, and pull a loop through.

2. Catch the loose yarn ends on the hook and pull them through the loop. Remove the crochet hoook, pull the tassel taut, and trim the ends even.

Making cords

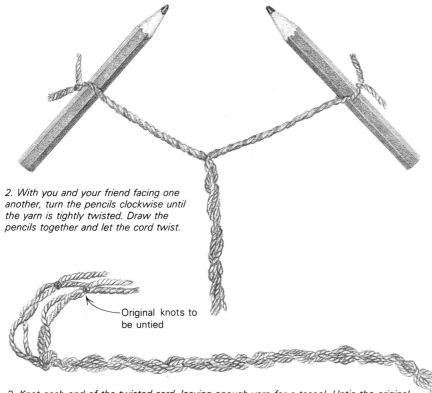

Two lengths of yarn four times the desired length of the cord, knotted at each end

Pencils inserted at each end to hold the yarn taut

1. Cut two lengths of yarn about four times as long as the desired cord and knot the two ends together. With the help of a friend, insert a pencil at each end and stretch the line taut.

2. With you and your friend facing one another, turn the pencils clockwise until the yarn is tightly twisted. Draw the pencils together and let the cord twist.

Original knots to be untied

3. Knot each end of the twisted cord, leaving enough yarn for a tassel. Untie the original knots at one end of the cord, cut open the other folded end, and untwist and trim the yarn for the tassels.

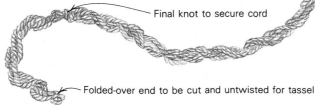

Final knot to secure cord

Folded-over end to be cut and untwisted for tassel

cil at each end in front of the knot, and stretch out the yarn until it is taut (see the drawing at left). With you and your assistant facing each other, each should hold the yarn between finger and thumb, just in front of the pencil, and turn the pencils clockwise until the two strands are tightly twisted. Bring the pencils together and allow the cord to twist. Remove the pencils and knot the ends of the cord, leaving enough extra cord on each end to form a tassel. Cut open the folded end, untie the original knots on the other end and trim the tassels to the same length.

Care for Shetland wool garments

To prevent a Shetland wool garment from getting misshapen when washed, thread a needle with yarn and loosely gather the neckline or the rim on a tammy or cap, or tack together the front opening on a cardigan. Wash the garment in warm water and a mild soap by squeezing, rather than rubbing it. Rinse it thoroughly in warm water. Remove as much moisture as possible either by rolling and squeezing the garment in towels or by giving it a short spin in the washing machine (remove it from the machine immediately).

Since Shetland wool tends to shrink and felt, care must be taken when drying the garment. The procedure used in Shetland, known as dressing, involves stretching the wet garment on a "woolly board" (see the drawing on the facing page) and allowing it to dry away from direct heat. All commercially produced Fair Isle knitwear is washed and dressed on the board before it is sent to the shop. Indeed, many knitters consider a garment to be properly dressed only when it has been on the board overnight. When the garment is removed from the board, the ribs of the garment are dampened either with a wet cloth or steam and pulled to tighten them.

If you do not own a woolly board like the one shown in the drawing, you can easily construct an alternative by cutting a flat board (I suggest a thin piece of plywood) into three pieces the size and shape of the garment's body and sleeves. Remember that the garment should remain stretched, not relaxed, on the board, so make the three parts of the board about ½ in. wider than the garment. Glove, mitten and beret boards can also be fashioned out of flat pieces of wood, though I have found that a dinner plate often substitutes nicely for a tammy board. (The glove board must have fingers, but a separate piece of wood can be inserted into the thumb.) If you faithfully follow these guidelines when washing Shetland wool garments, they will not shrink or felt and will give you many years of good service.

A woolly board

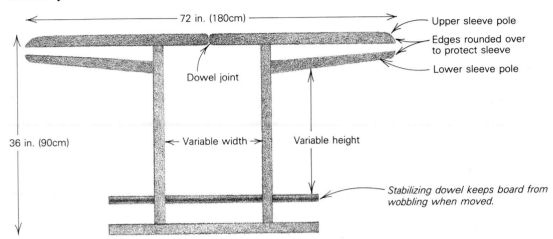

72 in. (180cm)

Upper sleeve pole

Edges rounded over to protect sleeve

Lower sleeve pole

Dowel joint

36 in. (90cm)

← Variable width →   Variable height

Stabilizing dowel keeps board from wobbling when moved.

Top dowel fits into hole in upper sleeve pole, bottom dowel fits into socket base.

Holes receive dowel in lower sleeve pole. The upper sleeve pole has a similar series of holes so that the distance between the vertical members can be varied to accommodate the body width of the sweater.

Vertical member of board

Holes for stabilizing horizontal dowel

The board does not stand alone, but must lean against another surface when in use. It is dismantled for storage.

When dressing a sweater, put the sweater on the board as you erect it. Put the two vertical members into the sweater, and attach the base according to the garment's width. Then insert the sleeve poles through the sweater sleeves and position them for the required width.

Integral to any wardrobe of Fair Isle patterns is the classic cardigan with underarm gussets, here translated in an oversize silhouette and worked

in pastels (see pp. 136-139 for knitting instructions).

A wardrobe of patterns

Many knitters find that they gain confidence in their skills by serving the apprenticeship of knitting designs from instructions. The collection of designs in this chapter—together with full working instructions—provides projects for knitters not yet confident enough to create their own original Fair Isle garments.

Most of the designs in this collection are classic in shape and are worked in both traditional and unusual patterns, colors and yarns. These shapes can be used again and again as canvases on which to paint your own colors and patterns. For some knitters, this exercise is the next step toward creating original designs.

In order to substitute yarns and patterns for those called for in these designs, three points must be observed. First, if you use an alternative yarn to that specified in the instructions, the gauge of your chosen yarn must be exactly the same as that in the directions. Second, make sure that your chosen pattern fits exactly into the total number of stitches in the garment. You can simplify this process by selecting a pattern of the same stitch count as the original. The number of rows in the pattern must also fit well into the garment length. Check this before starting a project, or use a pattern or patterns with the same number of rows as the original. Finally, adjust the yarn quantities required according to the patterns and colors chosen.

All instructions are given for working the designs in the traditional methods. These methods are fully described and illustrated in Chapter 4, "Technique."

With regard to the equipment you will need, a "set of needles" in the instructions refers to four double-pointed needles, which are traditionally used for working garments in the round. For very wide garments, it may be more practical to use five needles. For narrow areas such as sleeve wrists or for mittens and gloves, you will find that short needles are easier to work with than the longer needles used for other garments.

Many knitters prefer working with a circular needle rather than a set of double-pointed needles. However, I have not yet found a circular needle that is short enough for working very narrow areas. For these areas, it is necessary to have a set of short double-pointed needles in the appropriate size or sizes.

Sweaters and cardigans are worked flat at the shoulders, and for these areas, the instructions specify the use of double-pointed needles. However, you may also work these areas flat on a circular needle, placing the stitches not being knit on spare needles. Spare lengths of yarn can substitute for stitch holders, and contrasting yarn for stitch markers. Finally, for information on sources of yarn, see Sources of Supply, p. 194.

Knitting abbreviations		
	alt	alternate
	approx	approximately
	beg	begin(ning)
	cm	centimeters
	foll	following
	g	grams
	in.	inches
	K	knit
	M	make (see Lifted increase, p. 97)
	mm	millimeters
	no.	number
	P	purl
	patt(s)	pattern(s)
	PSSO	pass slipped stitch(es) over (see Decreases, pp. 98-100)
	rem	remain(ing)
	rep	repeat
	rnd(s)	round(s)
	SL	slip
	SSK	slip, slip, knit (see Decreases, p. 98)
	st(s)	stitch(es)
	tog	together
	yo	yarn over

Border-pattern gansey

This is a classic border-pattern gansey in mid-winter moorland colors. It has shaped armholes and is sized for both men and women.

Sizes

To fit bust/chest
32-34/35-37/38-39/40-42/43-44 in.
(81-86/89-94/97-99/102-107/109-112cm).

Knitted measurements

Bust/chest
37½/40/42½/45/47½ in.
(95/102/108/114/121cm).

Length from top of shoulder
24/24½/25½/26/27 in.
(61/62/65/66/69cm).

Sleeve length
19¼/20¼/21/22/22¼ in.
(50/52/53.5/56/57cm).

Materials

Shetland 2-ply jumper-weight yarn (Jamieson & Smith yarn used in this garment) in the foll shades:

1/2/2/2/2	2-oz. hanks in natural white (shade no. 1a)
2/2/2/3/3	1-oz. hanks in ocher (121)
2	2-oz. hanks in deep fawn (78)
5/5/5/6/6	1-oz. hanks in plum mix (87)
2/2/2/3/3	1-oz. hanks in corn yellow (FC43)
1/1/1/1/2	2-oz. hanks in Shetland black (5)
1/1/1/2/2	1-oz. hanks in green (141).

Set or circular needles in size 2 (2¾mm) and 3 (3¼mm).

7 stitch holders.

Stitch markers.

Gauge

16 sts and 16 rows to 2 in. (5cm), measured over patt, using size 3 (3¼mm) needles.

Border-pattern gansey

- natural white
- ◆ ocher
- ✿ deep fawn
- ✕ plum mix
- - corn yellow
- ● Shetland black
- ◇ green

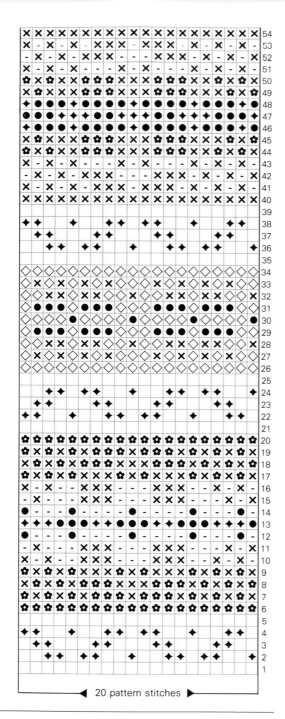

◀ 20 pattern stitches ▶

Body

With size 2 (2¾mm) needles and plum mix, cast on 264/280/300/312/332 sts. Place a marker at beg of rnd and work in corrugated rib as follows:

Rnds 1 and 2	K2 in plum mix, P2 in deep fawn; rep.
Rnd 3	K2 in plum mix, P2 in corn yellow; rep.
Rnd 4	K2 in Shetland black, P2 in corn yellow; rep.
Rnds 5 and 6	K2 in Shetland black, P2 in ocher; rep.
Rnd 7	As for rnd 4.
Rnd 8	As for rnd 3.

Rep these 8 rnds until rib measures 2¾/2¾/2¾/3¼/3 in. (7/7/7/8.5/8cm).

Next rnd: increase

With natural white—

First size: (M1, K7, M1, K8, M1, K7) rep to end. 300 sts.

2nd size: (M1, K7) rep to end. 320 sts.

3rd Size: (M1, K7, M1, K8) rep to end. 340 sts.

4th size: (M1, K6, M1, K7) rep to end. 360 sts.

5th size: (M1, K7) rep to the last 24 sts; (M1, K6) 4 times. 380 sts.

Change to size 3 (3¼mm) needles, place a marker at beg of rnd and, joining in and breaking off colors as required, work the patt from chart, repeating the 20 patt sts 15/16/17/18/19 times in the rnd.

Continue in this manner, repeating the 54 patt rnds and work 98/100/102/98/104 rnds in total.

Divide for armholes

Patt 11/6/12/7/13 sts and place these sts on a holder (left underarm); patt the next 139/149/157/167/175 sts (front); patt the next 11/11/13/13/15 sts and place these sts on a holder (right underarm); patt the next 139/149/157/167/175 sts (back); patt the rem 0/5/1/6/2 sts and place on first (left underarm) holder.

Shape armholes/work steeks

Keeping continuity of patt, work steeks between back and front at armholes, and decrease 1 st at each side of both armholes on the next 5 rnds. 129/139/147/157/165 sts rem on each of back and front.

Patt and steek 1 rnd straight, then continue working steeks and decrease 1 st at each side of both armholes on next and every foll alt rnd until 121/129/137/145/153 sts rem on each of back and front.

Continue straight, working patt and steeks as set, until 146/149/156/154/164 patt rnds have been worked from beg (rnd 38/41/48/46/2, inclusive, of 3rd/3rd/3rd/3rd/4th patt rep).

Note: If working knitted steeks, cast off each steek on this rnd.

Left front shoulder

Patt the first 45/49/52/56/59 sts (left shoulder); place the next 31/31/33/33/35 sts on a holder (front neck); leave the rem sts on spare needles.

Keeping continuity of patt, work the sts of left shoulder on 2 double-pointed needles, on right side only, breaking off yarns at end of each row, and decrease 1 st at end (neck edge) of next and every foll row until 40/44/45/49/52 sts rem.

Patt 1 row straight, then decrease 1 st at same edge of next and every foll alt row until 31/34/36/39/42 sts rem.

Place these sts on a holder.

Right front shoulder

With right side facing, rejoin appropriate yarns and, keeping continuity of patt, work the 45/49/52/56/59 sts of right shoulder as for left, reversing neck shaping. Place sts on a holder.

Back

With right side facing, rejoin appropriate yarns and, keeping continuity of patt, work the 121/129/137/145/153 sts of back on 2 double-pointed needles, on right side only, breaking off yarns at end of each row, and patt 16/18/16/18/18 rows straight. Then shape back neck as follows:

Right back shoulder

Patt the first 35/38/41/44/47 sts (right shoulder); place the next 51/53/55/57/59 sts on a holder (back neck); leave the rem sts on a spare needle.

Keeping continuity of patt, work the sts of right shoulder, decreasing 1 st at end (neck edge) of next and every foll alt row until 31/34/36/39/42 sts rem. Place these sts on a holder.

Left back shoulder

With right side facing, rejoin appropriate yarns and, keeping continuity of patt, work the 35/38/41/44/47 sts of left shoulder, as for right, reversing neck shaping.

Graft or cast off tog shoulder sts.

Cut open armhole steeks.

Sleeves

Place a marker on each center-underarm st. With size 3 (3¼mm) needles and plum mix, pick up and K the last 6/6/7/7/8 sts from underarm holder, beg with center-underarm st; then K up 139/145/155/163/171 sts evenly around armhole; pick up and K the rem sts from underarm holder. 150/156/168/176/186 sts total.

Begin at rnd 41 and patt sleeve as follows:

First rnd
>K1 background color (center-underarm st, to be worked in background throughout); patt the last 4/7/3/7/2 sts of chart, then rep the 20 patt sts 7/7/8/8/9 times, then patt the first 5/8/4/8/3 sts of chart.

Continue in this manner and patt 2 more rnds.

Next rnd
>Keeping continuity of patt, K1 background (center-underarm st), K2tog, patt to the last 2 sts, SSK. Patt 3 rnds straight. Rep these last 4 rnds until 82/84/116/132/158 sts rem.

3rd, 4th and 5th sizes only
>Patt 2 rnds straight, then decrease as before, on next and every foll 3rd rnd until 88/88/90 sts rem.

All sizes: decrease for wrist

With background color—

First size
>(K2tog, K2) 8 times, (K2tog, K1) 6 times, (K2tog, K2) 8 times. 60 sts.

2nd size
>(K2tog, K3) twice, (K2tog, K2) 16 times, (K2tog, K3) twice. 64 sts.

3rd and 4th size
>(K2tog, K3) 4 times, (K2tog, K2) 12 times, (K2tog, K3) 4 times. 68 sts.

5th size
>K2tog, K3; rep. 72 sts.
>
>Change to size 2 (2¾mm) needles and work in corrugated rib, as for body, for 2½/2½/2¾/2¾/2¾ in. (6/6/7/7/7 cm). Cast off all sts in background color.

Neckband

With size 2 (2¾mm) needles and plum mix, pick up and K the 51/53/55/57/59 sts from back neck holder; K up 27/28/30/33/33 sts to front neck holder; pick up and K the 31/31/33/33/35 from front neck holder; K up 27/28/30/33/33 sts along rem edge. 136/140/148/156/160 sts total.

K2, P2 corrugated rib in colors as for body, for 10 rnds.

Cast off evenly in plum mix.

Child's panel gansey

This child's panel gansey features all the elements of the classic panel garment, including stars, borders and seeding patterns.

Size

To fit chest 28 in. (71cm).
Approx age 8-9 years.

Knitted measurements

Underarm: 30 in. (76cm).
Length from top of shoulder: 20½ in. (52cm).
Sleeve seam: 15½ in. (39.5cm).

Materials

1-oz. hanks of Shetland 2-ply jumper-weight yarn (Jamieson & Smith yarn used in this garment) in the foll shades:

    6 dark blue (shade no. 135)
    2 each of light fawn (202), lemon (96), pink mix (FC6), peach (207) and pale lavender (FC21)
    1 flame red (129).

1 set or circular needles in sizes 2 (2¾mm) and 3 (3¼mm).

6 stitch holders.

Stitch markers.

Gauge

16 sts and 16 rows to 2 in. (5cm), measured over patt, using size 3 (3¼mm) needles.

Body

With size 2 (2¾mm) needles and dark blue, cast on 208 sts. Place a marker at beg of rnd and work K2, P2 corrugated rib as follows:

    K2 dark blue, P2 light fawn; for 4 rnds.

Rep these 4 rnds using each contrast color in turn (24 rnds altogether), and increase 1 st at beg and middle of last rnd. 210 sts.

Next rnd: increase

With dark blue, M1, K7; rep to end of rnd. 240 sts.

Note: Work Chart A in colors used for charts B and C.

Place a marker at beg of rnd, change to size 3 (3¼mm) needles, and set the patt as follows:

    Work the patt from Chart A over the first 33 sts, repeating the 8 patt sts 4 times, and working the last st as indicated on chart; Chart B over the next 13 sts; Chart C over the next 29 sts; Chart B over the next 13 sts;

Child's panel gansey

    dark blue
○ light fawn
✕ lemon
✿ pink mix
● peach
✦ pale lavender
◆ flame red
◇ pattern color

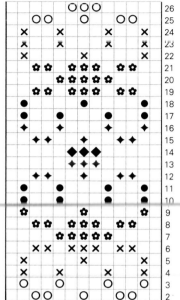

Chart B

◀ 13 pattern stitches ▶

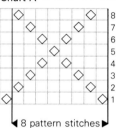

Chart A

◀ 8 pattern stitches ▶

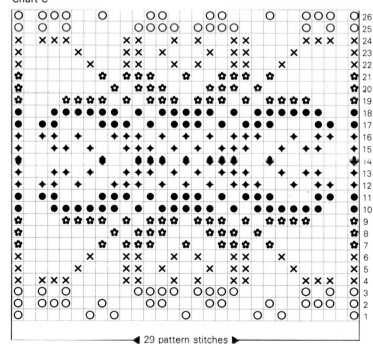

Chart C

◀ 29 pattern stitches ▶

Chart A over the next 65 sts, repeating the 8 patt sts 8 times, and working the 65th st as indicated on chart; Chart B over the next 13 sts; Chart C over the next 29 sts; Chart B over the next 13 sts; Chart A over the last 32 sts, repeating the 8 patt sts 4 times.

Joining in and breaking off colors as required, rep the 26 patt rnds and continue straight until 84 patt rnds have been worked altogether.

Next rnd: divide for armholes

Patt the first 5 sts of rnd and place on a holder (left underarm); patt the next 111 sts (front); patt the next 9 sts and place on a holder (right underarm); patt the rem sts, then place the last 4 sts of rnd onto left underarm holder, thus leaving 111 sts for back.

Shape armhole/work steeks

Keeping continuity of patt and working steeks over armholes, decrease 1 st at each side of armholes on next and every foll alt rnd 5 times. (101 sts rem on both back and front).

Working steeks over armholes, continue straight in patt until 130 patt rnds have been worked from beg (5 reps of Chart C). Cast off knitted steeks on last rnd.

Left front shoulder

Patt the first 34 sts of rnd; place the next 33 sts on a holder (front neck); leave rem sts on a spare needle.

Keeping continuity of patt, work the 34 sts of left shoulder on 2 double-pointed needles on right side only, breaking off yarns at end of each row, and decrease 1 st at neck edge of next and every foll alt row until 28 sts rem.

Patt 1 rnd straight. Place sts on a holder.

Right front shoulder

Rejoin appropriate yarns to the 34 sts of right front shoulder and work as for left, reversing shaping. Place sts on a holder.

Back

Rejoin appropriate yarns to the 101 sts of back and, keeping continuity of patt, work straight for 14 rows, working on right side only.

Place center 45 sts of back on a holder (back neck).

Graft or cast off together shoulder sts.

Neckband

With size 2 (2¾mm) needles and dark blue, pick up and K the 45 sts of back neck; K up 13 sts down left side of neck; pick up and K the 33 sts of front neck; K up 13 sts up right side of neck. 104 sts.

Change to size 3 (3¼mm) needles and work in K2, P2 corrugated rib as for body, but work 2 rnds of each contrast color (12 rnds altogether).

Cast off evenly in rib.

Turn neckband in half to the inside and stitch loosely and evenly in place.

Sleeves

Cut open armhole steeks.

With size 3 (3¼mm) needles and dark blue, pick up and K the 9 sts of underarm from holder; K up 107 sts evenly around armhole. 116 sts.

With dark blue, K4. Place a marker on next st (seam st). Now begin the rnd and set the patt as follows:

K1 dark blue (seam st); work sts 4 through 8 of Chart A, then rep the 8 patt sts 3 times, and work the last st as indicated; Chart B over the next 13 sts; Chart C over the next 29 sts; Chart B over the next 13 sts; rep the 8 patt sts of Chart A 3 times, then work the first 6 sts of Chart A once more.

Continue in this manner and patt 2 more rnds.

Next rnd: decrease

Keeping continuity of patt, K1 dark blue (seam st); K2tog; patt to the last 2 sts; SSK.

Patt 3 rnds straight.

Rep these last 4 rnds until 104 patt rnds have been worked altogether (4 reps of Chart C), and 64 sts rem.

Next rnd: work cuff decrease

With dark blue, K1, *K2tog, K7; rep from * to end of rnd. 57 sts.

Change to size 2 (2¾mm) needles, decrease 1 st at beg of next rnd (56 sts), and work 24 rnds in corrugated rib as for body, but beg with flame red and end with light fawn.

With dark blue, cast off evenly.

Allover-pattern sweater

This allover-pattern sweater is a loose-fitting style with deep, shaped armholes, turn-back cuffs and a neat collar—all worked in moorland colors in full bloom.

Sizes

To fit bust
32-33/34-36/37-39 in.
(81-84/86-91/94-99cm).

Knitted measurements

Bust
38½/41¼/44 in. (98/105/112cm).
Length from top of shoulder
23/24½/26¼ in. (59/62/67cm).
Sleeve length
20½/21/21½ in. (52/53/55cm).

Materials

1-oz. hanks of Shetland 2-ply jumper-weight yarn (Jamieson & Smith yarn used in this garment) in the following shades:

1/1/2	in corn yellow (shade no. FC43)
1	in deep plum mix (87)
1/1/2	in ocher (121)
1/2/2	in plum (19)
2/2/3	in honey gold (32)
1	in flame red (129)
3	in gold/rust mix (122)
3	in lavender mix (FC9)
1/2/2	in magenta (FC22)
3/3/4	in green mix (FC12)
2	in pale lavender (FC21)
1/2/2	in rust/blue mix (FC38)
1/2/2	in bright purple (123)
1/1/2	in rust (FC8)
1	in gold/green mix (1281)
1	in bright cornflower (131).

1 set or circular needles in size 2 (2¾mm) and size 3 (3¼mm).

6 stitch holders.

Stitch markers.

Gauge

16 sts and 16 rows to 2 in. (5cm), measured over patt, using size 3 (3¼mm) needles.

Body

With size 2 (2¾mm) needles and gold/rust mix, cast on 252/268/288 sts. Place a marker at beg of rnd and work in corrugated rib as follows:

Rnds 1 and 2	K2 in gold/rust mix, P2 in lavender mix.
Rnd 3	K2 in honey gold, P2 in flame red.
Rnd 4	K2 in honey gold, P2 in plum.
Rnd 5	K2 in ocher, P2 in plum.
Rnd 6	K2 in corn yellow, P2 in deep plum mix.
Rnd 7	As for rnd 5.
Rnd 8	As for rnd 4.
Rnd 9	As for rnd 3.
Rnds 10 and 11	As for rnds 1 and 2.
Rnd 12	K2 in gold/rust mix, P2 in magenta.
Rnd 13	K2 in green mix, P2 in magenta.
Rnd 14	K2 in green mix, P2 in corn yellow.
Rnd 15	K2 in green mix, P2 in pale lavender.
Rnd 16	K2 in rust/blue, P2 in pale lavender.
Rnd 17	K2 in rust/blue, P2 in bright purple.
Rnd 18	K2 in rust, P2 in bright purple.
Rnd 19	K2 in gold/green mix, P2 in bright cornflower.
Rnd 20	As for rnd 18.
Rnd 21	As for rnd 17.
Rnd 22	As for rnd 16.
Rnd 23	As for rnd 15.
Rnd 24	As for rnd 14.
Rnd 25	As for rnd 13.
Rnd 26	As for rnd 12.

Rep from rnd 1 until rib measures 3½ in. (9cm) from beg.

Next rnd: increase

With corn yellow—

1st and 3rd sizes only: K4, M1, K5, M1; rep to end of rnd. 308/352 sts.

2nd size only: (K4, M1, K5, M1) 10 times, (K4, M1) 11 times; rep once again. 330 sts.

All sizes:
Change to size 3 (3¼mm) needles, place a marker at beg of rnd and, joining in and breaking off colors as required, work the patt from chart, repeating the 22 patt sts 14/15/16 times in the rnd.

Repeating the 26 patt rnds, work 59/67/75 rnds altogether.

Next rnd: divide for armholes

Patt the first 6/12/8 sts and place these sts on a holder (left underarm); patt the next 143/153/161 sts; patt the next 11/12/15 sts and place these sts on a holder (right underarm); patt the next 143/153/161 sts; patt the rem 5/0/7 sts and place on left underarm holder.

Shape armholes/work steeks

Keeping continuity of patt, work steeks between back and front at armholes, and decrease 1 st at each side of both armholes on next 5/6/7 rnds. 133/141/147 sts rem on each of back and front.

Work patt and steek for 1 rnd straight, then continue working steeks and decrease 1 st at each side of both armholes on next and every foll alt rnd until 125/133/139 sts rem on each of back and front.

Continue straight, working patt and steeks as set, until 132/145/156 patt rnds have been worked from beg (rnd 2/15/26 inclusive, of 6th patt rep). Cast off knitted steeks on this rnd.

Allover-pattern sweater

	corn yellow
/	deep plum mix
-	ocher
◇	plum
O	honey gold
v	flame red
▪	gold/rust mix
⃝	lavender mix
✳	magenta
✕	green mix
✵	pale lavender
✢	rust/blue mix
●	bright purple
✿	rust
◆	gold/green mix
✦	bright cornflower

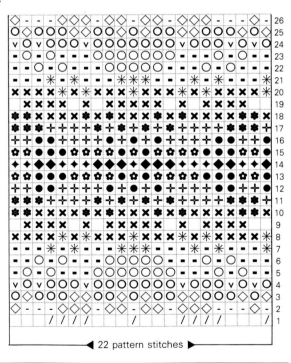

◀ 22 pattern stitches ▶

Left front shoulder

Patt the first 51/54/57 sts (left front shoulder); place the next 23/25/25 sts on a holder (front neck); leave the rem sts on spare needles.

Keeping continuity of patt, work the sts of left front shoulder on 2 double-pointed needles on right side only, breaking off yarns at end of each row, and place on a holder, 1 st at end (neck edge) of first 8 rows.

Patt 1 row straight, then decrease 1 st at neck edge of next and every foll alt row until 37/40/42 sts rem. Continue straight in patt to rnd 26/13/26, inclusive of 6th/7th/7th patt rep. Place these sts on a holder.

Right front shoulder

With right side facing, rejoin appropriate yarns and, keeping continuity of patt, work the 51/54/57 sts of right shoulder, as for left, reversing neck shaping. Place sts on a holder.

Back

With right side facing, rejoin appropriate yarns and, keeping continuity of patt, work the 125/133/139 sts of back on 2 double-pointed needles, as before, and continue straight in patt to rnd 26/13/26, inclusive of 6th/7th/7th patt rep.

Place the first 37/40/42 sts on a separate needle; place the next (center) 51/53/55 sts on a holder (back neck).

Graft or cast off together shoulder sts. Cut open armhole steeks.

Sleeves

Place a marker on 6th/6th and 7th/8th st(s) of underarm holder (center underarm).

With size 3 (3¼mm) needles and ocher, pick up and K the last 6/7/8 sts from underarm holder, beg with center-underarm st/sts/st; K up 191/201/211 sts evenly around armhole, pick up and K the rem 5/5/7 sts from underarm holder. 202/213/226 sts.

Joining in and breaking off colors as required, beg at rnd 1 of chart and work sleeve as follows:

K1/2/1 background color (center underarm to be worked in background throughout); patt the last 1/6/2 sts of chart over the next 1/6/2 sts; rep the 22 patt sts 9/9/10 times; patt the first 2/7/3 sts of chart over the last 2/7/3 sts.

Continue in this manner and patt 2 more rnds.

Next rnd: decrease

Keeping continuity of patt, K1/2/1 background (center underarm), K2tog, patt to the last 2 sts; SSK.

Patt 2 rnds straight.

Rep these last 3 rnds until 174/189/214 sts rem.

Patt 1 rnd straight, then decrease as before, on next and every foll alt rnd until 88/93/96 sts rem. Then continue straight in patt until sleeve measures 17½/18/18½ in. (45/46/47cm).

Next rnd: decrease for cuff

With background color, K2/3/0, (K2tog, K1) 28/29/32 times, K2/3/0. 60/64/64 sts.

Turn sleeve inside out (best to remove needles to do so), change to size 2 (2¾mm) needles and work K2, P2 corrugated rib in color sequence as for body for 6 in. (15cm).

Cast off in background color. Turn sleeve right side out and turn back cuff.

Neckband

With size 2 (2¾mm) needles and gold/rust mix, and beg at right shoulder, pick up and K the 51/53/55 sts from back neck holder; K up 15/15/16 sts down left neck edge, pick up and K the 8 sts from left neck holder; pick up and K the 23/25/25 sts from front neck holder and place a marker on center front st; pick up and K the 8 sts from right neck holder; K up 15/15/16 sts up right neck edge. 120/124/128 sts.

Work in K2, P2 corrugated rib in color sequence as for body, for 10 rnds.

Cast off evenly in gold/rust mix.

Collar

With size 2 (2¾mm) needles and gold/rust mix, cast on 122/126/130 sts.

Work in K2, P2 corrugated rib as flat knitting, working a K2 at end of every right side row, and using color sequence as for body, for 4½/4¾/5 in. (11.5/12/13cm). Cast off loosely and evenly in rib.

Pin cast-off edge of collar to inside of neck, placing ends of collar at each side of marked center front st. Slip st collar in place around neckband pick-up line.

Cotton sweater

This dropped-shoulder cotton sweater emphasizes pattern and color and evokes the movement of sea on sand. In the style of many fishermen's ganseys, a personal touch could be added by working the wearer's initials into the first lozenge on the left front.

Sizes

To fit chest
   38/40/42-44 in. (97/102/107-112cm).

Knitted measurements

Underarm
   42/44¼/47¼ in. (107/113/120cm).

Length from top of shoulder
   27/27½/28 in. (69/70/71cm).

Sleeve length
   21½/22/22½ in. (55/56/57cm).

Materials

50g balls (50g = approx 204m) of lightweight cotton yarn (DMC Splendida 4 Cotton used in this garment) in the foll colors:

   4 in navy blue (shade no. 5336)
   2 in pale turquoise (5828)
   4 in sand (5644)
   4 in deep turquoise (5806)
   3 in ivory (5712).

1 set or circular needles in sizes 1 (2¼mm) and 2 (3mm).

2 safety pins.

4 stitch holders.

Stitch markers.

Gauge

37 sts and 37 rows to 4 in. (10cm), measured over patt, using size 2 (3mm) needles.

Cotton sweater

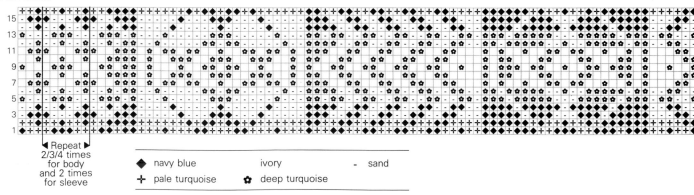

◀ Repeat ▶
2/3/4 times
for body
and 2 times
for sleeve

◆ navy blue   ivory   - sand

✦ pale turquoise   ✿ deep turquoise

Body

With set or circular size 1 (2¼mm) needles and navy blue, cast on 344/364/384 sts. Place a marker at beg of rnd and work K2, P2 corrugated rib as follows:

Rnds 1, 2, and 3	K2 in navy blue, P2 in pale turquoise.
Rnds 4 and 5	K2 in navy blue, P2 in sand
Rnds 6 and 7	K2 in deep turquoise, P2 in sand.
Rnds 8, 9, and 10	K2 in deep turquoise, P2 in ivory.
Rnds 11 and 12	As for rnds 6 and 7.
Rnds 13 and 14	As for rnds 4 and 5.

Rep these 14 rnds until rib measures 2¾/2¾/3 in. (7/7/8 cm).

Next rnd: increase

Using navy blue—

First size: (M1, K7) twice, *M1, K8, M1, K7; rep from * to end of rnd. 390 sts.

2nd size: (M1, K8) 14 times, *M1, K7; rep from * to end of rnd. 414 sts.

3rd size: (M1, K8) 6 times, *M1, K7; rep from * to end of rnd. 438 sts.

Place a marker on first and center (196th/208th/220th) st of rnd. These are the center-underarm sts. Change to size 2 (3mm) needles and, joining in and breaking off colors as required, work the patt from chart as follows:

*Patt the first 3 sts of chart; rep the next 6 sts of chart 2/3/4 times as indicated; patt next 165 sts of chart; rep next 6 sts of chart 2/3/4 times as indicated; work the last 3 sts of chart; rep from * once more.

Continue in this manner, repeating the 16 rnds of chart until body measures 16½/16¾/17 in (42/42.5/43cm) from beg.

Next rnd: divide for armholes

Place the first st of rnd on a safety pin (center underarm); work a steek (for a knitted steek, cast on at least 10 sts); increase 1 st in next st (armhole-edge st); continue in patt to st before

center-underarm st, and increase 1 st in this st (armhole-edge st); place center-underarm st on a safety pin; work a steek; increase 1 st into next st (armhole-edge st); patt to the last st of rnd and increase 1 st into this st (armhole-edge st).

Continue in patt and steek as set and work armhole-edge sts in background throughout, until body measures 24/24½/25 in. (61/62.5/64cm) from beg. Cast off knitted steeks on the last rnd.

Left front shoulder

Patt the first 86/91/96 sts (including armhole-edge st); place the next 24/26/28 sts on a holder (center front neck); leave the rem sts on spare needles.

Keeping continuity of patt, work the 86/91/96 sts of left front shoulder on double-pointed needles on right side only, breaking off yarns at end of every row, and place the last (neck-edge) st on a holder on every row for the next 13/12/11 rows. Then place the last 2 sts on the same holder on every row for the next 6/7/8 rows.

Place the rem 61/65/69 sts on a holder.

Right front shoulder

Rejoin appropriate yarns and, keeping continuity of patt, work the 86/91/96 sts of right front shoulder as for left, reversing shaping.

Place the rem 61/65/69 sts on a holder.

Back

Rejoin appropriate yarns and, keeping continuity of patt, patt the 196/208/220 sts of back, working on right side only, breaking off yarns at end of every row. Continue in this manner for 10 rows.

Right back shoulder

Patt the first 79/83/87 sts (including armhole-edge st); place the next 38/42/46 sts on a holder (center back neck); leave the rem sts on a spare needle.

Working on right side only, and keeping continuity of patt, work the 79/83/87 sts of right back shoulder, placing the last 2 sts on a holder on every row for the next 9 rows.

Place the rem 61/65/69 sts on a holder.

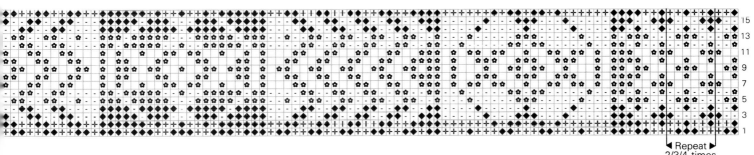

◀ Repeat ▶
2/3/4 times
for body
and 2 times
for sleeve

Left back shoulder

Rejoin appropriate yarns and, keeping continuity of patt, work the 79/83/87 sts of left back shoulder as for right shoulder, reversing shaping.

Back neck/shoulder rib

With right side facing, using size 1 (2¼mm) needles and sand, pick up and K across all sts of shoulders and neck. 196/208/220 sts. Work in K2, P2 corrugated rib as follows:

Row 1	K1 in navy blue, *P2 in pale turquoise, K2 in navy blue; rep from * to last 3 sts; P2 in pale turquoise, K1 in navy blue.
Row 2	As for row 1, but substitute P for K and K for P.
Rows 3 and 4	As for rows 1 and 2, substituting sand for pale turquoise.
Rows 5 and 6	As for rows 1 and 2, substituting deep turquoise for navy blue.
Rows 7 and 8	As for rows 3 and 4, substituting ivory for sand.
Rows 9-12	As for rows 5 and 6, substituting sand for ivory.

Cast off the center 74/78/82 sts (back neck); leave the rem sts of shoulders on spare needles.

Front neck/shoulder rib

Complete as for back rib and graft or cast off tog shoulder sts.

Sleeves

With size 2 (3mm) needles and sand, pick up and K the center-underarm st from safety pin; K up 194/198/202 sts evenly around armhole. Place a marker at beg of rnd.

Joining in and breaking off colors as required, and beg at rnd 14 of chart, set the sleeve patt as follows:

1st size:
K1 background (center-underarm st); work patt from chart, omitting first st of chart and repeating the 6 seeding patt sts twice at each end as indicated.

2nd and 3rd sizes:
K1 background (center-underarm st); K1/3 seeding; K1 patt; work patt from chart over the next 195 sts, repeating the 6 seeding patt sts twice as indicated on chart; continue seeding patt over the last 1/3 sts of rnd.

All sizes:
Patt 1 more rnd.

Next rnd: decrease

Keeping continuity of patt, K1 background (center-underarm st); K2tog; patt to the last 2 sts; SSK.

Patt 3 rnds straight.

Rep these last 4 rnds until 129/127/129 sts rem.

Patt 2 rnds straight, then decrease as before on next and every foll 3rd rnd until 105/107/109 sts rem.

Next rnd: decrease for cuff

First size:
(K2tog, K3) twice; (K2tog, K2) to the last 15 sts; (K2tog, K3) 3 times. 80 sts.

2nd size:
(K2tog, K2) to the last 3 sts; K2tog, K1. 80 sts.

3rd size:
(K2tog, K3) 4 times; (K2tog, K2) to the last 25 sts; (K2tog, K3) 5 times. 84 sts.

Change to size 1 (2¼mm) needles and K2, P2 corrugated rib as for body, but work colors from top to hem for 2¾/2¾/3 in. (7/7/8cm).

Cast off evenly in navy.

Border-pattern cardigan

This border-pattern cardigan presents another classic shape, a cardigan with shaped armholes, in colors taken from wild mimulus growing by a sandy stream.

Sizes

To fit bust
32-33/34-36/37-39/40-42 in.
(81-84/86-91/94-99/102-107cm).

Knitted measurements

Underarm
36/39/42/45 in.
(91/99/107/114cm).

Length from top of shoulder
24/24½/25½/26 in.
(61/62/65/66cm).

Sleeve length
17/17¼/17¾/18 in.
(43/44/45/46cm).

Materials

Shetland 2-ply jumper-weight yarn (Jamieson & Smith yarn used in this garment) in the foll colors:

4/4/5/5	2-oz. hanks in light fawn (shade no. 202)
3/3/4/4	1-oz. hanks in red (125)
2/2/3/3	1-oz. hanks in butter yellow (66)
2	1-oz. hanks in dark grey (54)
1/1/2/2	1-oz. hanks in wood green (118)
1	2-oz. hank in Shetland black (5)
1	1-oz. hank in each of mid-grey (27), gold/green(29), harebell blue (FC15), wine (55), gold (23).

1 set or circular needles in sizes 2 (2¾mm) and 3 (3¼mm).

9 stitch holders.

Stitch markers.

12/12/13/13 buttons.

Gauge

16 sts and 16 rows to 2 in. (5cm), measured over patt, using size 3 (3¼mm) needles.

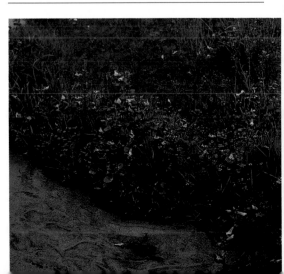

Border-pattern cardigan

light fawn
* mid-grey
✳ dark grey
◆ Shetland black
◇ wood green
✳ gold/green
✕ harebell blue
● wine
✿ red
- butter yellow
◆ gold

◀ 12 pattern stitches ▶

Body

With size 2 (2¾mm) needles and light fawn, cast on 258/278/302/322 sts. Work a steek between beg and end of each rnd. *Note:* If working a knitted steek, cast on an extra 8 sts.

Place a marker at beg of rnd and work in corrugated rib as follows:

Rnds 1 and 2	K2 in light fawn, P2 in dark grey; rep to last 2 sts; K2 in light fawn.
Rnd 3	K2 in light fawn, P2 in red; rep to last 2 sts; K2 in light fawn.
Rnds 4 and 5	K2 in butter yellow, P2 in red; rep to last 2 sts; K2 in light fawn.
Rnd 6	As for rnd 3.

Rep these 6 rnds until piece measures 2¾/3/2¾/3¼ in. (7/8/7/8.5cm).

Next rnd: increase

With light fawn, K 1/13/7/1; *M1, K 8/7/8/8; rep from * to last 1/13/7/1 sts; M1, K 1/13/7/1. 291/315/339/363 sts.

Change to size 3 (3¼mm) needles, continue working steek as set, and place a marker at beg of rnd. Joining in and breaking off colors as required, work the patt as follows:

K1 in background color (edge st); work the patt from chart, repeating the 12 patt sts 24/26/28/30 times in the rnd, then work the last st of chart; K the last st in background color (edge st).

Continue in this manner, working patt, edge sts and steek as set, and rep the 24 patt rnds until 98/96/102/98 patt rnds have been worked altogether.

Next rnd: divide for armholes

Patt the first 66/72/77/83 sts (right front); place the next 13/13/15/15 sts on a holder (right underarm); work a steek; patt the next 133/145/155/167 sts (back); place the next 13/13 15/15 sts on a holder (left underarm); work a steek; patt the rem 66/72/77/83 sts of rnd (left front).

Shape armholes

Keeping continuity of patt and working steeks at center front and armholes as set, decrease 1 st at each side of both armhole steeks on next 4/5/5/6 rnds.

Work patt and steek for 1 rnd straight, then decrease at armholes as before, on next and every foll alt rnd 4 times. 58/63/68/73 sts rem on each front, and 117/127/137/147 sts rem on back.

Continue straight in patt and steeks as set, until 150/153/156/156 patt rnds have been worked from beg (rnd 6/9/12/12 of 7th patt rep). Cast off knitted steeks on last rnd.

Right front neck

Patt the first 10/12/14/14 sts of rnd and place these sts on a holder; patt the rem 48/51/54/59 sts of right front; leave back and left front sts on spare needles.

Work right front sts with 2 double-pointed needles on right side only, breaking off yarns at end of each row, and shape neck as follows:

Keeping continuity of patt, work 1 row, then place the first (neck-edge) 2 sts of row onto front neck holder. Rep this row 2 more times.

Patt 4 rows, decreasing 1 st at neck edge of each row. Patt 1 row straight, then decrease 1 st at neck edge of next and every foll alt row 5/5/5/7 times. 33/36/39/42 sts remaining.

Continue straight and work to row 2/5/14/14 inclusive, of 8th patt rep. Place sts on a holder.

Back

With right side facing, rejoin appropriate yarns and, keeping continuity of patt, work the 117/127/137/147 sts of back with 2 double-pointed needles, as before, and continue straight in patt to row 19/22/7/7 of 7th/7th/8th/8th patt rep.

Shape neck

Patt 36/39/42/45 sts; place the next 45/49/53/57 sts on a holder; leave the rem sts on a spare needle. Patt these 36/39/42/45 sts, decreasing 1 st at end (neck edge) of next and every foll alt row until 33/36/39/42 sts rem.

Patt 1 row straight, then place sts on a holder. With right side facing, rejoin appropriate yarns and patt the rem 36/39/42/45 sts of back as for previous shoulder, reversing shaping.

Left front neck

With right side facing, rejoin appropriate yarns and, keeping continuity of patt, work as for right front neck, reversing shaping.

Graft or cast off together shoulder sts. Cut open armhole steeks.

Sleeves

With size 3 (3¼mm) needles and light fawn, pick up and K the last 7/7/8/8 sts from underarm holder; K up 139/149/155/163 sts evenly around armhole; pick up and K the rem sts from underarm holder. 152/162/170/178 sts total.

Mark the first st of rnd (center underarm) and work this st in background color throughout. Work the patt from chart over the rem sts as follows:

> Work the last 4/3/1/5 sts of chart over the next 4/3/1/5 sts; rep the 12 patt sts 12/13/14/14 times; work the first 3/2/0/4 sts of chart over the last 3/2/0/4 sts.

Continue in this manner and work 2 more rnds.

Next rnd: decrease

Keeping continuity of patt, K1 background (center-underarm st); K2tog; patt to the last 2 sts; SSK. Patt 3 rnds straight. Rep these last 4 rnds until 96/116/128/140 sts rem.

Then decrease as before on every foll 3rd rnd until 84/88/92/96 sts rem.

Next rnd: decrease

With light fawn—

First size: (K2tog, K1, K2tog, K2) rep to end. 60 sts.

2nd size: K3 *K2tog, K1, K2tog, K2; rep from * to the last st; K1. 64 sts.

3rd size: K4, *K2tog, K1; rep from * to last 4 sts; K4. 64 sts.

4th size: K6, *K2tog, K1; rep from * to last 6 sts; K6. 68 sts.

Change to size 2 (2¾mm) needles and work K2, P2 corrugated rib in colors as body, for 2¾ in. (7cm). Cast off evenly in background color.

Cut open center front steek.

Neckband

With right side facing, size 2 (2¾mm) needles and light fawn, pick up and K the 16/18/20/20 sts from right front neck holder; K up 19/19/21/21 sts to back neck holder; pick up and K the 45/49/53/57 sts from back neck holder, decreasing 1 st at center; K up 19/19/21/21 sts to left front holder; pick up and K the 16/18/20/20 sts from left front holder. 114/122/134/138 sts.

Work in corrugated rib as for body, for 10 rows. Cast off evenly in background color.

Button band

With right side facing, size 2 (2¾mm) needles and light fawn, K up 142/146/152/156 sts along left front opening. K2, P2 corrugated rib as for body, for 7 rows. Cast off evenly in light fawn.

Buttonhole band

Work as for button band, with the addition of 12/12/13/13 buttonholes, to be worked on the 4th row, as follows:

> Keeping continuity, rib 4/6/2/6, (K2tog, yo loosely, rib 10) 11/11/12/12 times; K2tog, yo loosely, rib 4/6/4/4.

Work 3 more rows of rib.

Cast off evenly in light fawn.

Sew on buttons to correspond with buttonholes.

Child's cardigan set

The child's cardigan set vividly illustrates how the same shape can serve as a framework for totally different pattern and color effects, the sources for which are worlds apart. The colors and patterns for the girl's set (below) were inspired by a piece of embroidery from the Thai highlands. The patterns and colors for the boy's set (facing page) were drawn from the first sight a Shetlander sees after the 14-hour sea passage from Lerwick to Aberdeen: oil-rig supply vessels in Aberdeen harbor.

Sizes

To fit approx ages 2-3/4-5/6-7/8-9/10-11 years.
Chest
22/24/26/28/30 in.
(56/61/66/71/76cm).

Knitted measurements

Underarm (buttoned)
26/28½/31¼/33¾/36¼ in.
(66/73/79/86/92cm).

Length from top of shoulder
13½/15½/17½/19½/21½ in.
(34/40/45/50/55cm).

Sleeve length
12½/14/15¼/17½/18¾ in.
(32/36/39/45/48cm).

Materials

Shetland 2-ply jumper-weight yarn (Jamieson &
Smith yarn used in this garment) in the foll colors:

Girl's set

1	2-oz. hank in natural white (1a) (shade no. 1a)
1	1-oz. hank in green (92)
2/2/3/3/3	1-oz. hanks in flame orange (FC7)
2/2/2/2/3	1-oz. hanks in pale turquoise (75)
2/2/2/2/3	1-oz. hanks in turquoise (48)
1	1-oz. hank in deep blue (FC48)
1/2/2/2/3	1-oz. hanks in sugar pink (95)
1	1-oz. hank in tangerine (90)
1/1/2/2/2	1-oz. hanks in bright pink (70).

Boy's set

2/2/2/2/3	1-oz. hanks red (125)
4/4/5/5/5	1-oz. hanks in bright blue (FC47)
1/1/1/2/2	2-oz. hanks in natural white (1a)
6/6/7/8/8	1-oz. hanks in deep blue (FC48)
1/2/2/2/2	1-oz. hanks in lemon (96)
2/2/2/3/3	1-oz. hanks in sky blue (FC49)
1	1-oz. hank in mid-gold (23)
1	1-oz. hank in deep gold (91)
1	2-oz. hank in Shetland black (5).

Set or circular needles in sizes 2 (2¾mm),
3 (3¼mm) and, for boy's scarf, 5 (3¾mm).

6 stitch holders.

Stitch markers.

2 safety pins.

7/8/10/10/10 buttons.

Gauge

16 sts and 16 rows to 2 in. (5 cm), measured
over patt, using size 3 (3¼mm) needles.

Cardigan

Note: The first color referred to is for the girl's cardigan; the second, in parentheses, for the boy's.

Girl's cardigan

natural white
✕ green
✻ flame orange
- pale turquoise
● turquoise
◆ deep blue
- sugar pink
/ tangerine
✿ bright pink

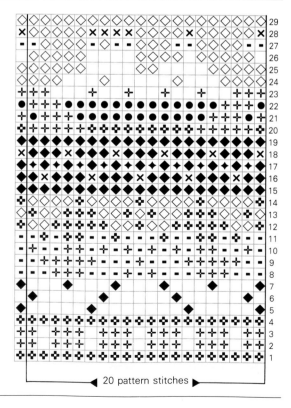

◀ 20 pattern stitches ▶

Boy's cardigan

✛ red
✛ bright blue
natural white
◆ deep blue
- lemon
◇ sky blue
✕ mid-gold
◆ deep gold
● Shetland black

◀ 20 pattern stitches ▶

Body

With size 2 (2¾mm) needles and turquoise (deep blue), cast on 178/198/214/230/250 sts. Work a steek between beg and end of every round. If working a knitted steek, cast on an extra 8 sts.

Place a marker at beg of rnd and work in K2, P2 corrugated rib as follows:

Rnd 1	K2 in turquoise (deep blue), P2 in deep blue (deep gold); rep to last 2 sts; K2 in turquoise (deep blue).
Rnds 2 and 3	K2 in turquoise (deep blue), P2 in flame orange (red); rep to last 2 sts; K2 in turquoise (deep blue).
Rnds 4 and 5	K2 in pale turquoise (bright blue), P2 in natural white (Shetland black); rep to last 2 sts; K2 in pale turquoise (bright blue).
Rnds 6 and 7	K2 in sugar pink (sky blue), P2 in tangerine (natural white); rep to last 2 sts; K2 in sugar pink (sky blue).
Rnds 8 and 9	K2 in bright pink (lemon), P2 in flame orange (bright blue); rep to last 2 sts; K2 in bright pink (lemon).
Rnd 10	K2 in bright pink (lemon), P2 in green (red); rep to last 2 sts; K2 in bright pink (lemon).
Rnds 11 and 12	K2 in sugar pink (sky blue), P2 in natural white (mid-gold); rep to last 2 sts; K2 in sugar pink (sky blue).

Rep these 12 rnds until piece measures 2/2/2¼/2½/2¾ in. (5/5/5.5/6/6.5cm).

Next rnd: increase

Natural white (sky blue), K 5/3/9/3/13, *M1, K7/8/7/7/7; rep from * to the last 5/3/9/3/13 sts; M1, K 5/3/9/3/13. 203/223/243/263/283 sts.

Change to size 3 (3¼mm) needles, continue working steek as set, and, if working a knitted steek, place a marker on first and last sts of rnd.

Joining in and breaking off colors as required, work the patt as follows:

K1 background color (edge st), work the patt from chart, repeating the 20 patt sts 10/11/12/13/14 times, then work the last st of chart; K the last st in background color (edge st).

Place markers on 52nd/57th/62nd/67th/72nd sts from beg and end of rnd (center-underarm sts).

Continue in this manner, repeating the 29 patt rnds, and work 43/55/64/78/87 patt rnds total.

Next rnd: begin armholes

Patt 51/56/61/66/71 sts, increasing 1 st on last st (armhole-edge st); place the next st on a safety pin (center-underarm st); work a steek; patt the next 99/109/119/129/139 sts increasing 1 st at each end (armhole-edge sts); place the next st on a safety pin (center-underarm st); work a steek; then increase 1 st on next st (armhole-edge st), and patt the rem sts of rnd.

Working all steeks as set, and all edge sts in background colors, continue straight in patt until 77/91/102/116/129 patt rnds have been worked in total, from beg. Cast off knitted steeks on the last rnd.

Right front neck

Patt the first 7/8/9/10/11 sts of rnd and place these sts on a holder. Patt the rem 45/49/53/57/61 sts of right front. Leave back and left front sts on spare needles and continue working right front sts with 2 needles on right side only, breaking off yarns at end of every row, and shape neck as follows:

Keeping continuity of patt, work the first 2 sts (neck edge) and place onto front neck holder; patt to end. Rep this row 2 more times.

Then place the first st of next 3/4/4/4/5 rows onto same holder.

Patt 1 row straight, then decrease 1 st at beg of next and every foll alt row 3/3/3/4/4 times. 33/36/40/43/46 sts rem.

Continue straight in patt until 91/107/120/136/149 patt rnds have been worked in total, from beg (rnd 4/20/4/20/4 of 4th/4th/5th/5th/6th patt rep). On 2nd and 4th sizes, work the last patt rnd in sugar pink (deep blue) straight.

Place right shoulder sts on a holder.

Back

Rejoin appropriate yarns and, keeping continuity of patt, work the 101/111/121/131/141 sts of back with 2 needles on right side only, and continue straight in patt until back corresponds in length with right front, at shoulder. Work the last rnd of 2nd and 4th sizes as for right front.

Place 33/36/40/43/46 sts at each side on holders for shoulders. Place the 35/39/41/45/49 center sts on a holder for back neck.

Left front neck

Rejoin appropriate yarns and, keeping continuity of patt, work rem sts as for right front neck, reversing shaping.

Graft or cast off shoulder sts tog.

Cut open armhole steeks.

Sleeves

With size 3 (3¼mm) needles and pale turquoise (sky blue)/ sugar pink (sky blue)/pale turquoise (natural white)/sugar pink (bright blue)/sugar pink (sky blue), pick up and K the center-underarm st from safety pin, then K up 93/101/109/113/121 sts evenly around armhole. 94/102/110/114/122 sts total. Place a marker at beg of rnd.

Beg at rnd 14/26/4/19/29 of chart and reading downward (turn chart upside down), patt sleeve as follows:

K1 background color (center-underarm st), work the last 7/1/5/7/1 st(s) of chart, then rep the 20 patt sts 4/5/5/5/6 times, then work the first 6/0/4/6/0 sts of patt rep.

Continue in this manner, and patt 2/2/2/3/3 more rnds.

Next rnd: decrease

Keeping continuity of patt, K1 background color (center-underarm st), K2tog, patt to the last 2 sts, SSK.

Patt 3/3/3/4/4 rnds straight.

Rep these last 4/4/4/5/5 rnds until 70/66/62/94/102 sts rem.

For 1st, 2nd, 4th and 5th sizes only:
On next rnd, work decrease rnd as before.

Patt 2/2/3/3 rnds straight.

Rep these last 3/3/4/4 rnds until 54/58/66/70 sts rem.

For all sizes: work wrist decrease

(K2tog, K 2/3/3/2/2) 6/1/3/6/8 times; (K2tog, K 1/2/2/1/1) 2/12/8/6/2 times; (K2tog, K 2/3/3/2/2) 6/1/3/6/8 times. 40/44/48/48/52 sts rem.

K2, P2 corrugated rib for 2/2/2¼/2½/2¾ in. (5/5/5.5/6/7cm), in color sequence as for body, but work from last rnd to first. Cast off evenly in turquoise (deep blue).

Cut open center front steek.

Neckband

With right side facing, size 2 (2¾mm) needles and sugar pink (sky blue), pick up and K the 16/18/19/20/22 sts from right-front neck holder; K up 6/6/6/9/9 sts to back neck holder; pick up and K the 35/39/41/45/49 sts from back neck holder, decreasing 1 st at center back neck; K up 6/6/6/9/9 sts to left-front neck holder; then pick up and K the 16/18/19/20/22 sts from this holder. 78/86/90/102/110 sts.

Work in K2, P2 corrugated rib (right side having a K2 at each end, and wrong side having a P2 at each end) in color sequence as for rnds 7/8/8/9/10 through to rnd 1 (inclusive) of body.

Cast off evenly in turquoise (deep blue).

Button band

With size 2 (2¾mm) needles and sugar pink (sky blue), K up 84/96/104/114/124 sts evenly along left (right) front opening.

K2, P2 corrugated rib in color sequence as for neckband.

Cast off evenly in turquoise (deep blue).

Buttonhole band

Work as for button band, with the addition of 7/8/10/10/10 buttonholes, to be worked on the 4th/4th/4th/5th/5th row, as follows:

1st and 2nd sizes:
Rib 2/1, (K2tog, yo loosely, rib 11) 6/7 times; K2tog, yo loosely, rib 2.
3rd, 4th, and 5th sizes:
Rib 1/2/2, (K2tog, yo loosely, rib 9/10/11) 9 times; K2tog, yo loosely, rib 2/2/3.

Girl's tammy

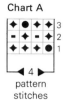

	natural white
✕	green
✳	flame orange
-	pale turquoise
●	turquoise
◆	deep blue
-	sugar pink
/	tangerine
✿	bright pink
s	SL1
▨	knit 2 tog, then PSSO

Girl's purse

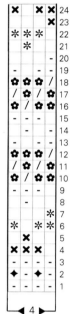

◀ 4 ▶
pattern
stitches

Chart A

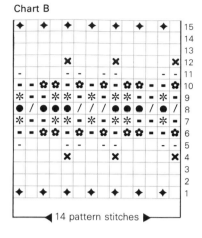

◀ 4 ▶
pattern
stitches

Chart B

◀ 14 pattern stitches ▶

Chart C

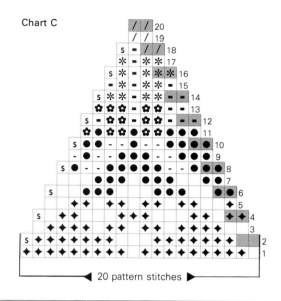

◀ 20 pattern stitches ▶

Girl's tammy

Sizes

To fit ages 2-4/5-8/9-11 years.

With size 2 (2¾mm) needles and deep blue, cast on 136/136/140 sts. Place a marker at beg of rnd and work K2, P2 corrugated rib as follows:

Rnds 1 and 2	K2 in deep blue, P2 in turquoise; rep to end.
Rnds 3 and 4	K2, in deep blue, P2 in pale turquoise; rep to end.
Rnds 5 and 6	K2 in deep blue, P2 in natural white; rep to end.

Repeat these 6 rnds, working 12/12/14 rnds altogether.

Next rnd: increase

1st and 2nd sizes only:
*(K4, M1) 3 times, K5, M1; rep from * to end of rnd. 168 sts.

3rd size only:
K5, M1; rep to end. 168 sts.

All sizes:
Change to size 3 (3¼mm) needles and K 3/4/5 rnds in deep blue.

Then joining in and breaking off colors as required, work the 3 rnds of patt from Chart A, repeating the 4 patt sts 42 times in the rnd.

Break off patt colors and with deep blue, K 1 rnd straight.

Next rnd: increase

K12, M1; rep to end. 182 sts.

K 2/3/4 more rnds in deep blue.

Then, joining in and breaking off colors as required, work the 15 rnds of patt from Chart B, repeating the 14 patt sts 13 times in the rnd.

K 1 rnd in deep blue.

Next rnd: decrease

With deep blue, K11, K2tog; rep to end. 168 sts.

Next rnd: K2tog, K19; rep to end. 160 sts.

K 0/1/3 more rnds in deep blue.

Then joining in and breaking off colors as required, work the 20 patt rnds from Chart C, double-decreasing where indicated on chart, as follows: SL1-K2tog-PSSO.

Draw yarn through rem 8 sts and fasten off securely.

Girl's purse

With size 3 (3¼mm) needles and sugar pink, cast on 88 sts. Place a marker at beg of rnd.

Joining in and breaking off colors as required, work the patt from chart, repeating the 4 patt sts 22 times in the rnd.

Rep the 24 patt rnds twice, then work rnds 1 through 3 once again.

Next rnd

With sugar pink, cast off the first 44 sts of rnd.

Keeping continuity of patt, work the rem 44 sts on 2 needles, decreasing on every row as follows: patt 1, SSK; patt to the last 3 sts; K2tog, patt 1.

Continue in this manner until 2 sts rem. Cast off.

Sew base along cast-on edge.

Using white, sugar pink and tangerine, make a twisted cord the desired length for handle, and 2 short cords for flap edges. (For information on making cords, see pp. 107-108.)

Knot the 2 short cords tog at one end and stitch along flap edges, with the knot at center front. Attach handle to purse. If desired, the purse may be lined with a suitable fabric.

Boy's scarf

Sizes

To fit ages 2-5/6-11 years.

With size 3 (3¼mm) needles and deep blue, cast on 96/120 sts. Place a marker at beg of rnd and K 6/8 rnds straight.

Change to size 5 (3¾mm) needles and, joining and breaking off colors as required, work the patt from scarf and mitten chart, repeating the 24 patt sts 4/5 times in the rnd. Work all 33 rnds of patt.

Change to size 3 (3¼mm) needles and, with deep blue, K straight until piece measures 38/42 in. (97/107cm) from beg.

Change to size 5 (3¾mm) needles and, joining in and breaking off colors as required, work the patt from chart as before, but read from rnd 33 to rnd 1 (turn chart upside down).

Change to size 3 (3¼mm) needles and with deep blue, K 6/8 rnds straight.

Place the first 48/60 sts on one needle and the rem 48/60 sts on another needle and cast off the sts tog. Sew cast-on edges tog.

Using 8 in. (20cm) lengths of yarn, make a fringe along each end. (For information on making fringe, see p. 107.)

Boy's scarf and mittens

- ✤ red
- ✛ bright blue
-   natural white
- ◆ deep blue
- ▪ lemon
- ◇ sky blue
- ✗ mid-gold
- ✦ deep gold
- ● Shetland black

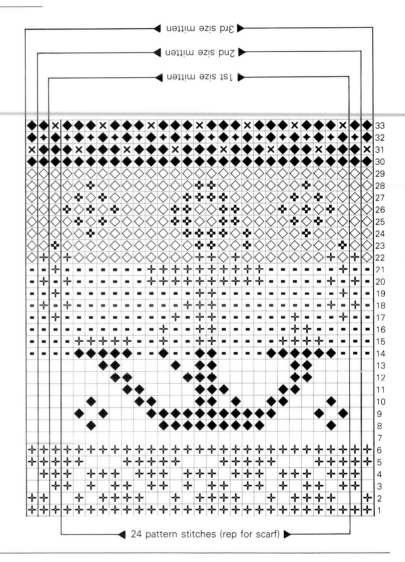

24 pattern stitches (rep for scarf)

Boy's mittens

Sizes

To fit age 2-4/5-8/9-11 years.

Left mitten

With size 2 (2¾mm) needles and red, cast on 38/40/44 sts. Place a marker at beg of rnd and work in corrugated rib as follows: K1 deep blue, P1 natural white; rep to end.

Rep this rnd until cuff measures 1¾/2/2¼ in. (4.5/5/5.5cm).

Next round: increase

With deep blue, (M1, K7) 1/2/2 time(s), (M1, K6/6/8) 4/2/2 times, (M1, K7) 1/2/2 time(s). 44/46/50 sts.

Change to size 3 (3¼mm) needles, place a marker at beg of rnd and, joining in and breaking off colors as required, work the patt as follows:

Turn scarf and mitten chart (p. 133) upside down, and patt the first 25/27/29 sts of rnd as

---

Boy's mittens, continued

- ✤ red
- ✚ bright blue
-    natural white
- ◆ deep blue
- - lemon
- ◇ sky blue
- ✕ mid-gold
- ✦ deep gold
- ● Shetland black

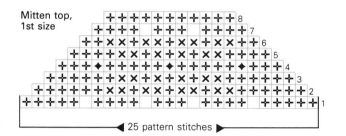

Mitten top, 1st size

◀ 25 pattern stitches ▶

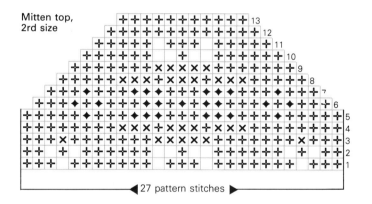

Mitten top, 2rd size

◀ 27 pattern stitches ▶

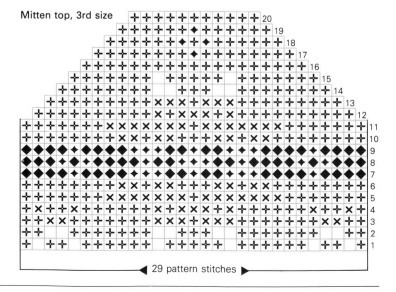

Mitten top, 3rd size

◀ 29 pattern stitches ▶

Indicated on chart; K the rem 19/19/21 sts (palm), working these sts in seeding patt on rnds with 2 colors, that is, K1 background, K1 patt, and rep to the last st, K1 background.

Continue working chart patt over first 25/27/29 sts and work the background color st in patt color and vice versa on all foll palm sts. Work 2/2/3 rnds.

Next round: begin thumb gusset

Keeping continuity of patt, work to the last st of rnd, and increase 1 st at each side of this st (3 sts represented in first row of thumb chart). Make these increases in the patt color if working a 2-color rnd.

Continue in this manner, increasing 1 st at each side of the increased sts on next 2/3/3 rnds (7/9/9 sts in thumb gusset) and patt these sts as illustrated on thumb chart.

Then continue straight in patts as set for a further 7/8/9 rnds.

Make thumb opening

Place the 7/9/9 thumb sts on a safety pin and continue in patts as set, casting on 7/9/9 sts at end of rnd.

Continue and work the 7/9/9 cast-on sts in seeding patt as for palm.

Patt straight to the last rnd of scarf and mitten chart.

K 1 rnd in deep blue, then work the patt from mitten top chart over the first 25/27/29 sts, and continue working the rem sts in seeding.

Patt 1/5/11 rnds in this manner. Then, keeping continuity of patt, decrease as follows:

K1, SSK; patt to the last 3 sts of mitten top chart; K2tog, K1, SSK; work seeding patt to the last 2 sts of rnd; K2tog.

Continue in this manner, working patt as set and decreasing 4 sts on every rnd until 11 sts rem on mitten top chart. 23 sts total.

Graft or cast off these sts tog.

Thumb

Rejoin appropriate yarns and patt the next rnd of thumb from chart over the 7/9/9 thumb gusset sts; K up 9/11/11 sts around opening. Place a marker at beg of rnd, and patt the first 7/9/9 sts as for thumb chart and patt the rem sts in seeding patt, working 11/13/15 rnds total.

Shape top

Next rnd:
   K1, SSK, K1/3/3, K2tog, K1, SSK,
   K5/7/7, K2tog.

Next rnd, for first size only:
   K1, SL1-K2tog-PSSO, K1, SSK,
   SL1-K2tog-PSSO, K2tog.

Draw yarn through rem sts and fasten off on the wrong side.

Next rnd, for 2nd and 3rd sizes only:
   K1, SSK, K1, K2tog, K1, SSK, K5, K2tog.

Work next rnd as for last rnd of first size, and fasten off rem sts.

Boy's mitten thumb chart

Chart shows length for largest size.

● pattern color
   background color

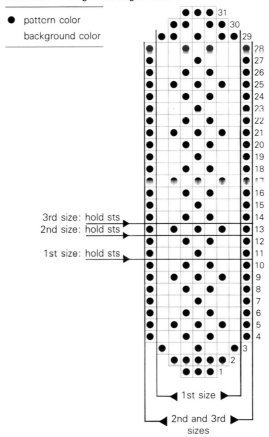

◄ 1st size ►

◄ 2nd and 3rd sizes ►

Oversize panel cardigan

This oversize panel cardigan in soft, pale colors with a touch of black is a loose, easy style. Large stars, borders, seeding and decorative gussets provide lots of interest to the patterning.

Sizes
To fit bust 34-38 in. (86-97cm).

Knitted measurements
Underarm (buttoned): 47¾ in. (121cm).
Length from top of shoulder: 27½ in. (70cm).
Sleeve length: 18 in. (46cm).

Materials
Shetland 2-ply jumper-weight yarn (Jamieson & Smith yarn used in this garment) in the foll colors:

    3 1-oz. hanks in ocher (shade no. 121)
    1 2-oz. hank in Shetland black (5)
    3 1-oz. hanks in mid-blue (FC49)
    6 1-oz. hanks in lemon (96)
    2 1-oz. hanks in light blue (14)
    2 1-oz. hanks in honey gold (32)
    1 2-oz. hank in light fawn (202)
    1 1-oz. hank in rust (FC8)
    2 1-oz. hanks in clover (FC10)
    2 1-oz. hanks in pink mix (FC6).

Oversize panel cardigan

Chart A

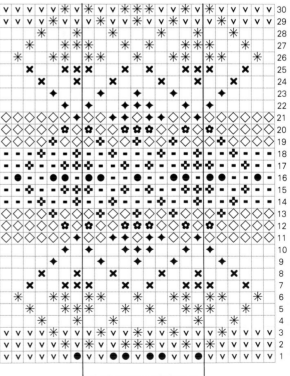

◀ 10 pattern stitches ▶

v	ocher	
●	Shetland black	
✳	mid-blue	
	lemon	
✕	light blue	
◆	honey gold	
◇	light fawn	
✿	rust	
✚	clover	
-	pink mix	

1 set or circular needles in sizes 2 (2¾mm) and
3 (3¼mm).

9 stitch holders.

Stitch markers.

13 buttons.

Gauge

16 sts and 16 rows to 2 in. (5 cm), measured
over patt, using size 3 (3¼mm) needles.

Body

With size 2 (2¾mm) needles and ocher, cast on
300 sts. Work a steek between beg and end of
each rnd. *Note:* If working a knitted steek, cast on
an extra 8 sts.

Place a marker at beg of rnd and work in
corrugated rib as follows:

Rnd 1	K1 in ocher, P1 in Shetland black.
Rnds 2 and 3	K1 in ocher, P1 in mid-blue.
Rnds 4, 5 and 6	K1 in lemon, P1 in mid-blue.

Rnds 7 and 8	K1 in lemon, P1 in light blue.
Rnds 9 and 10	K1 in lemon, P1 in honey gold.
Rnd 11	K1 in light fawn, P1 in honey gold.
Rnd 12	K1 in light fawn, P1 in rust.
Rnd 13	K1 in light fawn, P1 in clover.
Rnds 14 and 15	K1 in pink mix, P1 in clover.
Rnd 16	K1 in pink mix, P1 in Shetland black.
Rnds 17 through 30	As for rnds 15 through 2.

Next rnd: increase

With ocher, K6, *M1, K4; rep from * to the last
6 sts; M1, K6. 373 sts.

Change to size 3 (3¼mm) needles, continue
working steek as set, and place a marker at beg
of rnd.

Joining in and breaking off colors as required,
work the patt as follows:

Chart B

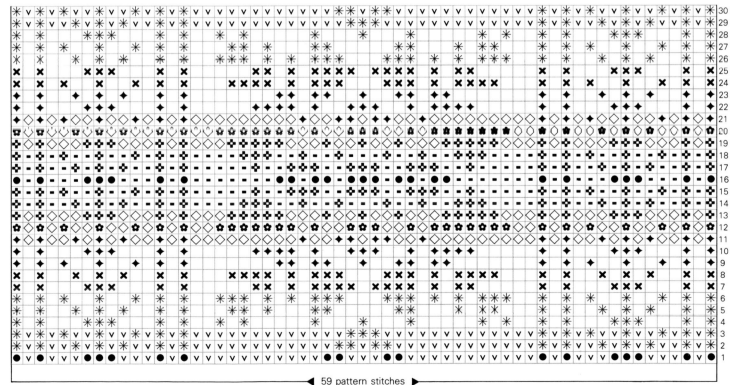

◀ 59 pattern stitches ▶

Chart C

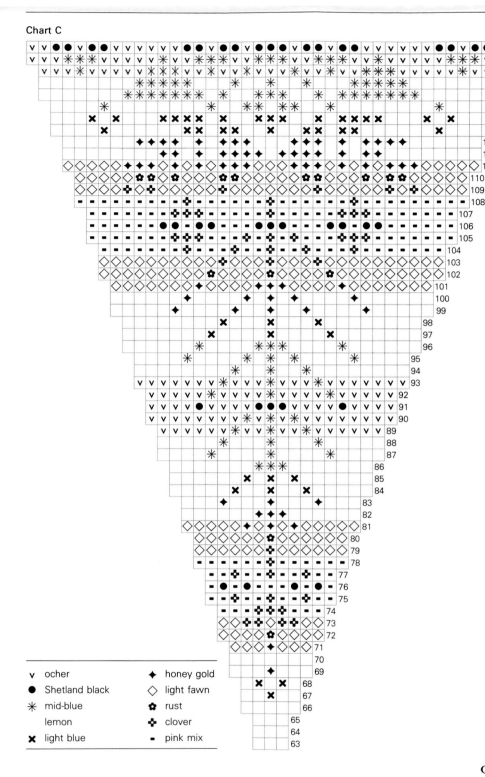

v ocher

● Shetland black

✳ mid-blue

   lemon

✖ light blue

◆ honey gold

◇ light fawn

✿ rust

✜ clover

- pink mix

K1 background color (edge st); Chart A over the next 23 sts; Chart B over the next 59 sts; Chart A over the next 23 sts, and place a marker on the 12th st of this panel (center right underarm); Chart B over the next 59 sts; Chart A over the next 43 sts, working the first 6 sts of chart, then repeating the 10 patt sts 3 times, then work the last 7 sts of chart; Chart B over the next 59 sts; Chart A over the next 23 sts, and place a marker on the 12th st of this panel (center left underarm); Chart B over the next 59 sts; Chart A over the next 23 sts; K1 background color (edge st).

Continue in this manner, working patt panels, edge sts and steek as set, and rep the 30 patt rnds twice. Then work rnds 1 and 2 once more (62 patt rnds altogether).

Next rnd: begin gussets

Work patt panels, edge sts and steek as set, and with background color, increase 1 st at each side of both right and left center-underarm sts. These 3 gusset sts are represented in rnd 63 of Chart C.

Continue working patt panels, edge sts and steeks as set, and work gussets from Chart C, reading from rnd 64 and increasing on every 3rd rnd as illustrated on chart. Work to rnd 120 inclusive (41 sts in each gusset).

Next rnd: begin armholes

Keeping continuity of patt, work 94 sts, increasing 1 st on last st (armhole-edge st); place the next 41 sts of gusset on a holder; work a steek; then increasing 1 st at each side (armhole-edge sts), patt the next 183 sts (back); place the next 41 sts of gusset on a holder; work a steek; then increasing on next st (armhole-edge st), patt the rem sts of rnd.

Continue working patt panels, center front and armhole steeks as set, and work all edge sts in background color throughout. Patt straight to rnd 21 inclusive, of 6th patt rep, casting off knitted steeks on rnd 21.

Right front neck

Keeping continuity of patt, work the first 12 sts of rnd and place on a holder; patt the rem 83 sts of right front. Leave the rem sts of back and left front on needles. Working with 2 double-pointed needles on right side only, breaking off yarns at end of each row and keeping continuity of patt, shape neck as follows:

> Place 3 sts on same holder at neck edge of next 2 rows.
>
> Place 2 sts on same holder at neck edge of next 4 rows.
>
> Place 1 st on same holder at neck edge of next 3 rows.
>
> Patt 1 row straight, then decrease 1 st at neck edge of next and every foll alt row 7 times, thus ending on row 15 of 7th patt rep, with 59 sts rem. Place these sts on a holder.

Back

Keeping continuity of patt, work the 185 sts of back on 2 double-pointed needles, as for front, and patt straight to row 7 inclusive of 7th patt rep.

Next rnd

Patt 63 sts; place the next 59 sts on a holder (back neck); leave the rem sts on a spare needle. Keeping continuity of patt, work the first 63 sts, on right side only, decreasing 1 st at end (neck edge) of next and every foll alt row 4 times, thus ending on row 15 of 7th patt rep, with 59 sts rem. Place these sts on a holder.

Rejoin appropriate yarns to the rem 63 sts of back and complete as for previous shoulder, reversing neck shaping.

Left front neck

Rejoin appropriate yarns and, keeping continuity of patt, work as for right front neck, reversing the shaping.

Graft or cast off tog shoulder sts. Cut open armhole steeks.

Sleeves

With size 3 (3¼mm) needles and ocher, K up 145 sts evenly around armhole. Join in Shetland black and patt the last rnd of Chart C (rnd 121) over gusset sts. 186 sts in rnd altog. Beg at rnd 1 on charts A and B, patt the sleeve as follows:

> Chart A over the first 43 sts, working the first 6 sts of chart, then repeating the 10 patt sts 3 times, then work the last 7 sts of chart; Chart B over the next 59 sts; Chart A over the last 43 sts, working as before; turn Chart C upside down and work rnd 120 over 41 gusset sts.

Continue in this manner, working all charts as set, and decrease 1 st at each side of gusset on rnd 119 of Chart C and every foll 3rd rnd as illustrated, until 1 st rem. Place a marker on gusset st and work this st in background color throughout. Patt 2 rnds straight.

Next rnd: decrease

Keeping continuity of patt, K1 background (gusset st); K2tog; patt to the last 2 sts; SSK. Patt 2 rnds straight. Rep these last 3 rnds until 106 sts rem (4 patt reps from beg of sleeve).

Next rnd: decrease

With ocher, (K2tog, K1) 9 times; (K2tog) 26 times; (K1, K2tog) 9 times. 62 sts.

Change to size 2 (2¾mm) needles and work 30 rnds of K1, P1 corrugated rib, as for body. Cast off evenly in ocher. Cut open front steek.

Neckband

With size 2 (2¾mm) needles and lemon, pick up and K the 29 sts from right-front neck holder; K up 17 sts to back neck holder; pick up and K the 59 sts from back neck holder; K up 17 sts to front neck holder; pick up and K the 29 sts from holder. 151 sts.

Work 11 rnds of K1, P1 corrugated rib in colors as rnds 20 through 30 of body.

Left front band

With right side facing, size 2 (2¾mm) needles and lemon, K up 163 sts evenly along left front opening. Work 11 rows in K1, P1 corrugated rib, as for neckband. Cast off evenly in ocher.

Right front band

Work as for left front band, with the addition of 13 buttonholes on row 6. Work buttonholes as follows:

Row 6	Rib 2; (cast off 2, rib 11) 12 times; cast off 2, rib 3.
Row 7	Keeping continuity, work in rib, casting on 2 sts over cast-off sts.

Rib for 4 more rows.

Cast off evenly in ocher.

Sew on buttons to correspond with buttonholes.

Wave-pattern cardigan

In this V-neck, dropped-shoulder, wave-pattern cardigan, bright patterns on shaded blue waves create the impact.

Sizes

To fit bust
32/34/36/38/40 in.
(81/86/91/97/102cm).

Knitted measurements

Underarm (buttoned)
41/43½/46/48½/51 in.
(104/111/117/123/130cm).

Length from top of shoulder
28/29/30/31/32 in.
(71/74/76/79/81cm).

Sleeve length
17½/18/18/18½/18½ in.
(45/46/46/47/47cm).

Materials

1-oz. hanks of Shetland 2-ply jumper-weight yarn (Jamieson & Smith yarn used in this garment) in the foll colors:

2/3/3/3/3	in pale blue mix (shade no. 1280)
2/3/3/3/3	in sky blue (FC49)
2/2/3/3/3	in dusky blue (33)
2/2/3/3/3	in bright blue (FC47)
4/4/5/5/6	in dark blue (135)
1	in tangerine (90)
1/1/2/2/2	in rust mix (FC38)
1/1/2/2/2	in pink mix (1289)
2/2/2/3/3	in flame red (129)
1/1/2/2/2	in turquoise (FC34)
1/1/2/2/2	in flame orange (FC7)
1/1/2/2/2	in bright turquoise (132)
1	in bright pink (70).

Set or circular needles in sizes 2 (2¾mm) and 3 (3¼mm).

6 stitch holders.

Stitch markers.

2 safety pins.

8/8/8/9/9 buttons.

Gauge

16 sts and 16 rows to 2 in. (5cm), measured over patt, using size 3 (3¼mm) needles.

Body

With size 2 (2¾mm) needles and dark blue, cast on 284/300/320/336/348 sts. Work a steek between beg and end of every rnd. If working a knitted steek, cast on an extra 8 sts.

Place a marker at beg of rnd and work corrugated rib as follows.

Rnds 1, 2, and 3	K2 in dark blue, P2 in pale blue mix.
Rnds 4 and 5	K2 in dark blue, P2 in sky blue.
Rnds 6 and 7	K2 in dark blue, P2 in dusky blue.
Rnds 8 and 9	K2 in dark blue, P2 in bright blue.
Rnd 10	K2 in dark blue, P2 in tangerine.
Rnd 11	K2 in dark blue, P2 in rust mix.
Rnd 12	K2 in turquoise, P2 in pink mix.
Rnds 13 and 14	K2 in turquoise, P2 in flame red.
Rnd 15	K2 in bright turquoise, P2 in flame orange.
Rnd 16	K2 in bright turquoise, P2 in bright pink.
Rnds 17 through 27/27/31/31/31	As for rnds 15 through 5/5/1/1/1, working in reverse.

Next rnd: increase

With pale blue mix, K9/3/13/7/12, *M1, K7/7/7/7/6; rep from * to the last 9/3/13/7/12 sts; M1, K9/3/13/7/12. 323/343/363/383/403 sts.

Place a marker at beg of rnd, change to size 3 (3¼mm) needles and continue working the steek as set.

Joining in and breaking off colors as required, work the patt as follows:

K1 in background color (edge st); work the patt from chart, repeating the 20 patt sts 16/17/18/19/20 times; work the last st from chart; K1 in background color (edge st).

Place markers on the 82nd/87th/92nd/97th/102nd sts from beg and end of rnd (center-underarm sts).

Continue in patt as set, repeating the 50 patt rnds, marking the center-underarm sts periodically and working 63 rnds altogether.

Next rnd: make pocket openings

Keeping continuity of patt, work 19/21/23/25/28 sts; place the next 45/45/47/47/47 sts on a holder (right pocket opening); with dark blue, cast on 45/45/47/47/47 sts; patt to the last 64/66/70/72/75 sts; place the next 45/45/47/47/47 sts on a holder (left pocket opening); with dark blue, cast on 45/45/47/47/47 sts; patt the last 19/21/23/25/28 sts.

Wave-pattern cardigan

pale blue mix
- **-** sky blue
- **◇** dusky blue
- **✕** bright blue
- **✿** dark blue
- **○** tangerine
- **●** rust mix
- **◆** pink mix
- **✛** flame red
- **✳** turquoise
- **v** flame orange
- **-** bright turquoise
- **/** bright pink

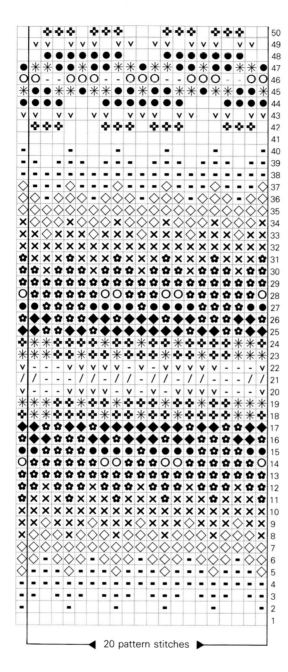

◀ 20 pattern stitches ▶

Working steek as set, and keeping continuity of patt, continue straight to rnd 38/38/38/38/42 (inclusive) of 2nd patt rep.

Next rnd: begin neck shaping

Continue working steek as set, K1 background; SSK; keeping continuity of patt, work to the last 3 sts of rnd; K2tog; K1 background.

Continuing to work steek as set and first and last sts in background color, patt 3 rnds.

Rep these last 4 rnds and patt to rnd 24/28/30/36/40 (inclusive) of 3rd patt rep.

Next rnd: begin armholes

Patt to the marked st of center underarm and increase 1 st on last st (right front armhole-edge st); place the marked st on a safety pin; work a steek; patt the next 159/169/179/189/199 sts (back), increasing 1 st at each end (back armhole-edge sts); place the next st (marked st) on a safety pin; work a steek; increase 1 st into the next st (left front armhole-edge st) and patt to end of rnd.

Working all steeks as set, and all edge sts in background color, continue in patt, decreasing at neck edges on every 4th rnd, as set, until 53/56/60/63/67 sts rem on each front.

Patt and steek straight to rnd 49/7/11/19/29 (inclusive) of 4th/5th/5th/5th/5th patt rep.

Next rnd

Keeping continuity of patt, K1 background; SSK; patt 51/54/58/61/65, then place these 53/56/60/63/67 sts on a holder; cast off steek; patt 53/56/60/63/67 sts and place these sts on a holder; patt 55/59/61/65/67 sts and place these sts on a holder (back neck); patt 53/56/60/63/67 sts and leave these sts on a needle; cast off steek; patt 51/54/58/61/65; K2tog; K1 background; cast off front steek.

Graft or cast off tog shoulder sts. Cut open armhole steeks.

Sleeves

With size 3 (3¼mm) needles and dusky blue/dark blue/bright blue/sky blue/pale blue mix, pick up and K the center-underarm st from safety pin; K up 147/155/159/163/171 sts evenly around armhole. 148/156/160/164/172 sts. Place a marker at beg of rnd.

Beg at rnd 7/13/11/5/1 of chart and patt sleeve as follows:

K1 background (center-underarm st); work the last 3/7/9/1/5 sts of chart patt; rep the 20 patt sts 7/7/7/8/8 times; work the first 4/8/10/2/6 sts of chart.

Continue as set and patt 6/2/2/2/2 more rnds.

Next rnd: decrease

Keeping continuity of patt, K1 background (center underarm st to be worked in background throughout); K2tog; patt to the last 2 sts; SSK.

Patt 3 rnds straight.

Rep these last 4 rnds until 92/96/100/102/110 sts rem.

Next rnd: decrease for wrist

With background, (K2tog, K1) 14/12/14/13/13 times, (K2tog) 4/12/8/12/16 times, (K2tog, K1) 14/12/14/13/13 times. 60/60/64/64/68 sts.

Work in K2, P2 corrugated rib in colors as for body from rnd 5 through rnd 31. Cast off in dark blue.

Cut open center front steek.

Neckband

With right side facing, size 2 (2¾mm) needles and dark blue, and using all needles to hold sts, K up 101/107/192/200/205 sts up right front; pick up and K the 55/59/61/65/67 sts of back neck; K up 182/188/193/201/206 down left front. 418/434/446/466/478 sts total.

Work K2, P2 corrugated rib as follows:

Row 1 (wrong side)	P2 in dark blue, K2 in dusky blue; rep to last 2 sts; P2 in dark blue.
Row 2	K2 in dark blue, P2 in dusky blue; rep to last 2 sts; K2 in dark blue.
Row 3	P2 in dark blue, K2 in bright blue; rep to last 2 sts; P2 in dark blue.
Row 4	K2 in dark blue, P2 in bright blue; rep, and make 8/8/8/9/9 buttonholes evenly spaced between hem and beg of neck shaping; end K2 in dark blue. (For information on making buttonholes, see p. 106.)
Row 5	P2 in turquoise, K2 in tangerine; rep to last 2 sts; P2 in turquoise.
Row 6	K2 in turquoise, P2 in tangerine; rep to last 2 sts; K2 in turquoise.
Row 7	P2 in turquoise, K2 in rust mix; rep to last 2 sts; P2 in turquoise.
Row 8	K2 in turquoise, P2 in flame red; rep to last 2 sts; K2 in turquoise.
Row 9	P2 in turquoise, K2 in flame red; rep to last 2 sts; P2 in turquoise.

Cast off in dark blue.

Pocket ribs

With size 2 (2¾mm) needles and dark blue, pick up and K the 45/45/47/47/47 sts of pocket opening, increasing 1 st at center

K2, P2 corrugated rib (1st and 2nd sizes having an extra K2 at end of right side rows) on 2 needles. Work color sequence as for rnds 10 through 16, then, working in reverse, as for rnds 15 through 10 of body.

Cast off evenly. Stitch ends of rib to front.

Pocket linings

With size 3 (3¼mm) needles and dark blue, K up 45/45/47/47/47 sts along cast-on edge of pocket opening.

Work straight in stockinette st until piece reaches top of rib when laid flat. Cast off. Press pocket linings lightly and stitch down.

Water-lily jacket

The water-lily jacket is a square, cropped style in quiet, vegetable-dyed shades. The use of silk in this garment adds a luxurious sheen to the water-lily panels and leaf borders.

Sizes

To fit bust 34-37 in. (86-94cm).

Knitted measurements

Underarm (including front edgings)
    45 in. (114cm).
Length from top of shoulder
    19¾ in. (50cm).
Sleeve length
    10 in. (26cm).

Materials

50g hanks (50g = approx 132 yd.) silk/wool mix yarn (Silkenwool by Silk City Fibers used in this garment) in the foll colors:

3	in dark green (shade no. 19)
3	in pale turquoise (01)
2	in indigo (88))
2	in grey (B)
3	in blue (03)
2	in ivory (A)
1	in yellow (91).

1 set or circular needles in size 6 (4mm).

6 stitch holders.

2 safety pins.

Stitch markers.

Gauge

12 sts and 12 rows to 2 in. (5cm), measured over patt, using size 6 (4mm) needles.

Body

With size 6 (4mm) needles and dark green, cast on 258 sts. Work a steek between beg and end of each round. *Note:* If working a knitted steek, cast on an extra 8 sts. Place a marker at beg of rnd and work checkered border as follows:

Rnd 1	K1 in indigo, *K2 in pale turquoise, K2 in indigo;** rep from * to last st; K1 in indigo.
Rnd 2	P1 in indigo, *P2 in pale turquoise, P2 in indigo;** rep from * to last st; P1 in indigo.
Rnds 3 and 4	As for rnds 1 and 2, substituting grey for indigo, and blue for pale turquoise.
Rnds 5 and 6	As for rnds 3 and 4, substituting blue for grey, and ivory for blue.
Rnds 7 and 8	As for rnds 3 and 4.
Rnds 9 and 10	As for rnds 1 and 2.

Continue to work steek as set and, with dark green, work rnd 1 from Chart A (p. 146), increasing 3 sts—1 at beg, 1 at center and 1 at end of rnd. 261 sts.

Joining in pale turquoise, work the rem rnds from Chart A, repeating the 12 patt sts 21 times in the rnd, and working the first 4 sts at beg, and last 5 sts at end of rnd, as indicated on chart.

Working steek as set, with dark green background and pale turquoise pattern, set patt panels as follows (see the charts on p. 146):

K1 background (edge st); Chart B over next 3 sts; Chart C over next 14 sts; Chart B over next 3 sts; Chart D over next 21 sts, Chart B over next 3 sts; Chart C over next 14 sts; Chart B over next 3 sts; next st background (right underarm st); Chart B over next 3 sts; Chart C over next 14 sts; Chart B over next 3 sts, Chart D over next 21 sts; Chart B over next 3 sts; Chart C over next 14 sts; Chart B over next 3 sts; turn Chart A on end and, reading rnds as sts and 12 patt sts as rnds, work over next 13 sts; Chart B over next 3 sts; Chart C over next 14 sts; Chart B over next 3 sts; Chart D over next 21 sts; Chart B over next 3 sts; Chart C over next 14 sts; Chart B over next 3 sts; next st background (left underarm st); Chart B over next 3 sts; Chart C over next 14 sts; Chart B over next 3 sts; Chart D over next 21 sts; Chart B over next 3 sts; Chart C over next 14 sts; Chart B over next 3 sts; K last st background (edge st).

Joining in and breaking off colors as required (working charts A and B in colors as for charts C and D), work the patts and steek as set, and continue straight until body measures 9½ in. (24cm) from beg.

Water-lily jacket

- ● dark green
- ▪ pale turquoise
- ✦ indigo
- ✿ blue
- ○ grey
-    ivory
- ◆ yellow
- ✚ pattern color
- / background color

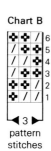

Chart B

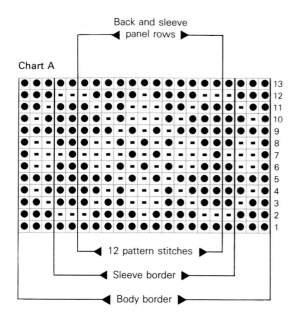

Back and sleeve
◀ panel rows ▶

Chart A

◀ 12 pattern stitches ▶

◀ Sleeve border ▶

◀ Body border ▶

◀ 3 ▶
pattern
stitches

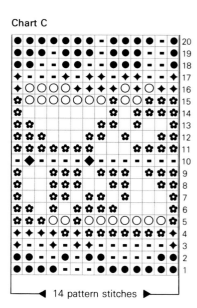

Chart C

◀ 14 pattern stitches ▶

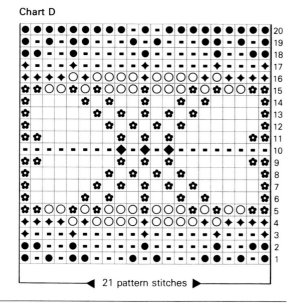

Chart D

◀ 21 pattern stitches ▶

FRANKLIN LAKES PUBLIC LIBRARY

Divide for armholes

Working steek as set, and keeping continuity of patt, work the first 62 sts of rnd (right front), increasing 1 st on last st (armhole-edge st); place the next st on a safety pin (right underarm st); work a steek; increase 1 st on next st (armhole-edge st), and continue in patt to left underarm st, increasing 1 st on last st (armhole-edge st); place left underarm st on a safety pin; work a steek; increase 1 st on next st (armhole-edge st) and continue in patt to end of rnd.

Working all edge sts in background color, continue working patt and steeks as set through rnd 2 of 5th repeat of patts C and D (82 panel patt rnds from beg). If working knitted steeks, cast off each on last rnd.

Shape right front neck

Using 2 double-pointed needles and keeping continuity of patt, work the first 8 sts of rnd and place these sts on a holder; patt the rem sts of right front; leave the rem sts of back and left front on a spare needle. Working on right side only, breaking off yarns at end of each row, shape neck as follows:

Keeeping continuity of patt, place the first 2 sts on neck holder at beg of next 3 rows. 49 sts rem. Decrease 1 st at beg of next 2 rows. Patt 1 row straight. Decrease 1 st at beg of next and every foll alt row until 42 sts rem.

Continue straight in patt to row 20 of charts C and D. Place sts on a holder.

Back

Using 2 double-pointed needles, join in appropriate colors and, keeping continuity of patt, work the 137 sts of back on right side only, breaking off yarns at end of every row, and patt straight through row 12 of of 5th rep of charts C and D.

Back right shoulder

Patt the first 46 sts of back; leave the rem sts on a spare needle. Then working on right side only, decrease 1 st at end (neck edge)) of next and every foll alt row until 42 sts rem (row 20 of charts C and D). Place sts on a holder.

Place the next 45 sts on a holder for back neck.

Back left shoulder

With right side facing, join in appropriate colors and work left shoulder to correspond with right, reversing shaping.

Shape left front neck

With right side facing, join in appropriate colors and, keeping continuity of patt, work the 63 sts of left front. Place the last 8 sts on a holder. Working on right side only, complete left front neck to correspond with right front neck, reversing shaping. Leave sts on needle.

Using dark green, graft or cast off tog shoulder sts.

Cut open armhole steeks.

Sleeves

With set or circular needles and dark green, pick up and K the underarm st from safety pin, then K up 127 sts around armhole.

Joining in pale turquoise as patt color, set patt panels as follows:

K1 dark green (center-underarm st); Chart B over next 3 sts; Chart C over next 14 sts; Chart B over next 3 sts; Chart A (turned on end) over next 13 sts; Chart B over next 3 sts; Chart C over next 14 sts; Chart B over next 3 sts; Chart D over next 21 sts; Chart B over next 3 sts; Chart C over next 14 sts; Chart B over next 3 sts; Chart A (on end) over next 13 sts; Chart B over next 3 sts; Chart C over next 14 sts; Chart B over last 3 sts.

Continue as set and work 1 rnd.

Keeping continuity of patt, and working in colors as charts C and D, decrease sleeve as follows:

K1 background (center-underarm st), K2tog, patt as set to the last 2 sts; SSK. Patt 2 rnds straight. Rep these 3 rnds until 102 sts rem.

Patt 1 rnd straight.

With dark green only, K1; K2tog; K to the last 2 sts; SSK. 100 sts.

Next rnd

K1 background (center-underarm st); join in pale turquoise and work the patt from Chart A, repeating the 12 patt sts 8 times across, and working the first st at beg, and last 2 sts at end of rnd as indicated on chart.

Keeping continuity of patt, complete Chart A, decreasing as before on next and every foll alt rnd until 88 sts rem.

Work 10 rnds of checkered patt in colors as for body, reading between * and **.

Cast off in dark green. Cut open center front steek.

Neck border

With right side facing and dark green, pick up and K the first 9 sts from right front neck holder; K2tog from holder, then K the rem 3 sts from holder; K up 16 sts to back neck; pick up and K the 45 sts of back neck (decrease 1st at center— 44 sts); K up 16 sts to left front neck holder; pick up and K 3 sts from holder, K2tog from holder, then K rem 9 sts. 102 sts.

Work 10 rows of checkered patt as for body, working flat and reading K instead of P on row 2 and every foll alt row. Cast off in dark green.

Front borders

With right side facing and dark green, K up 102 sts along front opening.

Work 10 rows in checkered patt as for neck. Cast off in dark green.

V-neck vest

Anchors, wheels and guiding stars are the symbols used in this V-neck, diced-pattern vest, worked in undyed Shetland colors.

Sizes

To fit chest
36-37/38-39/40-41/42-44 in.
(91-94/97-99/102-104/107-112cm).

Knitted measurements

Underarm
41/42¾/45/47¼ in. (104/109/114/120cm).

Length from top of shoulder
25¾/26¼/26½/27 in.
(65.5/66.5/67.5/68cm).

Materials

Shetland 2-ply jumper-weight yarn (Jamieson & Smith yarn used in this garment) in the foll colors:

2/2/3/3	2-oz. hanks in moorit (shade no. 4)
2/2/3/3	2-oz. hanks in natural white (1a)
2/2/2/3	1-oz. hanks in each of dark grey (54), and mid-grey (27)
1	2-oz. hank in each of light grey (203), light fawn (202), deep fawn (78), grey fawn (2), and Shetland black (5).

1 set or circular needles in sizes 2 (2¾mm) and 3 (3¼mm).

5 stitch holders.

Stitch markers.

Safety pin.

Gauge

16 sts and 16 rows to 2 in. (5cm) measured over patt, using size 3 (3¼mm) needles.

V-neck vest

/ light grey
● Shetland black
✳ moorit
▬ light fawn
  natural white
○ mid-grey
◆ dark grey
✖ grey fawn
✿ deep fawn

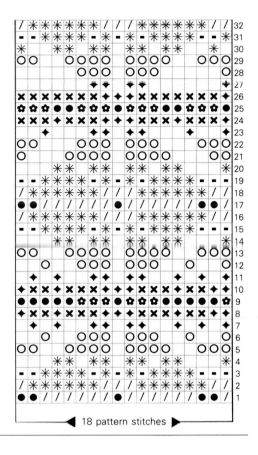

◀ 18 pattern stitches ▶

Body

With set or circular size 2 (2¾mm) needles and dark grey, cast on 288/304/320/336 sts. Place a marker at beg of rnd and work corrugated rib as follows:

Rnd 1	K2 in black, P2 in deep fawn; rep.
Rnds 2 and 3	K2 in dark grey, P2 in grey fawn; rep.
Rnds 4 and 5	K2 in mid-grey, P2 in natural white; rep.
Rnds 6 and 7	K2 in moorit, P2 in light fawn; rep.
Rnd 8	K2 in Shetland black, P2 in light grey; rep.
Rnds 9 and 10	As for rnds 6 and 7.
Rnds 11 and 12	As for rnds 4 and 5.
Rnds 13 and 14	As for rnds 2 and 3.

Rep these 14 rnds until rib measures 2¾/2¾/3/3 in. (7/7/8/8cm).

Next rnd: increase

With light grey, M1, K8; rep. 324/342/360/378 sts.

Change to size 3 (3¼mm) needles, place a marker at beg of rnd and, joining in and breaking off colors as required, work the patt from the chart (p. 149), repeating the 18 patt sts 18/19/20/21 times in the rnd.

Continue in this manner, repeating the 32 patt rnds, and work 96 rnds in total.

Next rnd: begin armholes/neck

Patt 12/17/13/18 sts and place these sts on a holder (left underarm); patt the next 69/73/77/81 sts (left front); patt the next st and place on a safety pin (center-front neck); patt the next 69/73/77/81 sts (right front); patt the next 23/24/25/26 sts and place on holder (right underarm); patt the rem sts of rnd, then place the last 11/7/12/8 sts onto left underarm holder, thus leaving 139/147/155/163 sts for back.

Shape armholes/neck

Working steeks over armholes and neck opening, shape as follows:

Keeping continuity of patt, decrease 1 st at each side of armhole edges on next 4/6/6/6 rnds, and at same time decrease 1 st at each side of neck on first and every foll 3rd rnd.

Continue decreasing 1 st at each side of neck on every 3rd rnd, and decrease 1 st at each side of armhole edges on every alt rnd 10/10/11/12 times.

Then work armhole straight and continue decreasing 1 st on each side of neck edge on every 3rd rnd until 27/28/30/32 sts rem on each of right and left front.

Continue straight in patt and continue working steeks until 88/92/92/96 rnds have been worked from beg of armhole/neck shaping. Cast off knitted steeks on the final rnd.

Place the center back 57/59/61/63 sts on a holder.

Cut open neck and armhole steeks. Graft or cast off tog shoulder sts.

Armhole bands

With set or circular size 2 (2¾mm) needles and light grey, pick up and K the 23/24/25/26 sts from holder, then K up 169/180/179/186 sts evenly around armhole. 192/204/204/212 sts.

Place a marker at beg of rnd and work in corrugated rib as follows:

Rnd 1	K2 in Shetland black, P2 in light grey; rep.
Rnds 2, 3 and 4	K2 in moorit, P2 in light fawn; rep.
Rnds 5, 6 and 7	K2 in mid-grey, P2 in natural white; rep.
Rnds 8 and 9	K2 in dark grey, P2 in grey fawn; rep.
Rnd 10	K2 in Shetland black, P2 in deep fawn; rep.

Cast off evenly in dark grey.

Neckband

With set or circular size 2 (2¾mm) needles and light grey, K up 83/88/89/92 sts evenly up right front neck edge; pick up and K the 57/59/61/63 sts of back neck from holder; K up 82/87/88/91 sts evenly down left front neck edge; then pick up and K the st from safety pin. 223/235/239/247 sts.

Working in corrugated rib in colors as for armhole bands, shape V-neck as follows:

Rnd 1	K2, P2; rep to the last 3 sts; K1; SL1-K2tog-PSSO (knitting tog the last and first st of rnd).
Rnd 2	K1, *P2, K2; rep from * to the last 4 sts; P2; SL1-K2tog-PSSO, as before.
Rnd 3	P2, K2; rep to the last 3 sts; P1; SL1-K2tog-PSSO as before.
Rnd 4	P1, *K2, P2; rep from * to the last 4 sts; K2; SL1-K2tog-PSSO as before.

Continue to work in colors as for armhole bands, and rep these 4 rnds once more. Then rep rnds 1 and 2 once again. 10 rnds total.

Cast off evenly in dark grey.

Long-line V-neck vest

This long-line V-neck vest is a longer, wider version of the classic V-neck, for a casual, sporty image.

Sizes

To fit bust
33-35/36-38 in. (84-89/91-97cm).

Knitted measurements

Underarm
39/42 in. (99/107cm).

Length from top of shoulder
28½/30½ in. (72.5/77.5cm).

Materials

Shetland 2-ply jumper-weight yarn (Jamieson & Smith yarn used in this garment) in the foll colors:

1	1-oz. hank in peach (shade no. 207)
2	1-oz. hanks in dark blue (135)
1/2	1-oz. hanks in lemon (96)
3/4	1-oz. hanks in sky blue (FC49)
1	2-oz. hank in light fawn (202)
2	2-oz. hanks in natural white (1a)
1/2	1-oz. hanks in pale green (FC24).

1 set or circular needles in sizes 2 (2¾mm) and 3 (3¼mm).

5 stitch holders.

1 safety pin.

Stitch markers.

Gauge

16 sts and 16 rows to 2 in. (5cm), measured over patt, using size 3 (3¼mm) needles.

Long-line V-neck vest

✿ peach
● dark blue
- lemon
O sky blue
■ light fawn
   natural white
✕ pale green

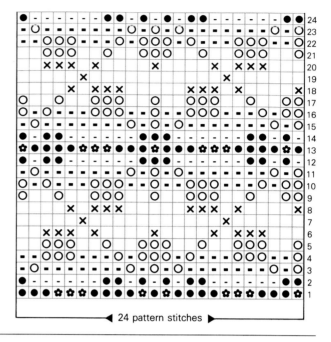

◀ 24 pattern stitches ▶

Body

With size 2 (2¾mm) needles and natural white, cast on 288/308 sts. Place a marker at beg of rnd and work corrugated rib as follows:

Rnds 1, 2, 3 and 4	K2 in natural white, P2 in sky blue; rep.
Rnds 5 and 6	K2 in natural white, P2 in dark blue; rep.

Rep these 6 rnds until rib measures 3 in. (8cm).

Next rnd: increase

With natural white, (K12/11, M1) rep to end of rnd. 312/336 sts.

Change to size 3 (3¼mm) needles and, joining in and breaking off colors as required, work the patt from chart, repeating the 24 patt sts 13/14 times in the rnd.

Continue in this manner, repeating the 24 patt rnds and work 124/136 patt rnds altogether (rnd 4/16 of 6th patt rep).

Next rnd: begin armholes/neck

Patt the first 17/12 sts of rnd and place these sts on a holder (left underarm); patt the next 67/72 sts (left front); patt the next st and place on a safety pin (center-front neck); patt the next 67/72 sts (right front); patt the next 21/23 sts and place on a holder (right underarm); patt the rem sts of round, then place the last 4/11 sts onto left underarm holder, thus leaving 135/145 sts for back.

Shape armholes/neck

Working steeks over armholes and neck openings, shape as follows:

Keeping continuity of patt, decrease 1 st at each side of armholes and neck on next and foll alt rnds 4/6 times (59/60 sts rem on each of left and right fronts, and 127/133 sts rem on back).

Now decrease 1st at each side of neck on every 3rd rnd and continue decreasing 1st at each side of armholes on every alt rnd 9 more times (109/115 sts rem on back).

Continue decreasing at each side of neck on every 3rd rnd and work armholes straight, until armhole measures 10/10½ in. (25.5/27 cm). Cast off knitted armhole steeks on last rnd.

Divide fronts and back

Break off yarns and place left and right fronts (and knitted steeks) on a spare needle.

Shape back neck

With right side facing, rejoin yarns and, keeping continuity of patt, work 31/32 sts; place the next 47/51 sts on a holder (center-back neck); leave rem sts on a spare needle.

Right back shoulder

Keeping continuity of patt, working on right side only and breaking off yarns at end of every row, patt the first 31/32 sts, decreasing 1 st at end (neck edge) of every row, 8 times. 23/24 sts rem. Place sts on a holder.

Left back shoulder

Rejoin appropriate yarns to the rem 31/32 sts of left shoulder and work as for right shoulder, reversing shaping. Place sts on a holder.

Left and right front

With right side facing, rejoin appropriate yarns and continue working left front, steek, and right front, decreasing as before on every 3rd rnd until 23/24 sts rem. Then patt straight until front corresponds in length with back at shoulders.

Cut open neck and armhole steeks. Graft or cast off tog shoulder sts.

Armhole bands

With size 2 (2¾mm) needles and natural white, pick up and K the 21/23 sts from underarm holder; K up 147/153 sts evenly around armhole. 168/176 sts. Place a marker at beg of rnd.

Work in K2, P2 corrugated rib as body for 10 rnds. Cast off evenly in natural white.

Neckband

With size 2 (2¾mm) needles and natural white, K up 92/96 sts evenly up right neck edge to back neck holder; pick up and K the 47/51 sts of back neck; K up 91/95 sts evenly down left neck edge; pick up and K the st from safety pin. 231/243 sts.

Place a marker at beg of rnd and work in K2, P2 corrugated rib as for armhole bands, decreasing at center front as follows:

Rnd 1	K2, P2, rep to the last 3 sts; K1; now work vertical double decrease—Sl next 2 sts together from left-hand needle to right, K the next st (first st of rnd, which means you must move marker to next st), then P2SSO. (See pp. 99-100 for more information on vertical double decrease.)
Rnd 2	K1, *P2, K2; rep from * to the last 4 sts; P2; work vertical double decrease over the next 3 sts as for rnd 1.
Rnd 3	P2, K2; rep to the last 3 sts; P1; work vertical double decrease over the next 3 sts as for rnd 1.
Rnd 4	P1, *K2, P2; rep from * to the last 4 sts; K2; work vertical double decrease over the next 3 sts as for rnd 1.

Continue to work in colors as for armhole bands and rep these 4 rnds once more. Then work rnds 1 and 2 once again. 10 rnds total. Cast off evenly in natural white.

Tammy, mittens and gloves set

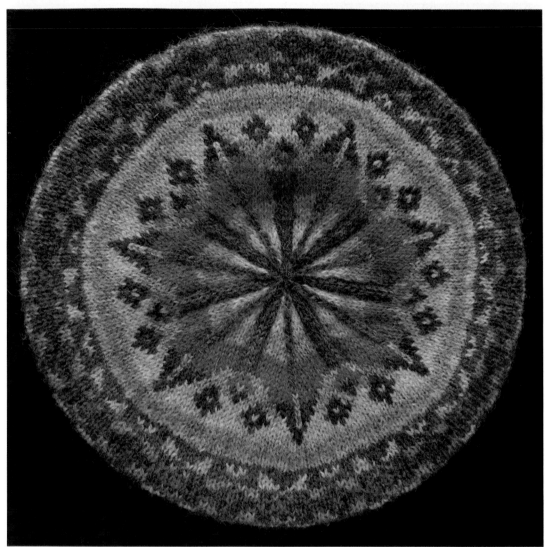

No Fair Isle collection is complete without a tammy, mittens and gloves. The patterns on these are traditional, and the colors flowery and bright.

Tammy

Sizes

To fit small to medium-sized head.

Materials

Shetland 2-ply jumper-weight yarn (Jamieson & Smith yarn used in all of these garments) in the foll colors:

1   2-oz. hank in light fawn (shade no. 202)
1   1-oz. hank in each of ocher (121), pale lavender (FC21), lavender mix (FC9), corn yellow (FC43), bright purple (123), honey gold (32), bright blue (FC47).

1 set or circular needles in sizes 2 (2¾mm) and 3 (3¼mm).

Stitch markers.

Gauge

16 sts and 16 rows to 2 in. (5cm), measured over patt, using size 3 (3¼mm) needles.

Rib to crown

With size 2 (2¾mm) needles and light fawn, cast on 140 sts. Place a marker at beg of rnd, and work in corrugated rib as follows:

Rnds 1 and 2   K1 in light fawn, P1 in honey gold.

Rnds 3 and 4   K1 in light fawn, P1 in bright blue.

Rep these 4 rnds until rib measures 1¾ in. (4cm).

Next rnd: increase

With light fawn, K5, M1; rep to end of rnd. 168 sts.

Change to size 3 (3¼mm) needles and, with light fawn, K 6 rnds.

Joining in and breaking off colors as required, work the 3 rnds of Peerie A, repeating the 6 patt sts 28 times in the rnd.

With light fawn, K 5 rnds.

Next rnd: increase

With light fawn, K12, M1; rep to end of rnd. 182 sts.

Place a marker at beg of rnd and, joining in and breaking off colors as required, work the 15 rnds of patt from border chart, repeating the 14 patt sts 13 times in the rnd.

With light fawn, K 3 rnds.

Next rnd: decrease

With light fawn, K2tog, K11; rep to end of rnd. 168 sts.

Place a marker at beg of rnd and, joining in and breaking off colors as required, work the patt from Peerie B, repeating the 6 patt sts 28 times in the rnd.

With light fawn, K 1 rnd.

Joining in and breaking off colors as required, work the 24 rnds of wheel patt, repeating the 24 patt sts 7 times in the rnd, and work a vertical double decrease on rnds as illustrated on chart. (For information on working a vertical double decrease, see pp. 99–100.)

Thread the yarn through a darning needle and pass it through the rem 14 sts, and fasten off securely.

Tammy

◇ lavender mix
○ corn yellow
✖ ocher
◆ bright purple
✿ honey gold
● bright blue
　 light fawn
- pale lavender
▦ sl 2 sts tog knitwise

Border

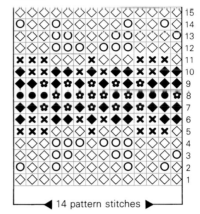

◀ 14 pattern stitches ▶

Peerie A

◀ 6 ▶
pattern stitches

Peerie B

◀ 6 ▶
pattern stitches

Wheel

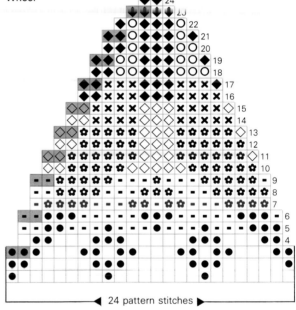

◀ 24 pattern stitches ▶

Mittens

Sizes

To fit small/medium/large hands.

Knitted measurements

Circumference at knuckles
7½/8/8½ in. (19/20.5/21.5cm).
Length
9½/9¾/10¼ in. (24/25/26cm).

Materials

One 1-oz. hank of Shetland 2-ply jumper-weight yarn in each of the foll colors:

> light fawn (shade no. 202), ocher (121), pale lavender (FC21), lavender mix (FC9), corn yellow (FC43), bright purple (123), honey gold (32), bright blue (FC47).

1 set of double-pointed needles in size 1 (2¼mm).

1 stitch holder.

Stitch markers.

Gauge

20 sts and 20 rows to 2 in. (5cm), measured over patt, using size 1 (2¼mm) needles.

Left mitten

Note: Asterisks (*) refer to instructions for gloves (see pp. 159-161).

*With light fawn, cast on 64/68/72 sts. Place a marker at beg of rnd and work K2, P2 corrugated rib as follows:

Rnds 1 and 2	K2 light fawn, P2 bright blue.
Rnds 3 and 4	K2 light fawn, P2 honey gold.

Rep these 4 rnds until rib measures 2½/2½/2¾ in. (6/6/7cm)**. On 3rd size only, increase 1 st at beg and middle of last rnd (74 sts).

***Place a marker at beg of rnd and, joining in and breaking off colors as required, patt as follows:

> Work back chart over the first 39/41/45 sts of rnd, working sizes as indicated on chart; work the palm patt over the next 23/25/27 sts, repeating the 4 patt sts 5/6/6 times, and rep first 3/1/3 sts of palm patt again; K1 background color; work the first st of thumb chart on last st of rnd.

Continue in this manner, and increase 1 st at each side of thumb gusset on next 6 rnds, as indicated on thumb chart, and work palm patt in colors as for back and thumb charts.

Continue as set and work straight through rnd 20 of patts.

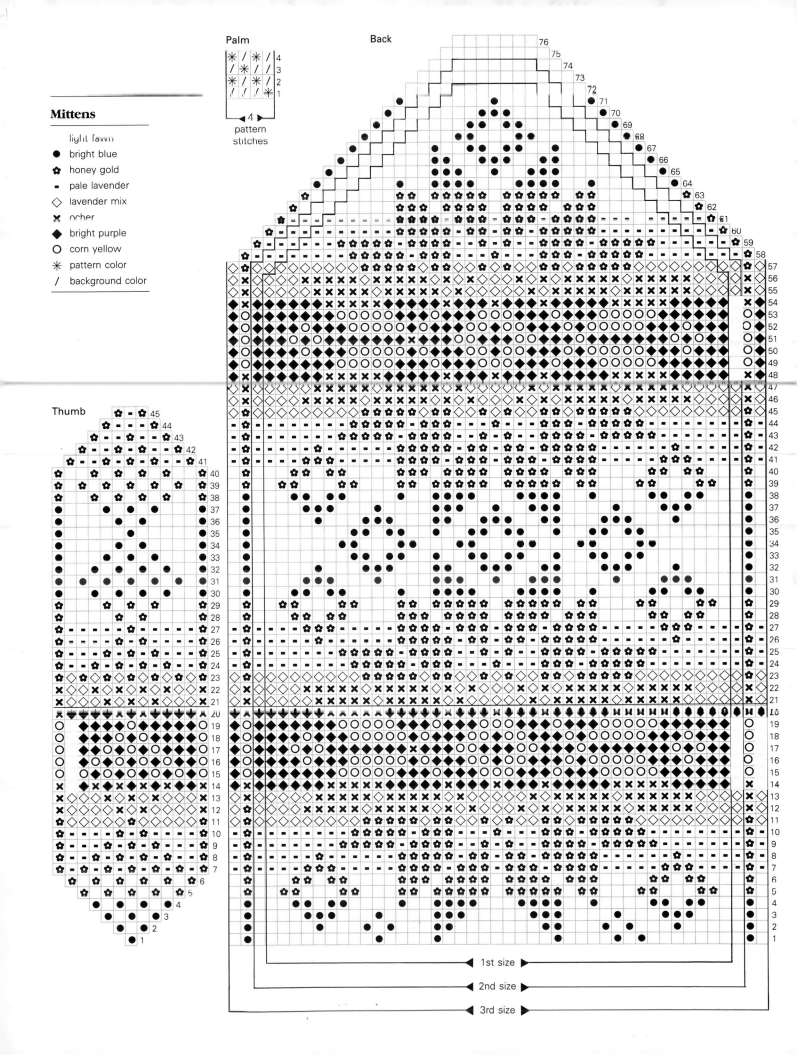

Mittens

- light fawn
- ● bright blue
- ✿ honey gold
- – pale lavender
- ◇ lavender mix
- ✕ ocher
- ◆ bright purple
- ○ corn yellow
- ✳ pattern color
- / background color

Palm

Back

Thumb

◄ 1st size ►

◄ 2nd size ►

◄ 3rd size ►

Make thumb opening

Place the 13 thumb gusset sts on a holder. Work rnd 21 of back and palm patt, then cast on 13 sts above thumb gusset sts.

Continue in patt as set and, keeping continuity of palm patt, work the extra 13 sts in palm patt.****

Patt straight through rnd 56/57/57.

Shape top

Patt 1, SSK; patt to the last 3 sts of back chart; K2tog, patt 1, SSK; keeping continuity of patt, work palm patt to the last 2 sts; K2tog.

Continue in this manner, decreasing 4 sts on every rnd and working back chart as indicated, to rnd 72/74/76.

With light fawn, graft or cast off tog back and palm sts.

Thumb

Pick up and patt (rnd 21 of thumb chart) the 13 sts of thumb gusset. Then using alt background and patt colors, K up 13 sts along thumb opening. Place a marker at beg of rnd and continue working the first 13 sts in patt as indicated on thumb chart, and work the last 13 sts in palm patt, repeating the 4 patt sts 3 times and working the first patt st once again.

Continue in this manner through rnd 40 of thumb chart.

Shape top

Patt 1, SSK; patt to the last 3 sts of thumb chart; K2tog, K1, SSK; patt to the last 2 sts of rnd; K2tog.

Continue in this manner, decreasing 4 sts on every rnd until 10 sts rem.

Next rnd

K1, SL1-K2tog-PSSO, K1, SSK, K1, K2tog.

Break off yarns and draw through the rem sts and fasten off on the wrong side.

Right mitten

Work as for left mitten, but begin patt and place thumb as follows:

Work back chart over the first 39/41/45 sts of rnd, working sizes as indicated on chart; work first st of thumb chart on next st; K1 background; work palm patt over the rem sts of rnd.

On rnd 21, cast on 13 sts above thumb gusset st.

Gloves

Sizes, knitted measurements, materials and gauge

As for mittens.

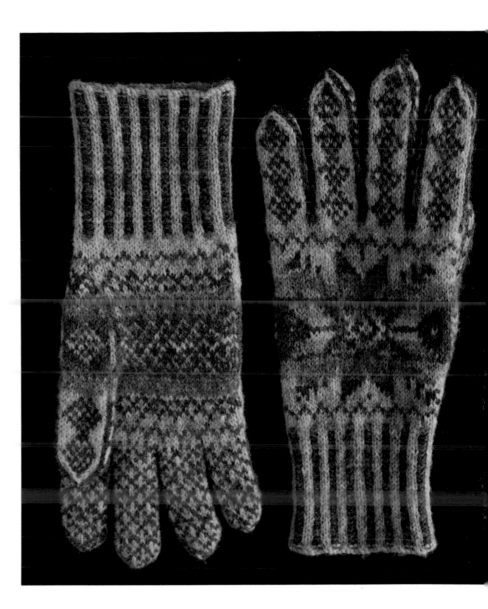

Left glove

Work as for mitten from * to ** (see instructions for mittens, pp. 156-158).

With light fawn, K 1/2/2 rnds. Then, joining in and breaking off colors as required, work the 3 rnds of border chart, repeating the 4 patt sts 16/17/18 times in the rnd.

K 1 rnd and, on 3rd size only, increase 1 st at beg and middle of this rnd (74 sts).

Now work as for mitten from *** to ****, reading glove back, thumb and palm charts (p. 160).

Patt straight through rnd 31 of back chart.

With light fawn, K1 rnd, and on 3rd size only, decrease 1 st at beg and middle of this rnd (84 sts).

Joining in and breaking off colors as required, work the 3 rnds of border chart, repeating the 4 patt sts 19/20/21 times in the rnd.

With light fawn, K1/2/2 rnds.

Index finger

Patt rnd 1 of finger chart over the first 11 sts of rnd; cast on 3 sts; place all rem sts, except last 9/10/11 sts of rnd, on a spare length of yarn; turn and work palm patt over the 3 cast-on sts and last 9/10/11 sts of rnd.

Place a marker at beg of finger rnd and continue in patt as set, repeating the 6 patt rnds of finger chart and working 24 rnds or to required length.

Shape top

K1, SSK; patt to the last 3 sts of finger chart; K2tog, K1, SSK; patt to the last 2 sts of rnd; K2tog.

Continue in this manner, decreasing 4 sts on every rnd until 11/12/13 sts rem.

Next rnd

With patt color, K1, SL1-K2tog-PSSO, K1, SSK twice, K 0/1/2, K2tog.

Then, for 3rd size only:

    With patt color, SL1-K2tog-PSSO, SSK, K1, K2tog.

All sizes:

    Draw yarn through rem sts and fasten off on the wrong side.

Second finger

1st and 2nd sizes only:

    With back of glove facing, K up 1 st from base of 11th st of index finger and work this st as first st of finger chart; patt the rem sts of finger chart over the next 9/10 sts from length of yarn.

Gloves

Thumb

Finger

Border

Palm

Back

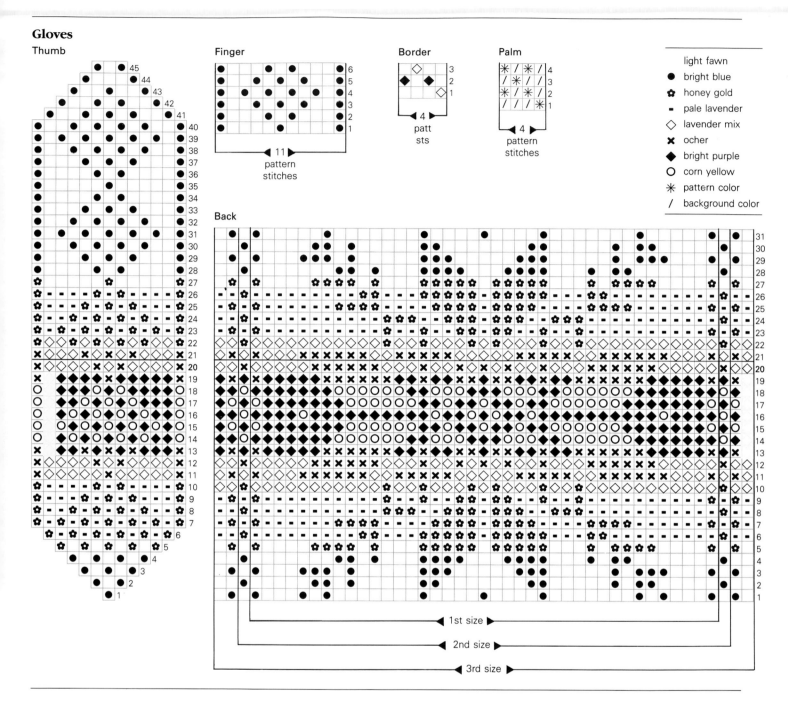

light fawn	
●	bright blue
✿	honey gold
-	pale lavender
◇	lavender mix
✕	ocher
◆	bright purple
○	corn yellow
✳	pattern color
/	background color

patt sts

pattern stitches

pattern stitches

◀ 1st size ▶

◀ 2nd size ▶

◀ 3rd size ▶

FRANKLIN LAKES PUBLIC LIBRARY

3rd size only:

With back of glove facing, patt the 11 sts of finger chart over the next 11 sts from length of yarn.

All sizes:

Cast on 2 sts, and for first size, work the 1st st cast on as 11th st of finger chart, and 2nd st cast on in palm patt. For 2nd and 3rd sizes, work the cast-on sts in palm patt; turn and work palm patt over the last 10 sts from length of yarn; K up 2/2/3 sts from cast-on sts of index finger, and work these sts in palm patt.

Place a marker at beg of rnd and continue in patt as set for 26/26/28 rnds or required length.

Shape top

1st and 2nd sizes only:

Work as for top of 2nd/3rd size index finger.

3rd size only:

K1, SSK; patt to the last 3 sts of finger chart; K2tog, K1, SSK, patt to the last 2 sts of rnd; K2tog.

Continue in this manner, decreasing 4 sts on every rnd until 14 sts rem.

Next rnd

With patt color, K1, SL1-K2tog-PSSO, K1, SSK, K1, SL1-K2tog-PSSO, K1, K2tog.

Then, in next rnd, SL1-K2tog-PSSO, SSK, K1, K2tog.

Draw yarn through rem sts and fasten off

Third finger

Work as for 2nd finger, but K up sts into base of cast-on st of 2nd finger; patt straight for 22/22/24 rnds or required length before shaping top.

Fourth finger

With back of glove facing, K up 1 st from base of cast-on st of 3rd finger and work this st as 1st st of finger chart; patt the rem 10 sts of finger chart over the next 10 sts from length of yarn; work palm patt over the last 8/9/10 sts from length of yarn. K up 2 sts from cast-on sts of 3rd finger.

Place a marker at beg of rnd and continue in patt as set for 16/17/18 rnds or required length.

Shape top

1st and 2nd sizes only:

Decrease as for index finger until 9/10 sts rem.

On next rnd, with patt color, K1, SL1-K2tog-PSSO, K1, SSK, K0/1, K2tog.

Draw yarn through rem sts and fasten off.

3rd size:

Shape top as for first-size index finger.

Thumb

Reading glove thumb chart, work as for mitten thumb.

Right glove

Work as for left glove, but place thumb as for right mitten and reverse position of fingers, beg with 4th finger as follows:

Work first 10 sts of rnd in finger chart; cast on 3 sts and patt first st cast on as 11th st of finger chart. Place rem sts, except last 8/9/10 sts of rnd, on a spare length of yarn; turn and work these last 8/9/10 sts in palm patt. Complete finger as for left glove.

3rd and 2nd fingers

Work as for left glove, but K up sts from base of cast-on sts of previous fingers.

Index finger

Work as for left glove, but patt finger chart over the next 11 sts from spare yarn, work palm patt over the rem 9/10/11 sts and K up 3 sts from cast-on sts of 2nd finger.

Thumb

Work as for left glove.

Sew in any gaps between fingers.

Creating original Fair Isle designs entails a logical, step-by-step process, which can be mastered with practice.

Creating your own designs

The knitters of Shetland do not need to draw up plans or write instructions before knitting a Fair Isle garment. They proceed from idea to finished garment with almost super-natural speed. Yet there is no magic involved. They have simply been immersed in knitting since childhood, produc-ing an average of one sweater a week for decades, using the same type of yarn and working continuously with Fair Isle patterns. The mathematical process of knitwear design has become second nature to these people, so much so that they barely regard it as mathematical—or, indeed, as a pro-cess—at all.

Yet the translation of an idea from a design into working instructions does, in fact, involve a step-by-step process. This process can be learned and, like any other, becomes easier with practice. In this chapter, I describe this process in seven steps, which apply to the design of Fair Isle gar-ments in general. Then I apply these steps to the design of particular garments—a cap and tammy, and a gansey.

Step 1: Measurements Take all the measurements required for your project and check them carefully for accuracy. If it is a garment intended for you, ask someone else to take your measurements—this is easier and more accurate than trying to do so yourself. If you have a garment the same size and shape as your intended project, check your measurements against it.

Step 2: Drawing a plan Draw a generously sized plan of the proposed design and plot all the measurements on it. This plan need not be drawn to scale, but it should be large enough so the plotted measurements and basic calculations can be read clearly (see, for example, the drawing on p. 180). The plan will greatly help you visualize the project and will be easier to work from than lists of numbers.

Step 3: Gauge Determine the exact knitting gauge for your project. This is absolutely crucial since all the calculations necessary to arrive at the correct shape and size for your garment are based on the gauge measurement. Therefore knit a gauge swatch using the yarn, needles and stitch intended for the project. The swatch must be blocked and the gauge measured precisely (see p. 89). If you intend to press the garment, block and press the swatch before you take its measurements.

Because stranded two-color knitting produces a closer fabric and therefore a tighter gauge than plain stockinette stitch, there are some special considerations in figuring gauge with Fair Isle work. If stranded knitting is to be worked on every row, the stitch and row gauge should be the same—for example, 8 stitches and 8 rows to 1 in. If plain rows are to be used between patterns, the row gauge will be greater than the stitch gauge, depending on the number of plain rows worked. Therefore, although swatches can be used to experiment with patterns and colors, make sure they contain the same stranded-knitting/ plain-row ratio as the design.

Also remember that because the gauge for plain stockinette work will be looser than the gauge for stranded knitting, any plain area of more than two rows should be worked on smaller needles than those that are used for stranded areas. Pick a needle size that will produce the same stitch gauge as the gauge for the stranded knitting.

Step 4: Calculating stitches and rows Once measurements and gauge are established, the number of stitches required for specific widths and the number of rows or rounds needed for given lengths can be calculated. To calculate the stitches required for width, multiply the width measurement by the stitch gauge. To calculate the rows or rounds required for length, multiply the length measurement by the row gauge.

For example, look at the tubular scarf in the drawing on the facing page, whose gauge has been established at 8 stitches and $8\frac{1}{2}$ rows to 1 in. and which is to be 18 in. wide by 60 in. long. The stitches required for width are: $18 \times 8 = 144$. The rows required for length are: $60 \times 8\frac{1}{2} = 510$.

Although this scarf is elementary in terms of design, the method for calculating the number of stitches and rows is the same for all designs, regardless of complexity.

Step 5: Fitting patterns into widths For circular designs, pattern repeats should divide an exact number of times into the total number of stitches in the round (see pp. 40-41). To calculate how many times a pattern repeat divides into a total number of stitches, divide the total number of stitches by the number of stitches in the repeat.

Example

Total number of sts = 144.

St repeat = 12.

$144 \div 12 = 12$ pattern repeats in the round.

The total stitch count of 144 in this scarf is convenient since it can be used with repeats of 2, 3, 4, 6, 8, 12, 16, 18, 24 and 36 stitches. It makes sense to use patterns with these repeats. Yet not all numbers offer quite so many possibilities.

Example

St gauge = 8 sts to 1 in.

Width = $40\frac{1}{2}$ in.

Total number of sts: $40\frac{1}{2} \times 8 = 324$.

St repeat = 20.

$324 \div 20 = 16$ pattern repeats, with a remainder of 4 sts.

To resolve this problem, there are several options: (A) Choose patterns that fit exactly into the total number of stitches. For instance, for the example above, use only patterns with repeats of 2, 3, 4, 6, 12, 18 or 36 stitches (see pp. 49-65 for some examples). (B) Adjust the pattern repeat to fit by moving the pattern elements closer or farther apart (see pp. 41-44). (C) Adjust the total stitch count to fit the pattern repeat. If the excess 4 stitches are subtracted from the total, the stitch count becomes 320, in which 16 pattern repeats fit exactly. This stitch count would produce a 40-in. width, and a decision would have to be made about the acceptability of losing ½ in. in width. Reducing the total stitch count should be done only when there is leeway in the measurement and the numbers involved are small. The alternative to reducing the stitch count is to add 16 stitches, which would accommodate exactly 17 repeats. However, adding 16 stitches would also add 2 in. to the width of the garment, which is significant and may be an unacceptable solution.

While increasing the total stitch count is not always the best solution, there are occasions when it is appropriate.

Example

Total number of sts = 324.

St repeat = 22.

324 ÷ 22 = 14 pattern repeats,
        remainder 16 sts.

Reducing the total stitches by 16 would result in an unacceptable loss of 2 in. in width. But adding 6 stitches would accommodate 15 repeats and add only ¾ in. to the width.

Sometimes a combination of options B and C provides the best solution.

Example

Total sts = 196, to be reduced or increased by a
        maximum of 2 sts.

St repeat = 20, to be adjusted as little as possible.

196 ÷ 20 = 9 repeats, remainder 16 sts.

Solution: Increase the total number of sts to 198 and reduce the st repeat by 2 to 18, giving 11 complete repeats.

Step 6: Centering patterns For perfect symmetry, patterns should be centered on flat pieces of knitting, like cardigans; on circular garments with a back and front; and on sleeves, which do not always accommodate patterns exactly.

Plan for tubular scarf

Gauge: 8 sts and 8½ rows to 1 in.
Width: 18 in. × 8 sts = 144 sts
Length: 60 in. × 8½ rows = 510 rows

 = knit in the round

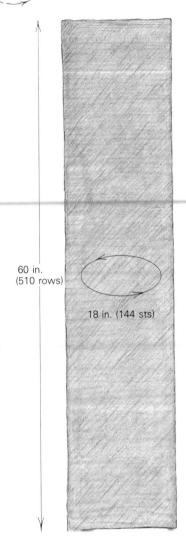

60 in.
(510 rows)

18 in. (144 sts)

Centering a pattern

↑   ↑
Last stitch   Center
added   stitch
to center
pattern

For the sake of visual symmetry, patterns should be centered on cardigans, on circular garments with a back and front, and on sleeves. To center a pattern, establish its midpoint and add a stitch or stitches, as needed, to make the pattern exactly the same on both sides of the center stitch.

In this baby's cardigan, the asymmetrical pattern repeat is centered to make the same vertical band fall on either side of the front-band opening.

In order to center a pattern, its midpoint must be placed at the center stitch of the piece. The chart at left illustrates a pattern repeated five times across. One stitch has been added to the last repeat, so that the pattern reflects exactly on each side of the center stitch. The addition of one or more stitches is the way garments with front openings are adjusted to make the pattern the same on each side of the opening. This type of adjustment is illustrated in the baby's cardigan shown in the photo below.

In this particular case, the 22-stitch pattern repeat is asymmetrical, with an 11-stitch vertical band of light background color alternating with an 11-stitch vertical band of dark background color. In order to make the pattern reflect on each side of the opening, the 22-stitch pattern is repeated X number of times plus 11 stitches, thus beginning and ending with the same vertical band. (For information on charting centered patterns, see pp. 40-41.)

The number of repeats in a circular garment needs further consideration if the garment is to be folded flat, like a tubular scarf, or divided into back and front, like a pullover sweater. The beginning of the round should always be placed at a folded edge of a circular piece, and at the underarm-seam stitch of a sweater. When an even number of repeats is worked in the round and the round starts at a central stitch in the pattern, the garment will contain complete patterns on back and front. For example, when the total number of pattern repeats in the round is 10, there will be 5 repeats on back and front (10 ÷ 2 = 5).

However, if the number of repeats is odd and the round begins as usual, the back and front will not contain complete patterns and those patterns will be off center. For example, when there are 9 total pattern repeats in a round, there will be 4½ repeats on both back and front (9 ÷ 2 = 4½).

To center a pattern that is off center on the back and front, the starting point of the pattern must be adjusted at the beginning of the round. The pattern is adjusted by starting the front with the last quarter of the pattern, working 4 repeats, and ending with the first quarter of the pattern. The back then begins with the last three-quarters of the pattern, works 3 repeats, and ends with the first three-quarters of the pattern. In short, the round begins with the last quarter of the pattern, works 8 repeats and ends with the first three-quarters of the pattern. The drawing at right illustrates the pattern correctly centered on front and back. (This means that the pattern will not match over the shoulder, and a small, simple pattern should be worked on the shoulder to separate front and back patterns.)

The only exception to this rule is the vertical asymmetrical pattern repeat. For example, the pattern for the baby's cardigan (see the facing page), when used in a pullover, should repeat an odd number of times in order to be centered on back and front.

In the case of centering patterns on a sleeve, there are two givens. First, the number of stitches knitted up around the armhole for a sleeve is fixed, as are the pattern repeats if they are to be the same as those worked on the body.

Second, it is unnecessary for the pattern repeats to fit the sleeve exactly because the pattern is gradually cut away by the sleeve de-

Uncentered pattern

A pattern that repeats an odd number of times in the round will be placed off center on a garment if the round begins at the center of the pattern repeat (in this case, at the center of the X).

Beginning of pattern round

Correctly centered pattern

To center an odd-numbered pattern repeat on a garment, the starting point of the pattern must be adjusted at the beginning of the round. The pattern is centered by beginning the round with the last quarter of the pattern.

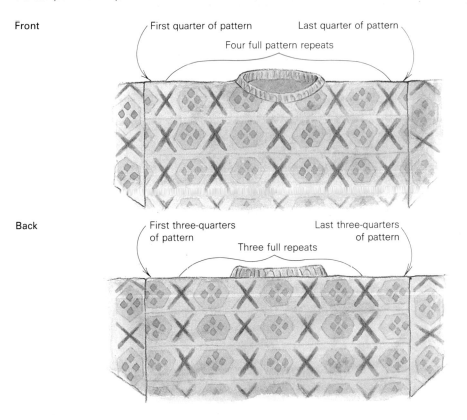

Front

First quarter of pattern   Last quarter of pattern

Four full pattern repeats

Back

First three-quarters of pattern   Last three-quarters of pattern

Three full repeats

Centering sleeve pattern at shoulder

Center the sleeve pattern at the shoulder by dividing the total number of stitches knit up by the stitch repeat and placing any left-over stitches at the beginning and end of the round.

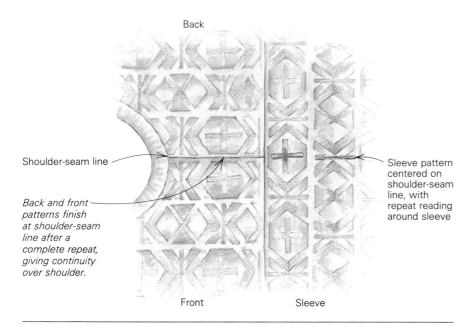

Back

Shoulder-seam line

Sleeve pattern centered on shoulder-seam line, with repeat reading around sleeve

Back and front patterns finish at shoulder-seam line after a complete repeat, giving continuity over shoulder.

Front   Sleeve

creases. However, it is important to center the pattern at the shoulder, as illustrated in the drawing above. To center the sleeve pattern, divide the total number of stitches knit up (not including the underarm-seam stitch, which is always worked in the background color) by the stitch repeat. Any remaining stitches are then placed at the beginning and end of the round. If the stitch repeat is an even number, the total number of stitches knit up should be odd, and vice versa. This ensures that the pattern is centered precisely.

Example

Total sts knit up around armhole = 143.

St repeat = 22.

143 ÷ 22 = 6 pattern repeats, remainder 11 sts.

To center the pattern and to take up the 11 remaining stitches, work the last 5 sts of the repeat over the first 5 sts of the sleeve, repeat the 22 pattern sts 6 times, and work the first 6 sts of the repeat over the last 6 sts of the sleeve. (For more on charting a pattern centered in this way, see the bottom drawing on p. 41.).

Note that on sleeves without gussets, you should always count the stitch to the left of the underarm-seam stitch as the first stitch of the sleeve. On sleeves with gussets, count the stitch to the immediate left of the gusset stitches as the first one.

Step 7: fitting patterns into lengths To calculate how many times a pattern repeats in a total number of rows/rounds, divide the number of rows/rounds by the row repeat.

Example

Total number of rows = 176.

Row repeat = 22.

176 ÷ 22 = 8.

Of course, not all patterns will fit a given row count so precisely, and, indeed, fitting the pattern into the total length should be considered in relationship to the design. Take, for example, the tubular scarf in the drawing on p. 165 and assume that it is to be worked with the same 19-row Fair Isle pattern repeated throughout. The calculation is as follows:

Total number of rounds = 510.

Row repeat = 19.

510 ÷ 19 = 26 pattern repeats, remainder 16 rounds.

In order to finish the scarf with a complete pattern, add 3 rounds to the total count, which produces 513 rounds and 20 complete row repeats.

However, if the same scarf were to be patterned with a 36-row repeat consisting of an 11/5/15/5 border-and-peerie arrangement, the pattern would need to be centered lengthwise in order for the scarf to start and finish with the same pattern. In other words, within the total number of rounds the 36-row repeat must be worked X number of times + 11 (11 being the number of rows needed for a final border to complete the arrangement). The calculation is as follows:

Total rounds = 510.

Row repeat = 36.

510 ÷ 36 = 14 pattern repeats, remainder 6 rounds.

Therefore, add 5 rounds to give 14 repeats + 11 rounds for the final border.

Since a scarf's length is not crucial, it is easy to adjust the number of rounds to fit patterns. Other garments have less leeway for adjustment in length, but patterns should nevertheless fit well at the shoulder, either on a complete repeat, as illustrated in the drawing above left, or at the center of a pattern, as illustrated in the drawing on the facing page.

If necessary, adjust the length of the rib so the total length of the garment remains as close as possible to the original requirement.

Example

Total length of garment = 25½ in.

Rib length = 2½ in.

Therefore, patterned length = 23 in.

Total patterned rounds = 176.

Row repeat = 19.

176 ÷ 19 = 9 pattern repeats, remainder 5 rounds.

Therefore, to finish at the center of the repeat, add 4 rounds, which produces 9 repeats plus 9 rounds. The actual center row of the pattern will be replaced by the grafting or casting off at the shoulder, and the other 9 rounds needed to complete the repeat will appear on the other side of the shoulder seam. Since 4 rounds will add ½ in. to the total length, reduce the rib to 2 in. to restore the original length.

In border arrangements, the full pattern need not repeat an exact number of times or fall at the center of the full repeat. You can finish at the end or at the center of an individual pattern within the arrangement.

Example

34-row repeat, consisting of a 3/15/3/13 arrangement.

Total pattern rounds = 176.

Row repeat = 34.

176 ÷ 34 = 5 pattern repeats, remainder 6 rows.

With 6 rows remaining, the knitting will thus finish on round 3 of the 15-row pattern. In order to finish at the center of this pattern, add 4 rounds. If total length is crucial, reduce the rib accordingly. Alternatively, subtract 3 rounds to finish at the end of the first 3-row peerie and increase the rib accordingly.

Large stars on panel garments should finish at the shoulder, either with a complete repeat or at the center of a repeat. Because of the stars' size, there is less variation possible in adjusting for length. If a large star panel is used on center front and back of a garment, the star should ideally finish on a complete repeat at center front (see the child's panel gansey on pp. 116-118).

Finally, a special note on horizontal sleeve patterns. If the sleeves on a garment are to be worked in the same horizontal pattern bands as on the body, the sleeve and body patterns should match. The sleeve pattern on

Body pattern meeting at shoulder on the center of a pattern

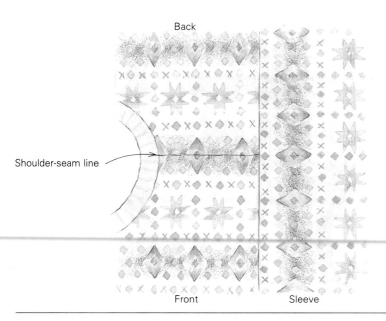

a dropped-shoulder garment should begin with the same pattern band as that worked directly below the armhole opening, and follow in order downward toward the hem (see the traditional gansey in the photo on p. 181). For a shaped armhole, the sleeve pattern should begin on the band directly above the armhole opening and follow downward.

From design to working instructions

Step 1

Take the body measurements needed for your project.

Step 2

Draw a plan of the project and plot the measurements on it.

Step 3

Establish your gauge.

Step 4

Calculate the number of stitches and rows needed for the garment's measurements.

Step 5

Fit the patterns into the garment's width.

Step 6

Center the patterns on the garment.

Step 7

Fit the patterns into the garment's length.

Plotted design for straight cap

A = circumference (average for women, 22 in./
    for men, 23 in.)
B = total length (average for women and men, 16 in.)
C = hem length (1 in.)
D = outer brim length (average for women
    and men, 3 in.)

 = knit in the round

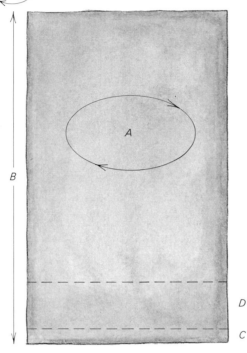

Straight cap

Designing a cap and tammy

A straight cap is a simple tube shape, gathered at the top and then hemmed and folded to form a brim, as illustrated in the drawing at left. To begin designing a Fair Isle cap, work through steps 1 and 2 by taking the measurements indicated in the drawing and plotting the design on paper.

Next proceed to steps 3, 4, 5 and 7. Note that the hem can be worked in plain stockinette stitch, and remember to use smaller needles on any plain areas in order to produce the correct stitch gauge. If you use horizontal pattern bands, fit them aesthetically around the brim.

A tammy is a beret knitted with a rib and border/peerie arrangement and distinctively shaped with a wheel-pattern crown. For those who have never knitted a Fair Isle tammy, the calculations will no doubt seem complicated and daunting. But do not be discouraged by this. Tammies are easy and fun to design and knit.

For beginners, perhaps the best introduction is to knit one from specific instructions (see the tammy project on pp. 154-155), which will give you a feel for the construction process. For those ready to design their own tammies, the generic instructions below will serve as a blueprint for a small to average-size adult tammy, provided you use the same gauge as that on which all the calculations are based. That gauge, worked out using Shetland 2-ply jumper-weight yarn, is 8 stitches and 8 rows to 1 in.

A tammy's wheel contains equal sections, whose stitch count and directions are calculated based on the number of points in the wheel. The drawing on the facing page shows an eight-pointed wheel and one section of the entire tammy. The wheel of a tammy might also have from six to ten points.

To begin designing a tammy, take the measurements called for in the drawing on the facing page and plot your design (steps 1 and 2). Next proceed to steps 3, 4, 5 and 7.

Work the rib with fewer stitches than are needed for the tammy's circumference (about 1 fewer for every 4 or 5 stitches), and on smaller needles (usually two sizes smaller, or one size if you rib tightly). Make sure to cast on an exact multiple of the stitches needed for the rib pattern. For example, a K2, P2 rib requires a multiple of 4 stitches.

Shaping a tammy from rib to wheel

There are two basic methods of shaping the tammy from the top of the rib to the wheel (measurement C), depending on the pattern arrangement. First, for a border/peerie/border arrangement, as illustrated in the drawing at right, increase from rib to circumference on one round, immediately after completing the rib, and work the pattern arrangement.

Example

Cast on 140 sts. Work rib. Increase evenly to 182 sts on next round. Work 15-row (14-st repeat) border pattern; work 1 round plain; work 3-row (7-st repeat) peerie; work 1 round plain; work same 15-row border pattern; work 1 round plain.

The second method produces a slight bit more shaping than the first. For a peerie/border/peerie arrangement, increase on the first round above the rib about two-thirds of the difference between the rib and circumference stitches. Then work the first peerie; increase to the total circumference and work the border pattern; decrease back to the peerie number and work the second peerie.

Example

Cast on 140 sts. Work rib. Increase evenly to 168 sts on next round. Work 4 rounds plain; work 5-row (12-st repeat) peerie; work 3 rounds plain; increase evenly to 182 sts on next round; work 15-row (14-st repeat) border; work 2 rounds plain; decrease evenly to 168 sts on next round; work same 5-row peerie; work 1 round plain.

Shaping a tammy's wheel   The wheel pattern must fit exactly into the total stitches left after working measurement C. In order to calculate the number of stitches needed for the pattern, divide the total number of stitches by the number of points in the wheel. For example, if there are 168 total stitches after working measurement C and the wheel has seven points, each point will consist of 24 stitches (168 ÷ 7 = 24).

If the number of points does not divide exactly into the total number of stitches, decrease evenly to fit. Do not increase, however, since this will spoil the tammy's shape.

The wheel is shaped by working double decreases in straight lines from each point to the crown. To work these decreases, use the mitered or the vertical double decrease, explained on pp. 97-100. The decrease rounds should be placed evenly from points to crown,

Tammy with eight-pointed wheel

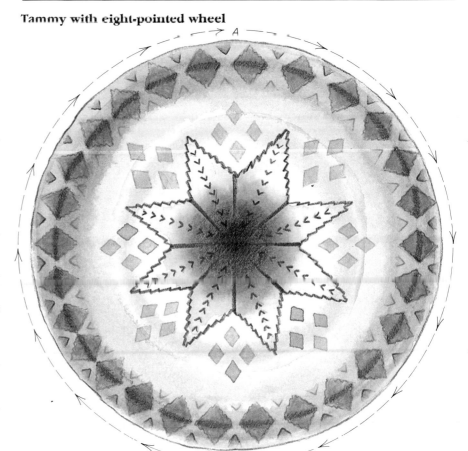

One section of eight-pointed tammy

A = circumference (average for child, 22 in./for small adult, 23 in./for large adult, 24 in.)
B = rib length (1/ 1¼/1½ in.)
C = length from top of rib to wheel (3¾/4/4¼ in.)
D = length of wheel (3¼/3½/3¾ in.)

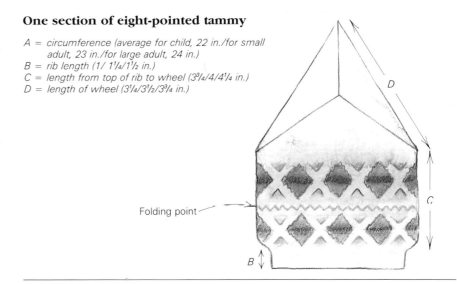

Folding point

as shown in the chart below left, or placed progressively closer toward the crown, as shown in the chart below right. Two stitches from each section should remain after shaping, and these are threaded through with yarn to fasten off the crown.

The length of the wheel (measurement D) determines how many rounds are to be worked in total, and the decrease rounds can then be placed accordingly. To make the necessary calculations for shaping the wheel, determine the following:

1. Total number of rounds in wheel;

2. Total number of sts at beginning of wheel;

3. Number of points in wheel;

4. Number of sts remaining after shaping wheel = number of points × 2;

5. Total sts to be decreased = total at beginning − sts remaining after shaping;

6. Number of sts to be decreased in 1 round = number of points × 2 (double decrease).

7. Number of decrease rounds required = total sts to be decreased ÷ number of decreases in 1 round;

8. Frequency of decrease rounds = total rounds ÷ number of decrease rounds.

The wheel-shaping calculations may look involved and complex, but, in practice, they are really quite simple.

Example

Total number of rounds in wheel = 26.

Total number of sts at beginning of wheel = 168.

Number of points in wheel = 6.

Number of sts remaining after shaping wheel:
6 × 2 = 12.

Total sts to be decreased: 168 − 12 = 156.

Number of sts to be decreased in 1 round:
6 × 2 = 12.

Number of decrease rounds required:
156 ÷ 12 = 13.

Frequency of decrease rounds: 26 ÷ 13 = 2.

Therefore, work a double decrease at each point on every second round (see the chart at bottom left).

Here is another slightly more complicated example. It is figured as follows:

Total number of rounds in wheel = 24.

Total number of sts at beginning of wheel = 168.

Number of points in wheel = 7.

Number of sts remaining after shaping wheel:
7 × 2 = 14.

Total sts to be decreased: 168 − 14 = 154.

Number of sts to be decreased in 1 round:
7 × 2 = 14.

Evenly spaced decrease rounds

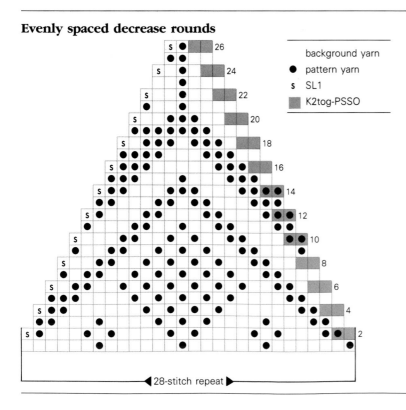

background yarn
● pattern yarn
s SL1
▨ K2tog-PSSO

◀28-stitch repeat▶

Progressively spaced decrease rounds

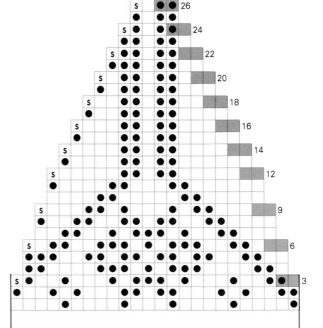

◀24-stitch repeat▶

Number of decrease rounds required:

154 ÷ 14 = 11.

Frequency of decrease rounds:

24 ÷ 11 = 2, remainder 2.

In this case, one cannot place the decrease rounds evenly from start to finish. But they can be placed in one of two ways. You could decrease on every 3rd round twice, then on every 2nd round 9 times. Or you could decrease on every 3rd round 3 times, every 2nd round 6 times, every round twice, and finally knit 1 round straight.

Wheel patterns can be varied enormously. Only two rules apply when designing a wheel pattern. First, the pattern must divide into equal sections. Second, the colors must be kept moving and hence small patterns should be used between the points. Always chart a single section of the wheel with pattern, as shown on the facing page, to be sure of knitting accurately.

Designing a gansey with gussets

The traditional gansey is a simple, dropped-shoulder shape with underarm gussets. The gansey has been around since the turn of the century and remains a classic base from which many variations can be worked.

Begin planning a traditional gansey by working through Step 1, taking the following measurements (see the drawing on p. 174):

(A) Chest circumference. This should be at least 2 in. more than the actual body measurement in order to allow for ease of movement. For a looser fit, increase the measurement accordingly.

(B) Length from top of shoulder to base of sweater.

(C) Body-rib length.

(D) Armhole depth.

(E) Length from underarm to base of sweater.

(F) Back-neck width. For a traditional gansey, this should be approximately one-third of the width from armhole to armhole, thus leaving the shoulders to measure equal thirds.

(G) Neck drop: 2 in. for a child; 2½ in. for a small adult; 2¾ in. for a medium-sized adult; and 3 in. for a large adult.

(H) Sleeve length.

(I) Sleeve circumference above rib.

(J) Sleeve-rib length.

Next proceed to steps 2, 3, 4, 5, 6 and 7. Before moving to the specific instructions be-low, acquaint yourself with the general knitting plan for a traditional gansey at the bottom of the drawing on p. 174.

Rib   Cast on fewer stitches and use smaller needles for the rib than for the body of the sweater. This prevents the garment from flaring and becoming misshapen at the hem. The stitches in measurement A should be reduced by approximately 1 in 7 to 1 in 10. The decision on the ratio to use depends on the hip size. For example, a large hip requires less difference between rib and body stitches than a small hip, and therefore a 1:10 ratio would give a better fit. In deciding on the ratio, make sure that the rib pattern will fit an exact multiple of times into the total stitch count so the patterning will be continuous.

Example

K2, P2 corrugated rib = 4 pattern sts.

Number of sts in chest circumference = 320.

Reduce sts by 1 in 8: 320 ÷ 8 = 40.

Number of sts for cast on and rib:

320 − 40 = 280.

Check rib pattern fit: 280 ÷ 4 = 70.

Not all calculations are quite so convenient.

Example

Number of sts in rib pattern = 4.

Number of sts in chest circumference = 330.

Reduce sts by 1 in 9:

330 ÷ 9 = 36, remainder 6.

In this case, taking the result to the nearest whole number, that is, 37, will produce an odd-numbered total, which will not fit the rib. The solution is to change the result to the nearest whole number that is divisible by 4:

330 − 38 = 292, and 292 ÷ 4 = 73, which means the rib pattern will fit.

Increasing from rib to chest stitches

After working the rib, increase the stitches as evenly as possible in 1 round to meet the total required for the chest measurement.

Example

Number of sts in chest circumference = 320.

Number of sts in rib = 280.

Number of sts to be increased = 40.

To place increases: 280 ÷ 40 = 7.

Therefore, to work increase round: K7, M1; repeat to end of round.

Basic gansey knitting plan

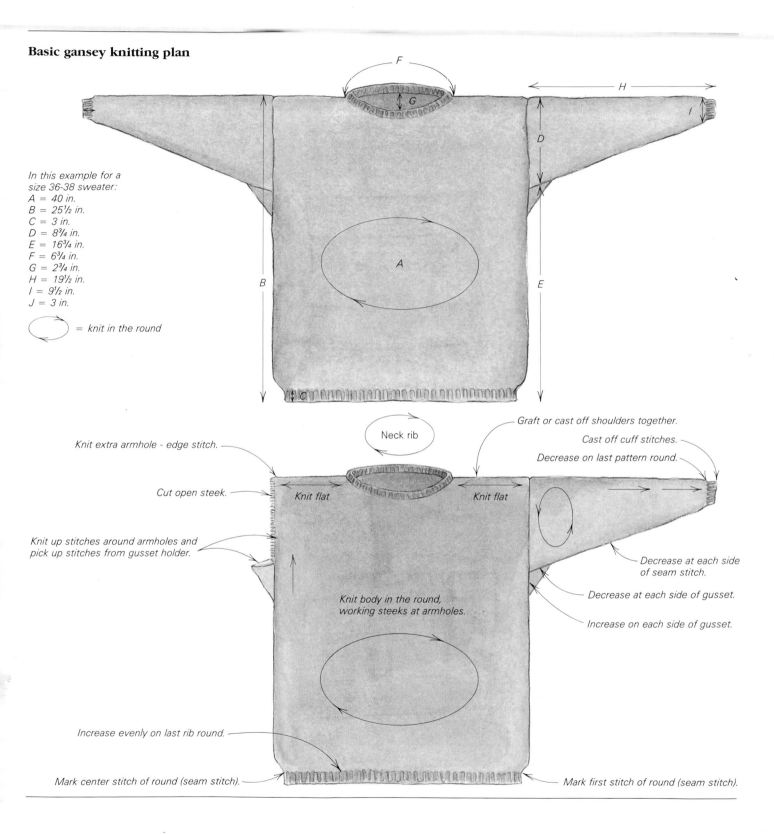

In this example for a
size 36-38 sweater:
A = 40 in.
B = 25½ in.
C = 3 in.
D = 8¾ in.
E = 16¾ in.
F = 6¾ in.
G = 2¾ in.
H = 19½ in.
I = 9½ in.
J = 3 in.

= knit in the round

Neck rib

Graft or cast off shoulders together.

Cast off cuff stitches.

Decrease on last pattern round.

Knit extra armhole - edge stitch.

Cut open steek.

Knit flat

Knit flat

Knit up stitches around armholes and
pick up stitches from gusset holder.

Decrease at each side
of seam stitch.

Decrease at each side of gusset.

Increase on each side of gusset.

Knit body in the round,
working steeks at armholes.

Increase evenly on last rib round.

Mark center stitch of round (seam stitch).

Mark first stitch of round (seam stitch).

Increasing evenly can be trickier.

Example

Number of sts in body circumference = 330.

Number of sts in rib = 292.

Number of sts to be increased = 38.

To place increases: 292 : 38 = 7, remainder 26.

This would mean K7, M1; repeat to last 26; K26, which is unacceptably uneven.

One solution would be: (K8, M1) 26 times, (K7, M1) 12 times. Or better still: (K8, M1, K7, M1) 12 times, (K8, M1) 14 times. Best of all would be: (K8, M1, K7, M1, K8, M1) 12 times; (K8, M1) twice.

The first solution is quite acceptable. If you are a stickler for evenness, however, you can juggle the numbers as I have done here, but it is by no means necessary.

The gusset   The diamond-shaped underarm gusset is started by increasing a stitch at each side of the body-seam stitch and then fashioned by increasing regularly on the outside of the increased stitches up to the armhole opening. This is the center and widest point of the gusset. The gusset stitches are then placed on a holder while the armhole and rest of the body are worked.

The stitches are picked up from the holder together with the stitches knit up around the armhole for the sleeve, and the gusset is decreased regularly while working the sleeve, until only the seam stitch remains (see the drawing on p. 176).

The traditional gusset is about 2½ in. wide at its center for a small adult, 2¾ in. for a medium-sized adult, and 3 in. for a large adult. The increases and decreases are worked on every fourth round.

In order to plan the size and starting point of the gusset, first determine the number of stitches required at its center (width at gusset center × stitch gauge + seam stitch). This number will always be odd because stitches are increased in pairs, starting on both sides of the seam stitch. The first increase will result in 3 gusset stitches, the next in 5, and so on.

To determine the number of rounds required from begininng of the gusset to its center, calculate as follows:

1. Divide the total stitches to be increased by 2.

2. Multiply the result of Step 1 by the frequency of increase rounds (4 for a traditional gansey).

3. Subtract the frequency of increase rounds minus 1 from the result of Step 2. This is necessary because the gusset begins with an increase round. For example, the gusset for the traditional gansey is increased on the first and every following fourth round rather than simply on every fourth round from beginning to center. The result of Step 3 is the number of rounds required from the beginning to the center of the gusset.

Example

Total sts at center = 23.

Therefore sts to be increased = 22.
22 ÷ 2 = 11.

Frequency of increase rounds: every 4th round.

11 × 4 = 44.

Frequency of increase (4) − 1 = 3.
    44 − 3 = 41.

Therefore, 41 rounds are required from the gusset's beginning to center.

The example above is for a traditional gusset, increased on every fourth round. Indeed, provided you increase on every fourth round, the above calculation can be reduced to this simple formula: Rounds required from beginning to center = (total number of increases × 2) − 3.

Here is the same example worked out using the shorter formula:

Totals sts at center = 23.

Therefore sts to be increased = 22.

(22 × 2) − 3 = 41.

If you wish, for aesthetic purposes, to make a gusset larger than the traditional one, it would be worked by increasing more frequently than every fourth round to a wider center, and the full formula must be used for the calculations. The angles of this gusset will be steeper than those in its traditional counterpart. While the gusset stitches are traditionally worked in a seeding pattern—that is, 1 stitch in pattern color, 1 stitch in background color, and vice versa—to keep the colors moving, more elaborate patterns can be worked inside a large gusset, making it both decorative and practical. For an example of a decorative gusset increased on every third round, see the oversize panel cardigan on pp. 136-139.

Gusset

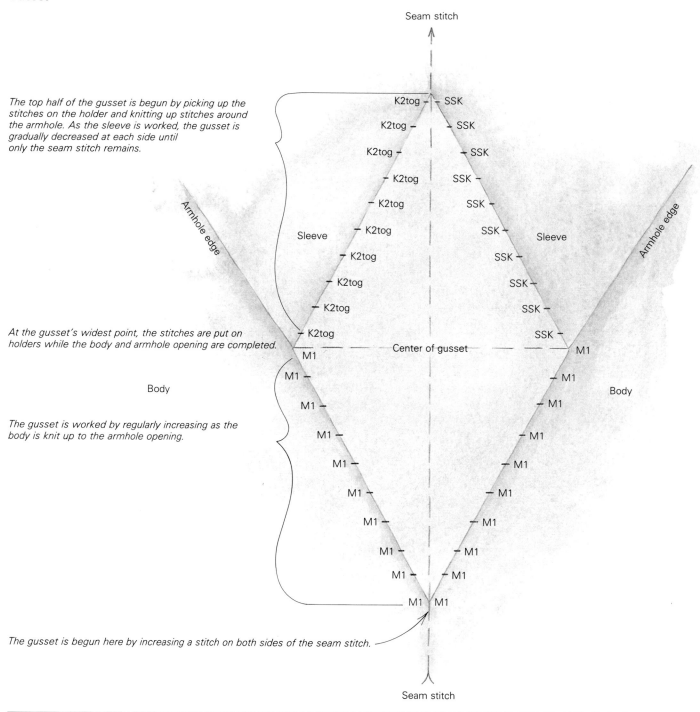

The top half of the gusset is begun by picking up the stitches on the holder and knitting up stitches around the armhole. As the sleeve is worked, the gusset is gradually decreased at each side until only the seam stitch remains.

At the gusset's widest point, the stitches are put on holders while the body and armhole opening are completed.

The gusset is worked by regularly increasing as the body is knit up to the armhole opening.

The gusset is begun here by increasing a stitch on both sides of the seam stitch.

Seam stitch

K2tog — SSK
K2tog — SSK
K2tog — SSK
K2tog   SSK
K2tog   SSK
Sleeve   K2tog   SSK   Sleeve
K2tog   SSK
K2tog   SSK
K2tog   SSK
K2tog   SSK
M1   Center of gusset   M1
M1   M1
M1   M1
Body   M1   M1   Body
M1   M1
M1   M1
M1   M1
M1   M1
M1   M1
M1 M1

Armhole edge

Armhole edge

Seam stitch

FRANKLIN LAKES PUBLIC LIBRARY

Dividing back and front at armholes To divide back and front, the gusset stitches must be placed on holders. Because the gusset stitches include the seam stitches, the back and front will be minus 1 stitch each. One stitch is increased at each side of both the back and front for armhole-edge stitches, so some minor calculations are necessary in order to work out the number of stitches on both back and front between the armholes.

Example

Number of sts in chest circumference = 334.

Subtract seam sts: 334 − 2 = 332.

Total + armhole edge sts = 332 + 4 = 336.

Number of sts in back and in front:
336 ÷ 2 = 168.

This calculation can be reduced to the following formula: (Total sts in body + 2) ÷ 2.

Neck shaping Traditional gansey necks are approximately one-third of the total width between armholes, which leaves an equal third for each shoulder. While the back neck is unshaped, the front neck is fashioned by placing roughly two-thirds of the number of stitches in the back neck on a holder at center front neck, and reducing the remaining stitches evenly at each side. The drawing below illustrates the traditional neck shaping.

Example

Total back-neck sts (measurement F) = 49.

Number of rows in neck drop (measurement G) = 20.

Approximately two-thirds of F = 33.

Number of sts to be decreased at sides:
49 − 33 = 16

Therefore, decrease 8 sts evenly at each side within 20 rows, as follows: every 2nd row 5 times; every 3rd row 3 times; and knit 1 row straight.

Make sure when knitting up the neck rib that the rib pattern fits exactly into the total number of stitches. If necessary, decrease to fit the pattern. Do not increase, since this will enlarge the rib and it will not lie flat.

Sleeve Calculate the number of stitches to be knit up around the armhole by multiplying the rounds in the armhole depth (measurement D) by 2. In practice, this number will be slightly too many stitches and therefore should be reduced by about ½ in. of stitches.

Example

Gauge: 8 sts and 8 rows = 1 in.

Number of rounds in armhole depth (D) = 73.

73 × 2 = 146.

Reduce by ½ in.: 146 − 4 = 142.

Traditional gansey neck shaping

The neck of a classic gansey is about one-third the total width between armholes. The front neck is shaped as shown, and the back neck is unshaped.

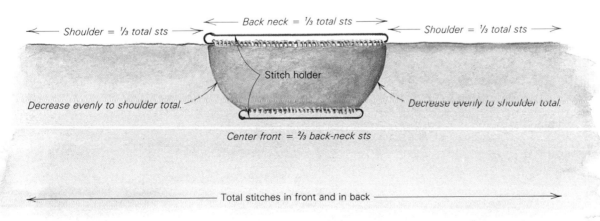

←— Shoulder = ⅓ total sts —→   ←— Back neck = ⅓ total sts —→   ←— Shoulder = ⅓ total sts —→

Stitch holder

Decrease evenly to shoulder total.   *Decrease evenly to shoulder total.*

Center front = ⅔ back-neck sts

←————————— Total stitches in front and in back —————————→

The sleeve stitches should be knit evenly into the armhole-edge stitch around the armhole. After knitting up the stitches and working a few rounds, check to make sure that the sleeve does not flare out from the shoulder (too many stitches) or that the armhole is not puckered (too few stitches). If you have knit up the wrong number of stitches, figure out how many fewer or more you need, rip out the work and knit up the adjusted number of stitches.

The gusset stitches should be decreased with the same frequency as they were increased, until the seam stitch alone remains. The sleeve is then decreased gradually to the top of the sleeve rib with K2tog and SSK decreases (see pp. 97-100). Calculate the number of sleeve decreases required as follows: (Total sts knit up around armhole + seam st) − stitches in measurement I.

Example

Total sts knit up around armhole
    + seam st = 143.

Total sts in measurement I = 77.

Number of sts to be decreased: 143 − 77 = 66.

The decreases are worked in pairs at each side of the seam stitch. In order to place the decreases evenly down the sleeve, use the following calculation: (Total patterned sleeve rounds − gusset rounds) ÷ half the number of sts to be decreased.

Example

Total patterned sleeve rounds (H − J) = 136.

Gusset rounds = 37.

136 − 37 = 99.

Half the number of sts to be decreased:
    66 ÷ 2 = 33.

99 ÷ 33 = 3.

Therefore, decrease 2 sts on every 3rd round.

A decrease round should also be worked immediately before beginning the sleeve rib, but make sure that the rib pattern fits exactly into the resulting number. If it is impossible to place the decreases evenly in this round, they should be positioned closer toward the center of the round.

Example

Total sts after sleeve decreases = 99.

Number of sts required for rib = 68.

Number of sts to be decreased = 31.

To place decreases: 99 ÷ 31 = 3, remainder 6.

Therefore, decrease as follows: (K2tog, K2) 3 times; (K2tog K1) 25 times; ((K2tog, K2) 3 times.

Gansey variations

The traditional gansey was originally designed as a practical working garment for fishermen. Inevitably it fell subject to the changes and developments in fashion once it was adopted for leisure wear by the general population. Because the gansey is a simple, basic shape, variations on it can be worked relatively easily. Some of these variations, like the shaped-armhole variation and V-neck vest, long ago became classics themselves.

Shaped armholes   With changes in fashion, the dropped shoulder with underarm gusset has largely given way to the shaped armhole, illustrated in the top drawing on the facing page. To work a shaped armhole, place the center-underarm stitches on a holder (approximately 1 in. of stitches for a small adult, 1½ in. for a medium-sized adult and 2 in. for a large adult), work a steek and decrease approximately 1 to 1½ in. at each side, within the first 3 in. of the armhole.

The underarm stitches are later picked up from the holder and worked with the stitches knit up around the armhole. The sleeve is then decreased gradually at each side of the underarm-seam stitch.

Shaped back neck   The traditional gansey neck is fairly small and basic in shape. For a more sophisticated line and an easier fit, shape the back neck by placing the center-back stitches on a holder approximately 1 in. to 1½ in. below the total length, and decrease evenly at each side to the required neck width. The front neck is worked as explained on p. 181 for the traditional gansey.

The entire neck can be made wider by simply adding more stitches to the total neck width, and the curve of the front neck shaping can be altered to suit. For example, as shown in the bottom drawing on the facing page, 2 stitches are placed on a holder at the neck edge of the first three rows and the remaining stitches decreased evenly.

(text continues on p. 182)

Shaped armhole and how to work it

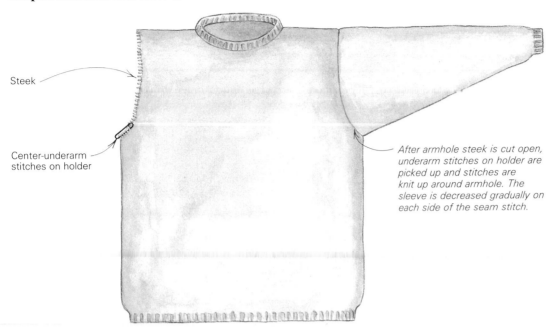

Steek

Center-underarm
stitches on holder

*After armhole steek is cut open,
underarm stitches on holder are
picked up and stitches are
knit up around armhole. The
sleeve is decreased gradually on
each side of the seam stitch.*

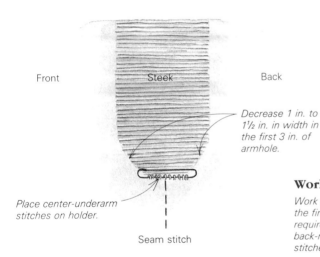

Front   Steek   Back

*Decrease 1 in. to
1½ in. in width in
the first 3 in. of
armhole.*

*Place center-underarm
stitches on holder.*

Seam stitch

Working a neck shaped back and front

*Work a shaped back neck by placing the back-neck stitches on holders 1 in. to 1½ in. below
the finished length of the body, and decrease evenly at each side to the
required width. The front neck is shaped by placing about two-thirds the number of
back-neck stitches on a holder and evenly reducing the remaining
stitches at each side.*

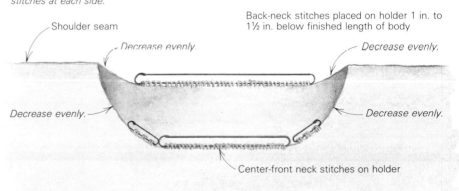

Shoulder seam

Decrease evenly.

Back-neck stitches placed on holder 1 in. to
1½ in. below finished length of body

Decrease evenly.

Decrease evenly.

Decrease evenly.

Center-front neck stitches on holder

Planning a gansey

The calculations below, for the traditional gansey shown in the photo on the facing page, illustrate the practical application of the guidelines set out on p. 169. The gansey is knit in 2-ply Shetland jumper-weight wool. If your gauge is exactly the same as in Step 3, you can use the calculations as a blueprint for a gansey of the same dimensions.

Step 1: Measurements

(A) 40 in.
(B) 25½ in.
(C) 3 in.
(D) 8¾ in.
(E) 16¾ in.
(F) 6¾ in.
(G) 2¾ in.
(H) 19½ in.
(I) 9 in.
(J) 3 in.

Step 2: Knitting plan

Study this knitting plan in conjunction with the drawing on p. 174

Step 3: Gauge

8 sts and 8 rows to 1 in., measured over Fair Isle patterns. Patterns are 17-row Fair Isle with 1 plain row at each side, giving 19-row bands. The lozenges in each band contain a different motif from the top of the rib to the shoulder. The stitch pattern repeat is 32.

Step 4: Calculating stitches and rows

Sts required for A: $40 \times 8 = 320$.
Patterned length of body (B − C):
  $25½ − 3 = 22½$ in.
Pattern rounds required: $22½ \times 8 = 180$.
Rounds required for D: $8¾ \times 8 = 70$.
Sts required around armhole for sleeve:
  $70 \times 2 = 140$.
Reduce by ½ in.: $140 − 4 = 136$.

Because the pattern repeat is even, the total number of armhole stitches must be odd, so the count is adjusted to 137 sts.

Pattern length from base to armhole (E − C):
  $16¾ − 3 = 13¾$.
Pattern rounds required: $13¾ \times 8 = 110$.
Sts required for F: $6¾ \times 8 = 54$.
Rows required for G: $2¾ \times 8 = 22$.
Pattern length of sleeve (H − J):
  $19½ − 3 = 16½$.
Pattern rounds required: $16½ \times 8 = 132$.
Sts required for I: $9 \times 8 = 72$.

Step 5: Fitting patterns into widths

St count of pattern repeat = 32.
Sts in A = 320.
$320 \div 32 = 10$.

Step 6: Centering patterns

The back and front are automatically centered, with 5 complete patterns on each. The calculations for the sleeve are as follows:

Armhole sts = 137.
$137 \div 32 = 4$, remainder 9.

Gansey knitting plan

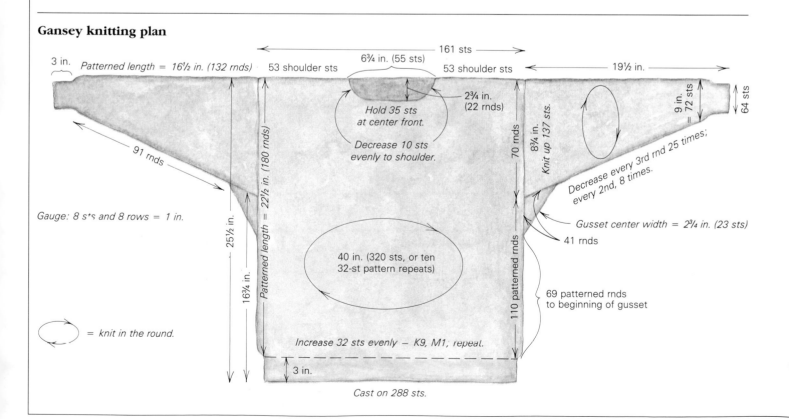

3 in.   Patterned length = 16½ in. (132 rnds)   53 shoulder sts   6¾ in. (55 sts)   53 shoulder sts   19½ in.

91 rnds

Gauge: 8 sts and 8 rows = 1 in.

Hold 35 sts at center front.

Decrease 10 sts evenly to shoulder.

2¾ in. (22 rnds)

Decrease every 3rd rnd 25 times; every 2nd, 8 times.

161 sts

25½ in.

16¾ in.

Patterned length = 22½ in. (180 rnds)

70 rnds

8¾ in. Knit up 137 sts.

9 in. 72 sts

64 sts

40 in. (320 sts, or ten 32-st pattern repeats)

Gusset center width = 2¾ in. (23 sts)

41 rnds

110 patterned rnds

69 patterned rnds to beginning of gusset

= knit in the round.

Increase 32 sts evenly — K9, M1, repeat.

3 in.

Cast on 288 sts.

To center the pattern, work last 4 sts of repeat, repeat the 32 pattern sts 4 times; work first 5 sts of repeat.

Step 7: Fitting patterns into lengths

Number of rows in pattern repeat = 19.
Total pattern rounds in body = 180.
Number of pattern repeats in body:
    180 ÷ 19 = 9, remainder 9, giving
    9 repeats and finishing at the center of
    the repeat.
Total pattern rounds in sleeve = 132.
Number of pattern repeats in sleeve:
    132 ÷ 19 = 6, remainder 18.

Adjust to 133 rounds, giving 7 complete repeats. Work the rib-decrease round on the last plain round.

Note that you should begin the sleeve pattern as the pattern band at the body underarm and work downward. There are only 6 pattern repeats worked in the body to the underarm; therefore the last sleeve repeat should be worked the same as the shoulder pattern band.

Additional calculations

Ribbing

Sts in A = 320.
Reduce by 1 st in 10: 320 ÷ 10 = 32.
Number of sts to cast on for rib = 288.
K2, P2 corrugated rib = 4 pattern sts.
Check fit: 288 ÷ 4 = 72.

Increase from rib to chest stitches

Number of sts to be increased = 32.
To increase evenly: 288 ÷ 32 = 9.
Therefore, on increase round, K9, M1; repeat to
    end of round.

Gusset:

Width at center = 2¾ in.
Sts required at widest point: 2¾ × 8 = 22.
Add 1 st to give odd total = 23.
Frequency of increase = every 4th round.
Rounds required from beginning to center, using
    short formula: (22 × 2) − 3 = 41.

Number of pattern rounds from base of sweater
    to armhole = 110.
110 − 41 = 69.
Therefore, work 69 pattern rounds, then begin
    the gusset.

Divide back and front at armholes

Place 23 sts of each gusset on holders.
Number of sts in each back and front:
    (320 + 2) ÷ 2 = 161.

Neck shaping

Back neck:

Sts in back neck (F) = 54.
Total sts in back = 161.
Sts remaining for shoulders: 161 − 54 = 107.

Adjust to give even total so that shoulders will have same number of sts. Therefore, 55 sts for neck; 53 sts for each shoulder.

Front neck:

Sts at center-front neck (odd number):
    approximately ⅔ rounds of F = 35.
Sts to be decreased: 55 − 35 = 20.

Therefore, decrease 10 sts at each side within 22 rows, that is, 1 st every 2nd row 10 times, then work 2 rows straight.

Neck rib:

Pick up and knit 55 sts from back neck; knit up 19 sts to front-neck holder; pick up and knit 35 sts of center-front neck; knit up 19 sts to complete. Total neck-rib stitches = 128.
Check 4-st rib pattern fit: 128 ÷ 4 = 32.

Sleeve

Number of sts to be knit up around armhole
    = 137.
137 + seam st = 138.
Number of sts in I = 72.
Number of sts to be decreased: 138 − 72 = 66.

To place decreases down sleeve [(132 patterned rounds in sleeve length − 41 rounds in gusset) ÷ 33]: 91 ÷ 33 = 2, remainder 25. Therefore decrease every 3rd round 25 times; then every 2nd round 8 times.

Number of sts for sleeve rib = 64.
Number of sts to be decreased: 91 − 64 = 27.

To place decreases in round: 91 ÷ 27 = 3, remainder 10. Therefore, work decrease round as follows:

    (K2tog, K2) 5 times; ((k2tog, K1) 17 times;
    (K2, K2tog) 5times.

This traditional dropped-shoulder gansey with under-arm gussets is a classic shape from which many variations can be worked.

Working a V-neck and shaped armhole

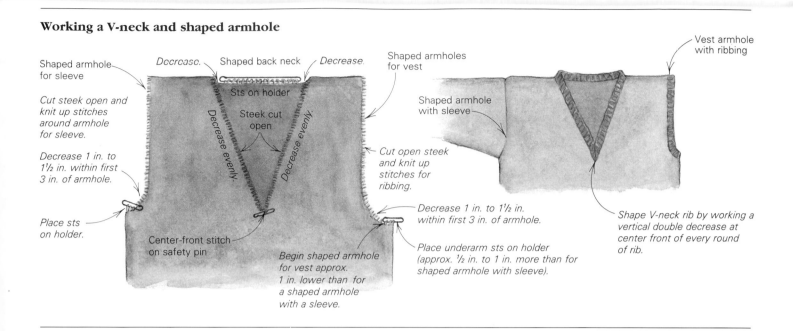

Shaped armhole for sleeve

Decrease.

Shaped back neck

Decrease.

Shaped armholes for vest

Vest armhole with ribbing

Cut steek open and knit up stitches around armhole for sleeve.

Sts on holder

Steek cut open

Decrease evenly.

Decrease evenly.

Shaped armhole with sleeve

Decrease 1 in. to 1½ in. within first 3 in. of armhole.

Cut open steek and knit up stitches for ribbing.

Place sts on holder.

Center-front stitch on safety pin

Begin shaped armhole for vest approx. 1 in. lower than for a shaped armhole with a sleeve.

Decrease 1 in. to 1½ in. within first 3 in. of armhole.

Place underarm sts on holder (approx. ½ in. to 1 in. more than for shaped armhole with sleeve).

Shape V-neck rib by working a vertical double decrease at center front of every round of rib.

V-neck The classic V-neck sweater is a popular variation on the traditional gansey and is quite simple to work. The V-shaping is usually started on the same round as the armholes begin (see the drawing above).

To work the V-neck, place the center-front stitch on a safety pin, work a steek and decrease evenly to the required width. It is important to place the decreases as evenly as possible in order to produce the straight lines of the V. Shaping the back neck also improves the look of the neckline. Finally, the rib is shaped by working a vertical double decrease at center front on every round.

The classic Fair Isle vest is a simple combination of a traditional gansey body with shaped armholes and a V-neck (see the drawing above). The armholes should be slightly deeper (approximately 1 in.) and wider (approximately ½ in. to 1 in.) than for a gansey in order to allow room for the armhole rib.

Classic cardigan

The classic cardigan is identical in shape to the gansey and differs only in that it has a front opening, which makes the calculations slightly more complex than for the gansey. Although the cardigan is knitted in the round, for the sake of clarity the measurement plan in the drawing on the facing page is drawn flat. The sleeve can be drawn separately (in this case, the sleeve is exactly the same as for the traditional gansey plan on p. 180 and is therefore omitted from the drawing). This plan is for a classic cardigan with gussets and a shaped back neck, like the one shown on pp. 136-139.

As for the gansey, the first step in designing a cardigan is taking the appropriate measurements:

(A) Chest circumference. This is the measurement of the buttoned cardigan and therefore includes one front band (I). The result should be at least 3 in. more than the actual body measurement.

(B) Length from top of shoulder to base.

(C) Body rib length.

(D) Armhole depth.

(B – D) Length from base to armhole.

(E) Length from center-front neck to base.

(F) Front-neck drop.

(G) Neck width.

(H) Back-neck drop.

(I) Front-rib width.

(A – I) Patterned width of body.

The sleeve measurements are the same as for the gansey.

Plan for cardigan

Next proceed to steps 2, 3, 4, 5, 6 and 7. Note, while working through these steps, that there are several points to remember when designing a cardigan:

1. When calculating the stitch count for the patterned width of the body, remember to add 1 stitch at each side for front-edge stitches.

2. When calculating stitches to cast on for the body rib, center the rib pattern. For example, a K2, P2 rib has a multiple of 4 stitches. Therefore, in order to center the pattern, cast on a multiple of 4 plus 2 stitches.

3. The round begins at the center of the front steek, and the position of the underarm-seam stitches must be calculated.

4. Work the neck rib, then knit up the stitches for front bands.

5. Space the buttonholes evenly, placing the first and last holes fairly close to the top and bottom of the cardigan. For example, if there are 164 stitches in the front band and 14 buttonholes, place the buttonholes by dividing the front-band stitches by the number of buttonholes minus 1: $164 \div 13 = 12$, remainder 8. Therefore, position the buttonholes as follows: Rib 3 (cast off 2, rib 10) 13 times; cast off 2, rib 3. (For information on making buttonholes, see p. 106).

Exploring shapes and styles

A good Fair Isle design sucessfully combines style, shape, pattern, color and materials. The traditional styles will always remain classic because they are very basic to the human shape and are comfortable and easy to wear. The classic shapes are therefore obvious and excellent starting points from which to work variations and create new styles.

Many knitters imagine that the circular knitting technique is very restrictive in terms of shaping and styling garments. Yet in practice, the basic techniques involved in shaping all knitted garments—increasing and decreasing—produce more streamlined and sophisticated results when applied to circular knitting, as exemplified by the tammy and underarm gussets. Openings can vary in size and shape as much as those worked in flat knitting, and steeks do not restrict shaping in any way. Indeeed, like some experienced Fair Isle knitters, you may choose to work steeks over wide openings like gansey necks in order to avoid knitting shoulders flat. The work will be bunched up while knitting, but once the steek is cut, the garment will assume its proper shape.

The drawings on pp. 184-185 offer some basic suggestions on varying a garment's neck, sleeve and length. These variations can be used either singly or in any combination

Neckline variations

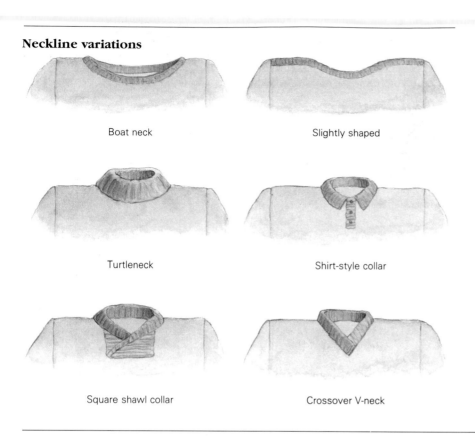

Boat neck

Slightly shaped

Turtleneck

Shirt-style collar

Square shawl collar

Crossover V-neck

to develop a particular design, or simply to serve as a starting point from which to explore your own ideas.

Necklines Six neckline variations are shown in the drawing at left. The boat neck is shaped at back and front. The shoulders for this neck are worked either flat or, for more experienced knitters, in circular fashion, with both the back and front neck bridged by a steek.

A wide, slightly shaped neck is accented by a continuous rib across the shoulders. The rib on back and front is worked flat (see the cotton sweater on pp. 122-124).

The classic turtleneck is effective worked in a corrugated rib, but remember to knit the rib inside out in order to have the right side facing outward when it is folded over.

For a shirt-style collar, cast off the stitches at the center-front neck and work a steek over the opening. Knit the collar flat, or if you sew very neatly, work a knitted steek, and fold and stitch it on the underside.

Sleeve variations

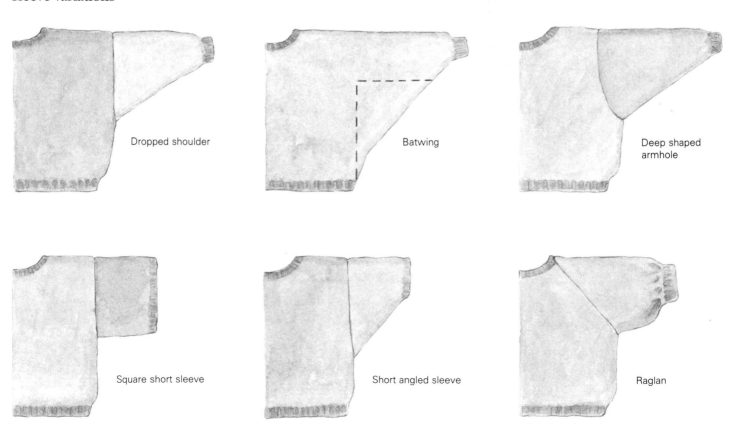

Dropped shoulder

Batwing

Deep shaped armhole

Square short sleeve

Short angled sleeve

Raglan

To create a square shawl collar, cast off the stitches at center front and work a steek over the opening. Separately knit the collar flat and sew it on. Since both sides of the rib show on this style of collar, corrugated ribbing is unsuitable. Instead, if you wish to carry the color theme throughout, work the ribbing in simple, narrow, colored stripes.

Finally, to create a short crossover V-neck, hold the center-front stitch and decrease sharply and evenly to the shoulder. Work the rib separately and sew it on.

Sleeves As shown in the bottom drawing on the facing page, the deep, dropped shoulder is basically a gansey sleeve without the gusset, whose armhole depth can be varied. The sleeve is decreased gradually on either side of the seam stitch, from the armhole to just above the rib.

The batwing sleeve can be produced in two very different ways. A large gusset (indicated by the dotted line) can be worked and filled with one or more suitable patterns. Alternatively, the entire garment can be knit from cuff to cuff, increasing the sleeve to the body opening and working steeks at the body and neck openings. The second sleeve is then decreased to the cuff, and body and neck ribs are knit up around the openings.

The deep, shaped armhole is simply an exaggerated classic-shaped armhole, with the sleeve steeply decreased to above the rib. For an example of this type of sleeve, see the allover-pattern sweater on pp. 119-121.

A square, short sleeve with a ribbed edge should be worked in the same gauge as the patterned area of the sleeve, using the same size needles and the same number of stitches, so that the rib does not pull in.

A short sleeve can be worked with a deep armhole and be steeply angled to the rib. This shape can be achieved by decreasing the sleeve sharply at each side of the seam stitch, or by working a gusset that finishes above the sleeve rib.

The raglan sleeve is worked in the same way as a circular-yoked garment. The body and sleeves are each knitted separately (though still in the round) up to the armhole opening. The underarm stitches are then placed on holders, and the sleeves and body are joined by working them together in one large circle. The raglans are decreased at each side of the "raglan line" stitch.

Lengths Circular knitting poses no restriction on garment length. The silhouettes illustrated in the drawing below give some suggestions for skirt, dress and coat or sweater

Length variations

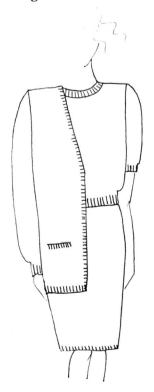

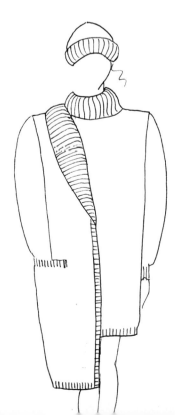

Playing pattern against pattern

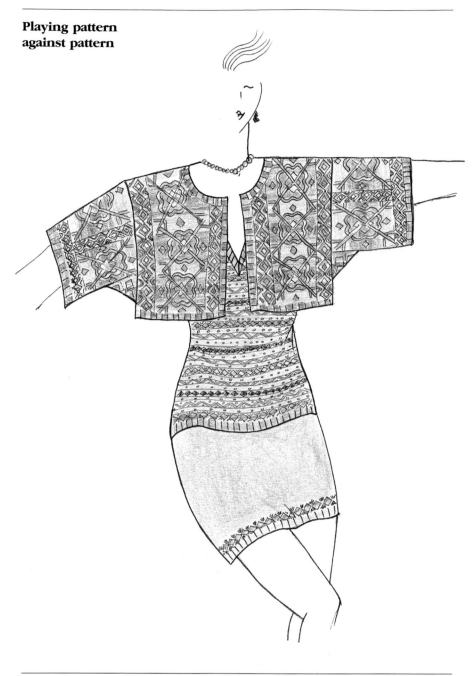

Sample swatches worked in heavy-weight yarn for the coat design in the drawing on the facing page.

lengths. Different lengths can sometimes work together and provide a "canvas" on which to combine complementary patterns and colors. The drawing at left illustrates a contemporary interpetation of this idea.

Choosing yarns

Two main points should be considered when choosing yarns for Fair Isle knitting: yarn weight and type. Since the knitted fabric is of double thickness, the yarns should be light in weight unless a heavy outdoor garment is desired. Yarn weight also considerably affects pattern and color. With lightweight yarns and small needles, the scale of the patterns is small, and there is a great deal of scope for changing pattern and color. The overall effect of working with a light-weight yarn can be intricate and subtle.

By contrast, heavier-weight yarns produce a larger, bolder scale. The swatches in the photo below left for the coat designs in the drawing on the facing page were worked in a heavy yarn (2-ply Shetland jumper-weight doubled) and illustrate the effect of heavy yarn on pattern and color.

With regard to yarn type, the most suitable for Fair Isle knitting are hairy rather than smooth and slippery yarns. The reason for this is that the individual fibers on hairy yarns cause the strands to cling together, thus producing a more stable fabric, which is also more suitable for cutting when steeks are involved.

Despite the above, it is still possible to use smoother yarns quite successfully for Fair Isle work, provided you choose patterns that change background and pattern yarns as frequently as possible. The cotton sweater on pp. 122-124 is a good example of the effective use of a smooth cotton yarn. The ripple-effect panels change continuously from background to pattern yarns every two stitches, thus giving stability to the fabric. However, because smooth cotton yarn is inelastic, it should be used only if you are certain of having a very uniform gauge. Wide knitted steeks should be worked with smooth yarns to give leeway for running when they are cut. Very slippery yarns like rayon are not suitable for cutting at all.

The yarn should work with the pattern and color you have selected. For best results, it should always be of high quality, which will enhance your workmanship. Fancy slubbed,

**Coat designs
to be worked
in heavy
yarn**

Although Shetland yarns are ideal for Fair Isle garments, various other yarn can be used for different effects, as, for example, in this sweater worked in mohair with a large allover pattern.

bouclé and multicolored yarns (unless used on a plain contrasting background) are generally unsuitable and tend to obscure patterns. Shetland 2-ply jumper-weight yarn is ideal in all respects and eminently suitable for all types of wool garments (see Sources of Supply, p. 194).

However, there is a host of yarns available to the knitter today, and it is well worth experimenting with any that fit the requirements mentioned above. For example, I was keen to knit a Fair Isle sweater quickly, using larger needles, although I did not want a heavy garment. Mohair fitted the bill perfectly. It is light, hairy and of excellent quality. Because the yarn's extreme hairiness tends to "fuzz" the patterns, I used a large Norwegian allover pattern in medium-bright colors on soft, pale backgrounds for a well-defined effect (see the photo at left).

Yarn quantities   It is always difficult to judge the quantity of yarn required for a design, since this depends very much on the size and shape of the garment as well as on the amount of stranded knitting called for. Because of its double thickness, stranded knitting uses more yarn than does plain knitting. As a rough guideline, a garment worked entirely in stranded knitting will use approximately half again as much yarn as the same garment knitted in plain stockinette stitch. A traditional gansey worked entirely in stranded knitting in 2-ply Shetland jumper-weight yarn uses roughly 16 oz. to 18 oz., 18 oz. to 20 oz. and 20 oz. to 22 oz. respectively for small, medium and large sizes. Amounts of specific colors can be estimated by determining the approximate ratio of their use in the patterns. It is well worth being generous in your calculations. A few balls of assorted colors left over will be a very positive addition to the yarn collection of a keen and serious Fair Isle knitter.

A final word

In the past, Shetland women were forced to endure a lifetime of often ill-rewarded toil to attain their mastery of Fair Isle knitting. This book is intended to replace those hard years of apprenticeship for the new Fair Isle knitter and provide a comprehensive guide for anyone who wishes to practice the art. I emphasize the word "practice," for that is the key to mastery of technique and to creative development.

In writing any book, the author gives the reader insight into his or her own personality. Whether the view is just a glimpse or a complete panorama, it always contains an element of the private and personal. In this book, I have sought to explore in depth the artistic possibilities of Fair Isle knitting. I have also tried to provide an inspirational guide to help readers develop their own creative skills with all aspects of pattern, color and design. This

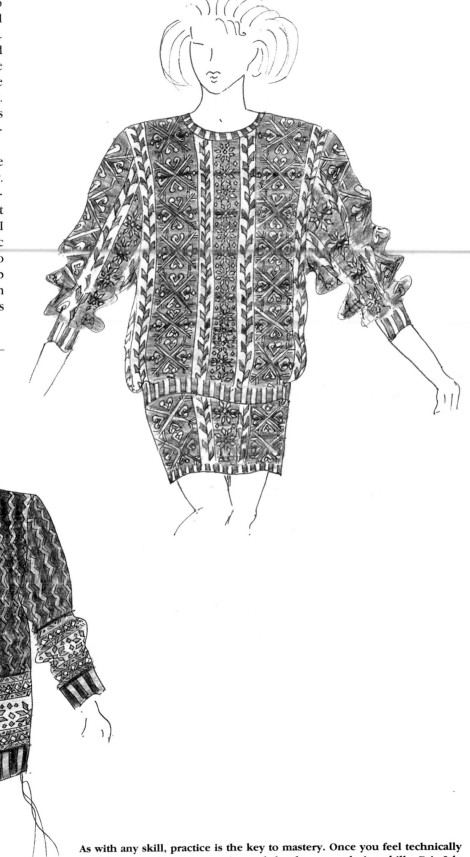

As with any skill, practice is the key to mastery. Once you feel technically confident, continue to exercise and develop your design skills. Fair Isle patterns and designs offer endless creative possibilities.

strand of the book has been intensely personal, revealing my own thought processes, working methods and sources of inspiration.

The other main strand of the book reflects my belief that aesthetic satisfaction and creativity proceed best from a sound technical base. To this end, I have endeavored to provide a complete instruction manual of Fair Isle knitting technique. All technicalities have been fully dealt with, and all trade secrets revealed.

The story began with a small island, remote, yet in haphazard contact with world-wide sea traffic. The story ends with an art that has become world famous. But in fact, the story does not really end at all, for the art long ago spread from that island and remains, as it always has been, a dynamic, creative process. It will continue to develop as long as there are knitters diligent enough to master its techniques and sufficiently imaginative to put them to interesting use. This book puts *you* at the forefront of that continuing development, for, used correctly, it places the art in *your* hands. Use it well.

In a 1956 photo, a young boy carrying rhubarb wears a Fair Isle sweater with patterning typical of the period.

Credits

Photos

Cover: Joseph Kugielsky.

Unless otherwise noted, all outdoor photography by Alice Starmore.

p. vi: Courtesy Trustees of National Library of Scotland.

pp. 2-3, 5, 22: Courtesy G.W. Wilson Collection, Aberdeen University Library.

pp. 4, 30 (center): Courtesy Shetland Tourist Organization.

pp. 8, 17, 193: Courtesy National Museums of Scotland.

p. 23 (top): Courtesy Leeds City Art Galleries, Leeds, England.

pp. 23 (bottom), 25, 26: Courtesy Shetland Museum.

p. 82 (bottom left): Courtesy Zona, New York.

Illustrations

pp. vii, 11, 13, 162-184: Mark Kara.

pp. 88-109: Marianne Markey.

Sources of supply

The Shetland yarn used in the garments and swatches in this book was supplied by:

Jamieson & Smith, Ltd.
90, North Road
Lerwick
Shetland Isles
Scotland, UK
ZE1 OPQ
Phone: 011-33-595-3579

Unlike most brands of 100% Shetland yarn, Jamieson & Smith yarn is available in a wide range of colors. You can order directly from Jamieson & Smith, requesting a single hank or as much yarn as you like. Delivery is prompt, and a sample card is available upon request.

From time to time Jamieson & Smith yarn is available in the United States. At the time of publication, it was carried by the shops listed below. The range of colors and price may vary from store to store.

Blue Hill Yarns
Box 201
Blue Hill, ME 04614
(207) 374-5631

Bluenose Wools
407 N. Columbia
Chapel Hill, NC 27516
(919) 967-8800

Dream Weaver
650 Miami Circle NE
Atlanta, GA 30324
(404) 237-4588

Great Scot
5606 Mohican Rd.
Bethesda, MD 20816

Kaleidoscope Yarns
16 Church St.
Belfast, ME 04915

Renee-Yarn
4801 Montgomery Dr.
Santa Rosa, CA 95409
(707) 538-1519

Schoolhouse Press
6899 Cary Bluff Rd.
Pittsville, WI 54466
(715) 884-2799

Tomato Factory Yarn Co.
8 Church St.
Lambertville, NJ 08530
(609) 397-3475

The Wool Shop
25 The Plaza
Locust Valley, NY 11560
(516) 671-9722

The Wooly West
208 South 13th East
Salt Lake City, UT 84102
(801) 583-9373

Yarn Galore
5428 MacArthur Blvd. NW
Suite 102
Washington, DC 20016
(202) 686-5648

Renaissance Yarns' new Baa-Baa's Best is suitable for Fair Isle knitting and is available in many local U.S. yarn stores. Although it is a blend of wools rather than a pure Shetland yarn, Baa-Baa's Best handles beautifully for Fair Isle work and is available in numerous colors. It can also be ordered directly from:

Renaissance Yarns
P.O. Box 937
Norwalk, CT 06856
(800) 544-2290

The cotton yarn used for the sweater on pp. 122-124 was supplied by:

The DMC Corporation
107 Trumbull St.
Elizabeth, NJ 07206

The silk yarn used for the water-lily jacket on pp. 144-147 was supplied by:

Silk City Fibers
155 Oxford St.
Paterson, NJ 07522.

Bibliography

Brand, Rev. John. *A Brief Description of Orkney, Zetland, Pightland and Caithness*. 1701.

Description of Ye Countrey of Zetland by Parish Ministers. Circa 1680.

Don, Sarah. *Fair Isle Knitting*. New York: St. Martin's Press, 1983.

Edmonston, Dr. Arthur. *View of the Ancient and Present State of the Zetland Isles*. 1809.

Edmonston, Eliza. *Sketches and Tales of the Shetland Isles*. 1856.

Kiewe, Heinz Edgar. *The Sacred History of Knitting*. Oxford, England: Art Needlework Industries Limited, 1971.

Linklater, Eric. *Orkney & Shetland*. 3rd ed. Philadelphia: International Publications Service, 1980.

O'Connor, Kaori. *Creative Dressing*. Boston: Routledge and K. Paul, 1981.

The Poor Knitters of Shetland: A short account of them by a Lady Resident. Anonymous pamphlet, 1861.

Scott, Sir Walter. *Northern Lights: A voyage in the lighthouse yacht to Nova Zembla and the Lord knows where, in the summer of 1814*. Written in 1814, published in 1982.

Scottish History Society. *Macfarlane's Geographical Collections*. Vol. III. 1908.

Standen, Edward. *On the Shetland Isles*. Pamphlet, 1845.

The Statistical Account of Scotland, 1791 to 1799. Orkney & Shetland Volume.

Index

Numbers in italics refer to drawings, charts and photos.

Managing editor	Deborah Cannarella
Editor	Christine Timmons
Copy/production editor	Ruth Dobsevage
Indexer	Harriet Hodges
Editorial assistant	Maria Angione
Design director	Roger Barnes
Designer/art director	Ben Kann
Art assistants	Cindy Nyitray, Rosanne Shea
Production manager	Peggy Dutton
Composition systems manager	Dinah George
Systems operator	Nancy-Lou Knapp
Technician	Margot Knorr
Production coordinator	Robert Marsala
Production assistants	Lisa Carlson, Mark Coleman, Priscilla Rollins, Tom Sparano

Typeface	ITC Garamond
Paper	Warrenflo, 70 lb., neutral pH
Printer and Binder	W.A. Krueger Co., New Berlin, Wis.

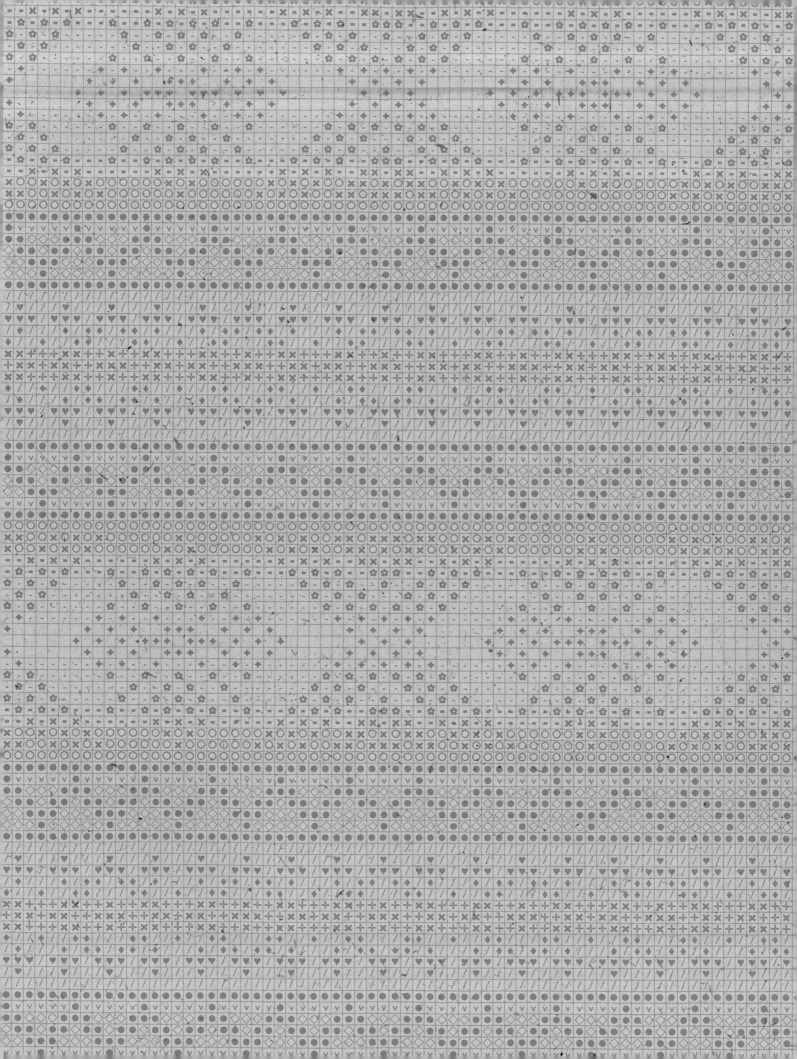